AXONOMETRIC AND OBLIQUE DRAWING
A 3-D Construction, Rendering, and Design Guide

AXONOMETRIC AND OBLIQUE DRAWING
A 3-D Construction, Rendering, and Design Guide

M. Saleh Uddin

McGraw-Hill
New York San Francisco Washington, D.C. Auckland Bogotá
Caracas Lisbon London Madrid Mexico City Milan
Montreal New Delhi San Juan Singapore
Sydney Tokyo Toronto

Library of Congress Catalog-in-Publication Data

Uddin, M. Saleh, 1955-
Axonometric and Oblique Drawing: A 3D Construction, Rendering and Design Guide
P. cm.
ISBN 0-07-065775-1
1. Architectural Drawing-Catalogs.   2. Technical Drawing-Catalog.
3. Contemporary Architects

1 2 3 4 5 6 7 8 9 0   QKP/QKP 9 0 2 1 0 9 8 7

ISBN 0-07-065755-6

McGraw-Hill books are available at special quantity discounts to use as premiums and sales promotions, or for use in corporate training programs. For more information, please write to the Director of Special Sales, McGraw-Hill, 11 West 19th Street, New York, NY 10011. Or contact your local bookstore.

This book is printed on acid-free paper.

Design, electronic layout and composition by M. Saleh Uddin.

Cover drawing: Author M. Saleh Uddin

AXONOMETRIC AND OBLIQUE DRAWING
A 3-D Construction, Rendering, and Design Guide

CONTENTS

Dedicated to my mother
who died in a tragic road accident.

ACKNOWLEDGMENTS

I would particularly like to extend my appreciation to all the architects who have participated in this book with their contributions of drawings. Architects and illustrators from Japan, Australia, and Malaysia need special mention for their prompt response to my many queries and for maintaining deadlines.

I thank my many students of the past nine years for their direct and indirect contributions to this book. Several projects in this book are the works of students from the Savannah College of Art and Design, Savannah, Georgia, and the Southern University at Baton Rouge, Louisiana.

Bryan Cantley of Cal Poly Fullerton, Steven House of House + House, Tom Sofranko of Louisiana State University, George Loli of the University of Southwestern Louisiana, Nan Blake of the University of Texas at Austin, and Lonnie Wilkinson of, the Southern University deserve special thanks for their enthusiasm and trust in this project.

My special gratitude is extended to my colleague Professor Douglas Schneider who not only edited the text, but reviewed and critiqued the entire contents of the book.

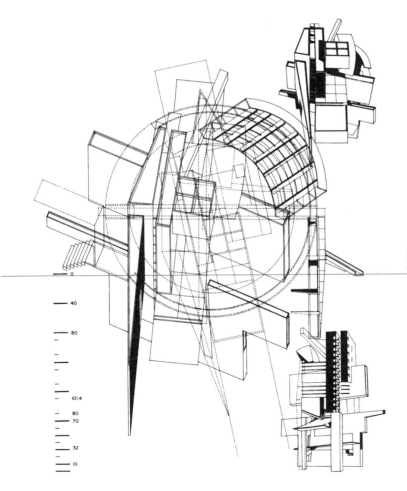

Drawing by Pomchai Boonsom (student), Southern California Institute of Architecture.
Neil Denari, Faculty Advisor. The Automated Spectacle: A Fictional Reopening of a Closed Space.

Axonometric is a generic term commonly used for all "paraline drawing." Sometimes architects and interior designers may incorrectly refer to any paraline drawing as either an "axonometric" or an "isometric." But actually all paraline drawings fall into two basic categories: axonometric and oblique. There is also a difference between an axonometric drawing and an axonometric projection.

A wide range of terminologies such as paraline, parallel projection, axonometric, oblique, isometric, dimetric, trimetric, transmetric, transoblique, planometric, cavalier, cabinet and military perspective may seem to be overly confusing. However, foreshortening of proportions and change of angles are the key factors that differentiate paraline drawings.

Since the term Axonometric is widely used in the profession, this book continues to use it from Chaps. 3 through 8, for purposes of convenience.

A clear subdivision of paraline, or axonometric and oblique drawings, are explained with examples in Chap. 2 of this book.

. . . .

Introduction

Axonometric Versus Perspective

Redrawn by author after a 4th century B.C. artwork

INTRODUCTION

AXONOMETRIC VERSUS PERSPECTIVE

The extraordinary attention given to perspective drawing in the field of design representation has always prevented consideration of the other equally important modes of representation. Although axonometric and oblique drawings are by no means recent developments in graphic representation, only in the later part of the twentieth century have they become more widely used techniques of design and presentation.

Seeing in oblique views is essential to us for depth perception. For common perception oblique views are perhaps the most comfortable ones since our brain is accustomed to seeing objects in three dimension.

The scientific nature of the images generated by paraline drawings, and their compatibility with prevailing ideological preferences, has attracted the interest of modern and contemporary architects and designers.

Although it is relatively easy to follow the application and perfection of parallel projection in the course of the sixteenth century and onward, it is not so easy to locate its theoretical and technical beginnings. Its constant presence in the ancient world obliges us to go back many centuries with little hope of finding written sources to enlighten us. There are contradictory dates in the historical record and the potential for debate regarding the discovery and operational knowledge of parallel projection systems.

Some authors have mentioned that orthographic projections or descriptive geometry did not come along until the end of the eighteenth century, having been discovered by French mathematician and physicist, Gaspard Monge (1746-1818), whereas principles of perspective were understood in the early part of the fifteenth century, although numerous documents contradict this claim. And if the science of descriptive geometry was discovered as late as the eighteenth century, the extensive use of precise axonometric or paraline drawings found earlier in Europe, and used for the purpose of fortification, contradicts the assumed evolution of the paraline drawings even further.

It is very clear that although Leonardo da Vinci knew the laws of perspective perfectly well, to the point of transgressing them with the aerial perspective, he seems to have given precedence to the older system of parallel projection in many of his sketches.

The use of parallel projection by Leonardo da Vinci and the unknown author of the "Codex Coner" during the perspective oriented Renaissance period is significant, for it indicates the continuity of a mode of representation other than the pictorial view throughout the history of architectural drawing.

Parallel projection appeared in Western culture as early as the fourth century B.C. and it was once the predominant form of representation in China. It is often found together with convergent projection. Perhaps the most noticeable and appropriate use of parallel projection is seen in the military drawings of the sixteenth century.

After 1550 in Europe, the essence of an architectural design was for the purpose of fortification and the creation of geometric impenetrability. The precision of the drawing was vital, because an imperfection of a line could mean the loss of an army. There was no logic for drawing seductive perspectives and conical projections. Parallel projection became the expedient method, capable of illustrating construction principles, which was of paramount importance and took precedence over aesthetics.

In 1564 a work explicitly contrasting parallel projection with Renaissance central projection (perspective) was published. The book mentioned "No one should expect to see in these works the methods or rules of the perspective: firstly, because it is not part of a soldier's profession to produce them, and secondly, because the foreshortening involved would remove too much from the plans, whereas the entirety of these works lies in such plans and outlines as shall be called perspectiva soldatesca."

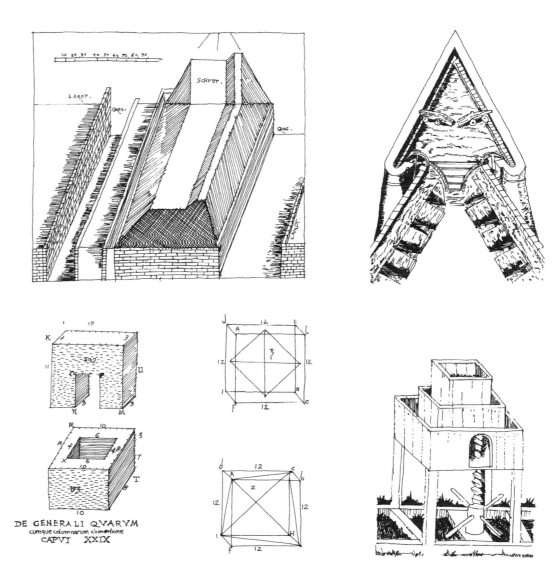

Redrawn by author based on drawings from printed materials

The noticeable comeback of paraline drawings during the early modern period linked with the De-Stijl movement (1917-1931) in Holland is significant for the fact that the roots of the contemporary trends of axonometric drawing inherently lie in it. The extensive use of axonometric drawings by Theo van Doesburg, the founder of the movement, to express the composition of forms brought a new phenomenon in architectural design presentation.

In its departure from Modernism (mid 70's) the Post-Modern period and the New-Age sought new intentions toward architectural ideas. Drawings produced by Aldo Rossi in Milan, Oswald Mathias Ungers in Berlin, Leon Krier in London, Aldolfo Natalini in Florence, and OMA (Office for Metropolitan Architecture) in Amsterdam, Rotterdam, and London, and Raimund Abraham and Rob Krier in Vienna, during the decades of the 60's, 70's, and 80's to communicate their new ideas through axonometrics once again repositioned the axonometric drawing as one of the primary methods of graphically communicating the design ideas of the contemporary thoughts. Among American architects John Hejduk, Michael Graves, Peter Eisenman, Richard Meier, Bernard Tschumi, and Steven Holl are the pioneers. Most of these architects used axonometric drawings as the primary means to communicate their design ideas in the early stages of their career.

There is no doubt that axonometric drawings have always played an undeniable role in communicating the ideas throughout the history of architectural presentation. Occurrences and reoccurrences of paralines in various forms are noticeable with the change of sociopolitical conditions that have some impact on the built environment whether in the form of fortification or in mere aesthetics.

Since parallel projection is becoming more and more preferable for architectural representation, due to its versatility, flexibility, and capability to show more information in one drawing, it is significant that this type of drawing gets appropriate attention.

There is no doubt that understanding the mechanism of perspective is much more difficult than understanding that of parallel projection. Students always tend to struggle to memorize station point, cone of vision, picture plane, horizon line, and so forth to start a mechanical perspective. It seems that the total understanding of the concept of the perspective projection is not that easy to grasp. Once understood there is a tendency to forget the process if not practiced enough. For studio projects students often end up with unsatisfactory views. In addition to this problem someone needs to be really good in drawing landscaping elements (trees, ground cover, people, etc.) to render a believable environment in the drawing. It is undeniable that students do a superb job on constructing the drawing of the building, but when the time comes for some imaginative freehand work, they are often lost. If the contextual entourage is not drawn properly, the drawing may portray weaknesses of the designer or renderer. The basic advantage of parallel projection from the viewpoint of a designer is that he or she does not need to have

Redrawn by author after original drawing by Theo van Doesburg

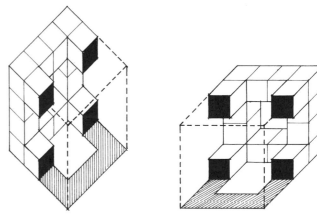

Paraline drawings can combine information that are usually illustrated individually in plan, elevation, and section.

these special skills to produce a drawing that will show the confidence of the renderer, as well as enough information to understand the three-dimensional nature of the project.

Paraline drawings are usually illustrated individually in plan, elevation, and/or section. They are capable of creating a variety of three-dimensional illustrations having different emphasis, using the same plan and elevation/section. This may be done by varying the combination of change of viewpoint and emphasis of the design element. Change of viewpoint refers more to types of paraline, i.e., isometric, elevation-oblige, plan-oblique, whereas emphasis refers to selection of the illustration, i.e., exploded, transparent, and so forth. An effective paraline drawing should consider appropriate combinations of both, for the expression of the specific design work.

Architects generally refer to any paraline drawing as either an "axonometric" or "isometric." These terms are usually used incorrectly, and a specific system of categories has been developed. The nomenclature of existing categories are perhaps overly and unnecessarily complicated with such names as cavalier, cabinet, isometric, dimetric, trimetric, transmetric, axonometric, paraline, and oblique. Since their application can influence the design process to a great extent, some alternative to simplify the basic divisions used in architectural representation may be advisable.

Since architects do not use the process of foreshortenings in their paraline drawings, this book tends to emphasize oblique paraline projections (refer to Chap. 2) over other systems, where actual plan or elevation is used without foreshortening, to produce the three-dimensional paraline. The strength of parallel projection methods as a tool to explore and represent architectural design is represented in Chap. 5.

In addition to explaining types of paralines, step-by-step methods of the construction process, shadow casting, and exploration and emphasis of paralines by improvised methods, this book documents a variety of axonometric drawings and renderings by the leading professionals in the field of architecture.

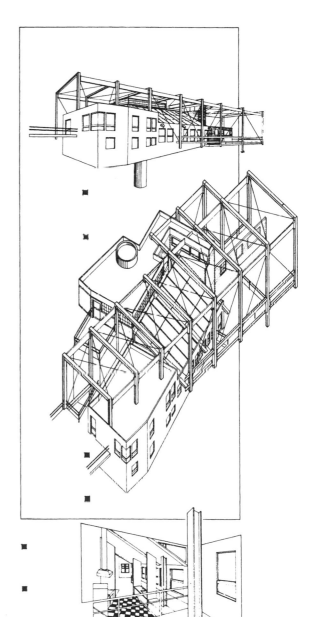

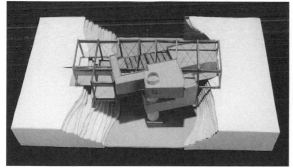 

Dwelling with a bridge. Design represented in models, parallel projection and perspective drawings. Student: Gary Coccoluto. Studio Critic: M. Saleh Uddin

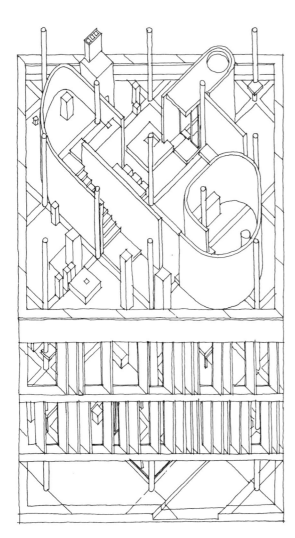

Redrawn by author after original drawing by John Hejduk

Conventions and Construction of Paralines

2.1 Types of Paraline Drawings

Before explaining the axonometric and oblique paralines, it is important to illustrate such drawing types in context with other drawing types and projection systems used to construct them.

All technical drawings are constructed on the basis of a common systems of Projection. The *projection* is the relationship between a point in space and its representation on a selected plane.

The four principal types of projection illustrated in the drawing are:
1. ORTHOGRAPHIC PROJECTION: Plan, Elevation, and Section (Multiview)
2. AXONOMETRIC PROJECTION (PARALINE): Isometric, Dimetric, Trimetric (Single-view)
3. OBLIQUE PROJECTION (PARALINE): Plan Oblique, Elevation Oblique (Single-view)
4. CENTRAL PROJECTION: Perspective (Single-view)

1 and 2

In both multiview projection (1) and axonometric projection (2) the observer is considered to be at infinity, and the visual rays are parallel to each other and perpendicular to the plane of projection.

3

In oblique projection (3), the observer is considered to be at infinity, and the visual rays are parallel to each other but oblique to the plane of projection.

4

In central (perspective) projection (4), the observer is considered to be at a finite distance, and the visual rays form a cone of vision, connecting sight lines from the observer's eye to the various points of the object.

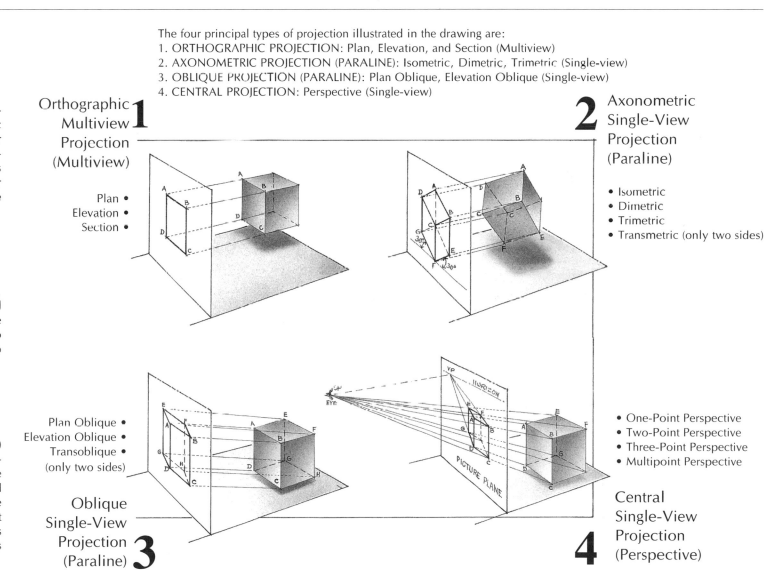

Orthographic Multiview Projection (Multiview) 1

Plan •
Elevation •
Section •

Axonometric Single-View Projection (Paraline) 2

• Isometric
• Dimetric
• Trimetric
• Transmetric (only two sides)

Plan Oblique •
Elevation Oblique •
Transoblique •
(only two sides)

Oblique Single-View Projection (Paraline) 3

• One-Point Perspective
• Two-Point Perspective
• Three-Point Perspective
• Multipoint Perspective

Central Single-View Projection (Perspective) 4

SINGLE-VIEW DRAWING AND PARALLEL PROJECTION

Depending on the nature of the projections all drawings may be divided into two basic categories; 1. multiview drawings and 2. single-view drawings. Plan, elevation, and section drawings are multiview drawings where several coordinated images are necessary to communicate the complete visualization of the object.

Single-view drawings are three-dimensional projections where one drawing illustrates several surfaces of the object, facilitating the understanding of the overall form of the object. *Parallel projection* and *central projection* are the two systems that are capable of portraying the three-dimensional nature of an object. *Axonometric* and *oblique* drawings fall under parallel projection, whereas *perspectives* fall under central projection.

Single-View 3-D Drawing	
Central Projection (Perspective)	**Parallel Projection (Axonometric and Oblique)**

Axonometric

Isometric 1:1:1
Dimetric (any two dimensions adjusted)
Trimetric (all three dimensions adjusted)
Transmetric (shows two sides)

Oblique

Plan Oblique (Planometric)
Elevation Oblique
Transoblique (shows two sides)
(Obliques have options of being Cavalier, General, and Cabinet depending on the foreshortening process)

FORESHORTENING IN PROJECTION

Both the axonometric and oblique projections employ the method of foreshortening in constructing the three-dimensional paraline drawing. In the axonometric projection the object is considered to be in an inclined position resulting in foreshortening of all three axes. In an oblique projection the surface parallel to the picture plane remains to its true size while the other two visible surfaces of the object become foreshortened.

Drawings show a projected line on the picture plane at three different conditions; vertical, parallel, and inclined.

NOTE: While technically all paraline projections employ the method of foreshortening, for simplicity and ease of construction architects and designers do not favor foreshortening of dimensions along the axes.

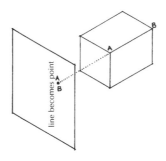

Lines perpendicular to the plane of projection appear as a point

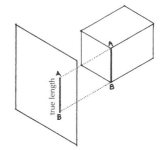

Lines parallel to the plane of projection will appear as their true length

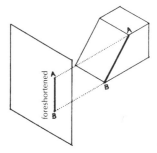

Lines inclined to the plane of projection will appear to be foreshortened

PROJECTIONS OF LINES PERPENDICULAR, PARALLEL, AND INCLINED TO THE PICTURE PLANE

2 . . . . Conventions and Construction of Paralines

2. PARALINE DRAWING

Paralines are single-view, three-dimensional drawings where parallel lines of the object remain parallel and do not converge to vanishing points, as they do in a perspective drawing. Paraline drawings are sometimes referred to as AXONOMETRIC (Greek) or AXIOMETRIC (English) drawings. To be technically correct, axonometrics are one of the two main divisions of paraline drawings. Obliques constitute the other type of paralines. As the name indicates, all divisions of this group use parallel lines to represent the parallel lines of the object.

Paraline drawings offer a suitable alternative to perspective projection for design illustrations and diagrams, where the drawing can easily be constructed entirely with the aid of a set square or adjustable triangle and scale rule using known dimensions. This particular type of drawing can combine information that otherwise would be shown in several drawings. Paralines can combine plan, elevation, and section in one three-dimensional drawing where lines are drawn to a scale. For illustrating the interior information of a building in context to the exterior form or spatial enclosure, paralines provide enough options in their range of types and techniques of presentation. For sketching quick three-dimensional ideas, and analyzing a design by its constituent parts, paralines offer more effective options than other types of drawings.

TECHNICAL NOMENCLATURE OF PARALINE DRAWINGS

Architects and interior designers usually incorrectly refer to any paraline drawing as either an axonometric or an isometric. Even though the divisions of paralines are developed on the basis of mathematical proportion, they may seem overly confusing if not understood well. A wide range of terminologies such as these exists:

    Paraline
    Axonometric
    Oblique
    Isometric
    Dimetric
    Cavalier
    Cabinet
    Military Perspective
    Planometric
    Transmetric
    Transoblique

The specific classification of paralines are based on the variation of angles of axes and foreshortening of dimensions along the axes. A clear subdivision of paralines are shown in the diagram to the right. Clarification of each type is explained in the last section of this chapter.

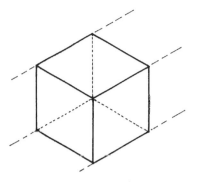
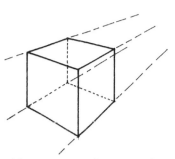

Lines remain parallel to axes in paralines   Lines converge in perspectives

Subdivisions of Paralines	True Plan/ Elevation	Drawing	Foreshor- tening	Main Divisions	
Isometric	No		No	Axonometric	PARALINE
Dimetric	No		Yes	Axonometric	PARALINE
Trimetric	No		Yes	Axonometric	PARALINE
Transmetric	No	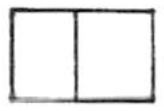	Yes	Axonometric	PARALINE
Plan Oblique	Yes	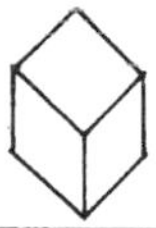	No	Oblique	PARALINE
Elevation Oblique	Yes	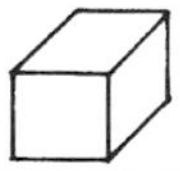	Yes/No	Oblique	PARALINE
Transoblique	Yes/No	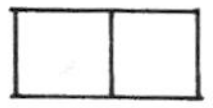	Yes/No	Oblique	PARALINE

Classification of Paralines

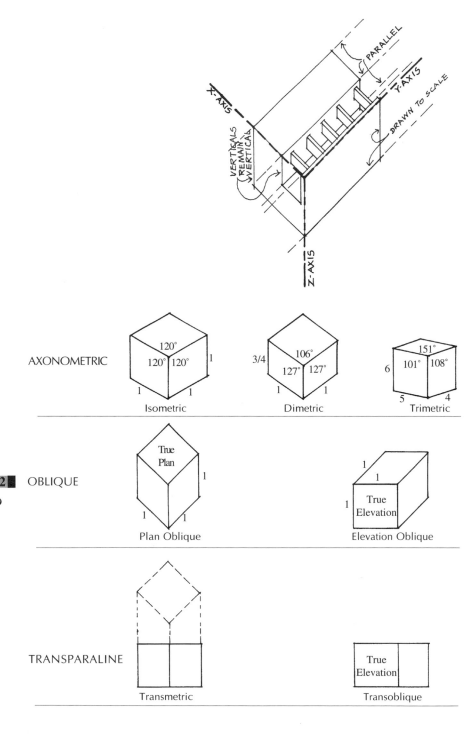

AXONOMETRIC

Isometric — 120° 120° 120° 1 1 1

Dimetric — 3/4 106° 127° 127° 1 1

Trimetric — 151° 6 101° 108° 5 4

OBLIQUE

True Plan — Plan Oblique — 1 1 1

True Elevation — Elevation Oblique — 1 1 1

TRANSPARALINE

Transmetric

True Elevation — Transoblique

FACTORS COMMON TO ALL PARALINE DRAWINGS

• Allparalines include three axes that correlate to width, height, and depth.
• All lines parallel to each other in the object remain parallel to each other in the drawing.
• All lines parallel to the axes can be drawn to scale.
• All vertical lines may be kept vertical.

TYPES OF PARALINE DRAWINGS

By the nature of its projection system paralines may be divided into two basic categories:

1. Axonometric drawing
2. Oblique drawing

TRANSMETRIC and TRANSOBLIQUE are the two types of paralines where two faces of the object are shown, instead of the usual three. They fall under the category of TRANSPARALINE drawing, and usually are not included under three-dimensional paraline types (lacks the third face).

TRANSMETRIC

In a transmetric drawing both visible faces are foreshortened as a result of projections from a rotated plan view. Transmetric drawings are one type of axonometric drawing where the vertical axis is parallel to the picture plane, resulting in a nonexistent view of the third surface.

TRANSOBLIQUE

In a transoblique drawing either the plan or one of the elevations retains its true shape, while the other adjacent side may be foreshortened or left to its full scale. Transoblique drawings are one type of oblique drawing where the receding lines do not create a third axis, resulting in a nonexistent view of the third surface.

TYPES OF PARALINES USED BY ARCHITECTS

The most commonly favored paralines are the ones that use either the actual floor plan or the elevation to construct the three-dimensional drawing, by projecting the scaled drawing to its respective heights or depths. Foreshortening or proportionate reduction of axes is not a common practice by architects and designers. The most commonly used paraline drawings by architects and interior designers (without scale reduction) are:
• Plan Oblique
• Isometric
• Elevation Oblique
These paralines do not require foreshortening of the surfaces.

3. AXONOMETRIC DRAWING

The primary characteristics of axonometric projection is the inclined position of the object with respect to the plane of projection. Since the principal edges are inclined to the plane of projection, the lengths of the lines, the size of the angles, and the general proportions of the object vary in an infinite number of proportions.

The word *axonometric* simply means dimensions along the axes.

AXONOMETRIC DRAWING AND AXONOMETRIC PROJECTION

Axonometric drawing in general may not consider foreshortening of edges since it is not a projected image, whereas axonometric projection refers to the image being foreshortened as a result of inclined and rotated position of the object with respect to the picture plane. Except for the orthographic multiview projection, all other projection systems use foreshortening in order to illustrate the three-dimensional nature of the object (refer to the section on Projection Systems discussed earlier). But for convenience, foreshortening is not being practiced in axonometrics and obliques for buildings and other complex objects.

DEFINITION OF AXONOMETRIC

[Greek: *axon* means axis + *E* means metric]
being or prepared by the projection of objects on the drawing surface so that they appear inclined with three sides showing and with horizontal and vertical distances drawn to scale but, diagonal and curved lines distorted. (Webster's Ninth New Collegiate Dictionary, 1991)

Axonometric (adjective)
Designating a method of projection (axonometric projection) in which a three-dimensional object is represented by a drawing (axonometric drawing) having all axes drawn to exact scale, resulting in the optional distortion of diagonals and curves.
(The Random House Dictionary of the English Language, 2nd Edition, Unabridged, 1983)

Axonometric Projection
The representation on a single plane (as a drawing surface) of a three-dimensional object placed at an angle to the plane of projection.
(Webster's Third New International Dictionary, 1986)

TYPES OF AXONOMETRIC DRAWING

Depending upon the number of foreshortening of proportions, axonometric drawings are classified into the following three divisions:
1. Isometric
2. Dimetric (Symmetrical and Unsymmetrical)
3. Trimetric

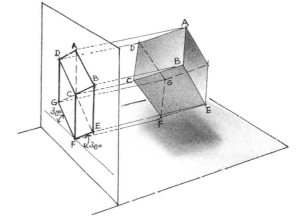

Axonometric   Projection

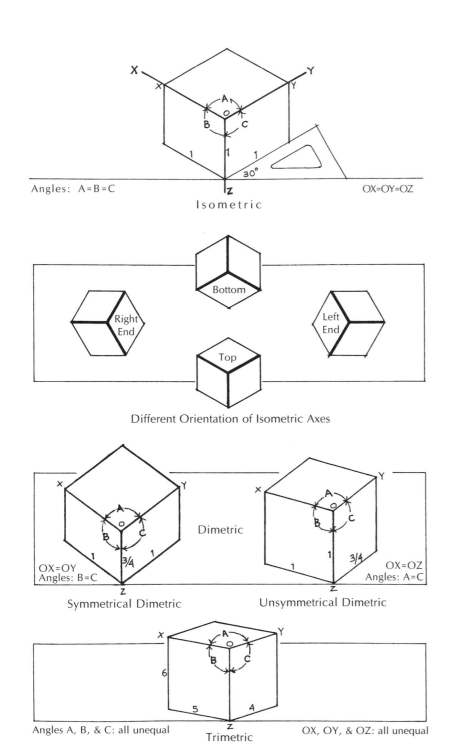

Angles: A=B=C   OX=OY=OZ

Isometric

Different Orientation of Isometric Axes

Dimetric

OX=OY
Angles: B=C

Symmetrical Dimetric

OX=OZ
Angles: A=C

Unsymmetrical Dimetric

Angles A, B, & C: all unequal   OX, OY, & OZ: all unequal

Trimetric

4. ISOMETRIC

The word *isometric* means equal measure. Isometric is a type of axonometric projection where the object is tilted in such a way that all the three axes create equal angles with the picture plane, the resultant drawing having 120-degree angles between all three axes at the front corner. The axes of the object may be oriented differently to create the desired effect as long as the angles are spaced 120 degrees with each other.

Iso means equal. *Metric* means pertaining to distance. Thus, a definition of *isometric* would be: designating a method of projection (isometric projection) in which a three-dimensional object is represented by a drawing (isometric drawing) having the horizontal edges of the object usually drawn at a 30-degree angle and all verticals projected perpendicularly from a horizontal base, all lines being drawn to scale.

Characteristics of an isometric drawing:
• All three visible surfaces have equal emphasis.
• All lengths are true lengths, but not the shapes. There is no foreshortening of proportions.
• Orthographic plans and elevations cannot be used.
• Receding lines are drawn in 30-degree angles making it possible to use a 30-degree/60-degree triangle to construct the drawing.

5. DIMETRIC

In a dimetric drawing the object is turned so that two of its axes make the same angle and the third axis makes a different angle with the picture plane. Depending on the orientation of the angles, such types may be catagorized into symmetrical dimetric and unsymmetrical dimetric.

Characteristics of a dimetric drawing:
• Two of the adjacent surfaces have equal emphasis.
• Foreshortening in proportion is used to minimize apparent distortion.
• Orthographic plans and elevations cannot be used.

6. TRIMETRIC

In a trimetric drawing the object is turned so that all three axes make different angles with the picture plane.

Characteristics of a trimetric drawing:
• All three adjacent surfaces have unequal emphasis.
• Foreshortening in proportion (all three sides) is used to minimize distortion.
• Orthographic plans and elevations cannot be used.

7. OBLIQUE DRAWING

In an oblique drawing, one set of planes of the object is always presented in its true shape. From these true shapes, parallel lines are drawn at any angle to represent the perpendiculars to those true planes. All planes parallel to the picture plane retain their true shape and are drawn at the same scale. An oblique drawing is based on an orthographic view of one plane of a building or object, usually the plan or a facade, and an oblique view of the space behind.

Oblique drawings are a result of oblique projection, where an observer is considered to be at an infinite distance and looking toward the object in such a way that the projectors are parallel to each other and oblique to the plane of projection. The resulting drawing is an oblique projection. As a common rule one of the principal faces remains parallel to the plane of projection, making it identical to a plan or elevation.

The biggest advantage of such a drawing is that it uses a true plan or an elevation to produce the three-dimensional oblique view.

Oblique drawing is divided into two major divisions:
1. Plan oblique: Actual plan projected upward, downward, or in an angle.
2. Elevation oblique: Actual elevation projected in an angle or upward.

ANGLES OF RECEDING LINES IN OBLIQUES

The receding lines may be drawn at any convenient angle. Examples of obliques with the receding lines drawn in various angles are shown in the illustration to the right. The angle that should be selected will depend on the shape, feature of the object, and the surface to be empasized.

FORESHORTENING OF RECEDING LINES IN OBLIQUES

Our eyes are accustomed to seeing objects with all receding parallel lines appearing to converge. An oblique without foreshortening may often present apparent degrees of distortion in its proportions. Usually when receding lines are drawn in full length, they seem to appear too long and to diverge toward the rear of the object. Varying degrees of foreshortening of the receding lines are available to minimize the distortion of an oblique drawing.

Foreshortening in oblique drawings is not usually practiced by architects for two reasons:
1. It consumes more time since conversion of scale is required.
2. True dimensions are not retained.

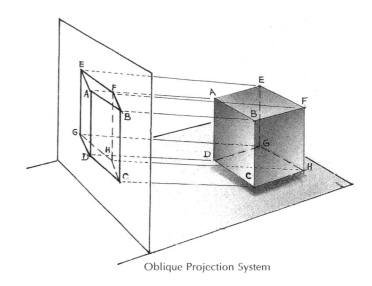

Oblique Projection System

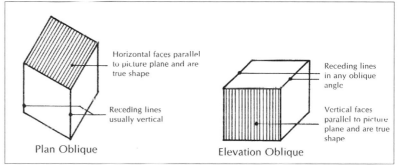

Horizontal faces parallel to picture plane and are true shape

Receding lines usually vertical

Plan Oblique

Receding lines in any oblique angle

Vertical faces parallel to picture plane and are true shape

Elevation Oblique

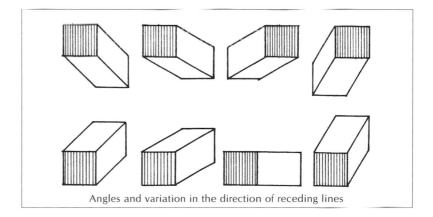

Angles and variation in the direction of receding lines

SCALE OF RECEDING LINES;
CAVALIER, GENERAL, AND CABINET TYPES

When the receding lines maintain their true length in an oblique drawing the drawing is called a *cavalier oblique*. As a historical reference it may be mentioned that cavalier projections are noticeable in the drawings of medieval fortification.

When the receding lines are foreshortened three-quarters of their true lengths the oblique drawing is called a *general oblique*.

When the receding lines are drawn to half size, the oblique drawing is generally called a *cabinet oblique*. The term may be attributed to the early use of this type of oblique drawing in the furniture industries. Cabinet oblique is more commonly associated with elevation oblique drawing.

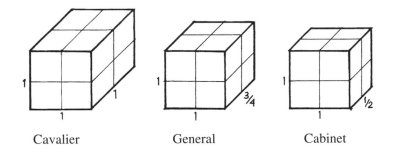

Cavalier   General   Cabinet

USE OF OBLIQUE DRAWING

- Obliques are the type of paralines most commonly used by architects. They offer the distinct advantage of drawing one principal face of the building or object in true scale.
- Any complex shapes, circles, ellipses, or arcs can be drawn in true shape if they are in the principal plane.
- Orthographic drawings such as site plan, roof plan, floor plan, elevation, and section can be used as the principal surface from which obliques can be projected.
- Obliques can successfully illustrate the overall volumetric aspects ranging from object design to large scale urban design.
- Longer sides of the objects are not recommended to be placed along the direction of the receding lines since they may appear distorted.

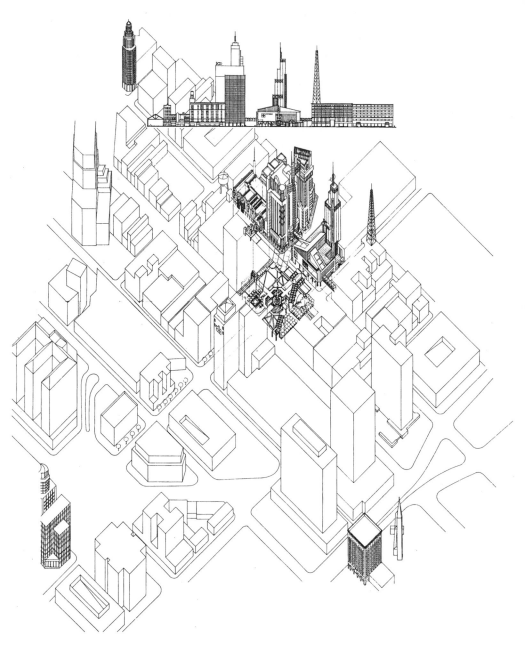

Use of plan oblique drawing in a large-scale urban design proposal. Site plan projected upward to produce 45-degree/45-degree plan oblique. Drawing illustrates new design proposal for urban revitalization within the context of existing city blocks. Courtesy: M. Saleh Uddin.

8. PLAN OBLIQUE

In a plan oblique drawing, the plan view of an object or building retains its true size and shape. The drawn building plan can be used directly to construct the paraline. Usually the plan is tilted at a desirable angle and the wall planes are projected vertically upward or downward to their respective heights. For convenience and to save time 45-degree/45-degree or 30-degree/60-degree obliques are the most common ones favored by architects and designers. Shapes that are on planes parallel to the plan surface retain their true shape and size.

The desired appearance of a plan oblique will depend on three factors:

1. Orientation of the plan
2. Angle or direction of the receding lines
3. The ratio of foreshortening for vertical planes

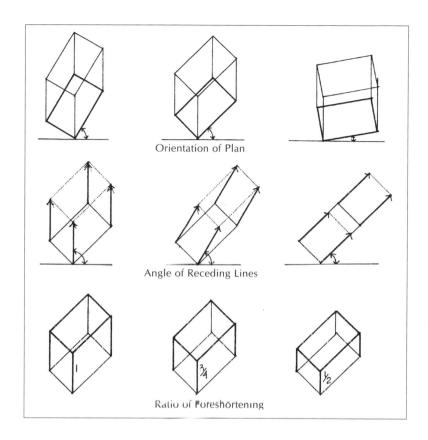

Orientation of Plan

Angle of Receding Lines

Ratio of Foreshortening

9. ELEVATION OBLIQUE

In an elevation oblique drawing, the orthographic elevation view of an object or building retains its true size and shape. The drawn elevation can be used directly to construct the paraline. Usually one of the elevations forms the front vertical wall, and receding lines at desirable angles form other adjacent surfaces. For convenience and to save time, receding lines are usually drawn at 30-degrees, 45-degrees, 60-degrees, or 90-degrees.

The desired appearance of an elevation oblique will depend on two factors:

1. The angle or direction of the receding lines.
2. The ratio of foreshortening between the true elevation and the receding planes.

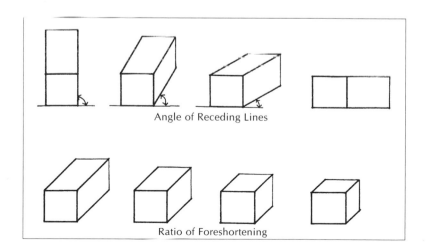

Angle of Receding Lines

Ratio of Foreshortening

10. ILLUSTRATIVE COMPARISON OF AXONOMETRIC TYPES

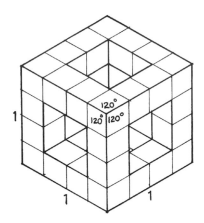

ISOMETRIC

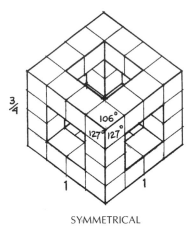

SYMMETRICAL

UNSYMMETRICAL

DIMETRIC

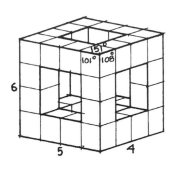

TRIMETRIC

Isometric projection is a form of axono-metric projection where all three visible surfaces are given equal importance. The object is turned so that all three axis lines are at the same angle with the picture plane. Dimensions of height, width, and depth remain constant in the ratio of 1:1:1. All circles and arcs lying in the faces become elliptical. Because of the change of angles, true plan or elevation cannot be used.

Dimetric projection is an axonometric projection and a modified form of isometric, where any two dimensions of height, width, or depth are adjusted to create greater realism, usually in the ratio of 2:2:1 or 3/4:1:1. The object is turned so that two of its axes make the same angle and the third axis makes a different angle with the picture plane. All circles and arcs lying in the faces become elliptical. Because of the change of angles true plan or elevation cannot be used.

SYMMETRICAL

Symmetrical dimetric is similar to isometric where both sides are drawn at the same angle. The difference is that the object is either tilted backward to show less of the top or tilted forward more than isometric in order to show a greater amount of the top. The object may be tilted forward or backward as much as desired. The drawn object should be symmetrical to the vertical axis.

UNSYMMETRICAL

Unsymmetrical dimetric is turned in such a way that either of the two visible sides can be given a larger or smaller area than the other. The drawn object is not symmetrical on the vertical axis.

Trimetric is an axonometric projec-tion and a modified form of isometric, where all three dimensions of height, width, or depth are adjusted to create greater realism, usually in the ratio of 6:5:4. All circles and arcs lying in the faces become elliptical. Because of the change of angles, actual plan or elevation cannot be used.

The object is placed in such a way that no two axes make equal angles with the plane of projection. Each of the three axes and lines parallel to them, respectively, create different ratios of foreshortening when pro-jected to the plane of projection. If a drawing has three unequal axes and none of the angles are less than 90 degrees, and if it is neither an isomet-ric nor a dimetric, the result will be a trimetric projection.

2 . . .Conventions and Construction of Paralines

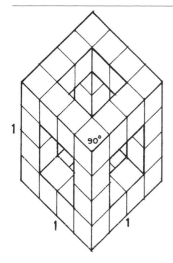

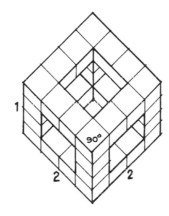

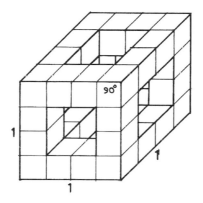

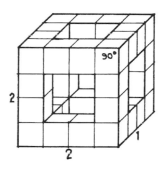

PLAN OBLIQUE, 1:1:1
(Full Scale)
PLANOMETRIC
CAVALIER

PLAN OBLIQUE, 1:2:2
(Reduced Vertical Scale)
MILITARY PERSPECTIVE
CABINET

ELEVATION OBLIQUE, 1:1:1
(Full Scale)
CAVALIER

ELEVATION OBLIQUE, 2:2:1
(Reduced Oblique Scale)
CABINET

Plan oblique or planometric is a modified form of scale plan, where the plan is rotated to a suitable angle and the elevations or side planes are projected vertically. Dimensions of height, width, and depth remain constant in the ratio of 1:1:1. The main advantage of this type of oblique is the use of actual plan to construct the three dimensional drawing.

All circles and arcs lying in the vertical planes become elliptical, but retain their true shape in horizontal planes or in plans.

Reduced vertical scale plan oblique or military perspective is a modified form of 1:1:1 plan oblique, where vertical dimensions are reduced to give a greater realism. Usually the dimensions of height, width, and depth are drawn in the ratio of 1:2:2.

All circles and arcs lying in the vertical planes become elliptical, but retain their true shape in horizontal planes or in plans.

Elevation oblique is a modified form of scale elevation, where the principal surface becomes the true elevation and is drawn parallel to the picture plane. The adjacent planes are projected obliquely at any suitable angle. A full scale elevation oblique or cavalier oblique is drawn in the ratio of 1:1:1 for the height, width, and depth.

All circles and arcs lying in the receding planes become elliptical, but retain their true shape in vertical planes.

Reduced elevation oblique is a modified form of full scale elevation oblique where oblique dimensions are reduced to give a greater realism. Usually the dimensions of height, width, and depth are drawn in the ratio of 2:2:1. In the cabinet or elevation oblique the principal surface becomes the true elevation and is drawn parallel to the picture plane. The adjacent planes are projected obliquely at any suitable angle, foreshortening to half of the full scale.

All circles and arcs lying in the receding planes become elliptical, but retain their true shape in vertical planes.

CAVALIER, GENERAL, AND CABINET (applies for both plan and elevation oblique)
In cavalier obliques, the receding axes are drawn in full scale.
In general oblique, the receding axes are usually foreshortened to three-quarters of full scale.
In cabinet oblique, the receding axes are drawn to half of full scale.

2.2 Construction of Paraline Drawings

1. OPTIONS FOR PARALINE CONSTRUCTION

All architectural drawings are produced to serve specific purposes. Since paralines give a variety of viewpoint options, it must be decided beforehand what the construction of the drawing intends to show. Paraline drawings provide more options of desired viewpoints to communicate design information than any other drawing type that is used in architectural design presentation. Following are some of the options that may be used for construction of a paraline drawing to suit some specific purpose.

1. Overall building form and exterior configuration by constructing a down-view paraline.

2. Overall building form and interior configuration by constructing an up-view paraline.

3. Building details by drawing specific elements in a larger scale with appropriate details.

4. Highlight both interior and exterior by:
   a) taking the roof off.
   b) cut-away of specific areas to access the interior elements, keeping the exterior profile.
   c) showing a vertical section cut.
   d) removing walls or making them transparent.
   e) separating the building shell or enclosure from the plan footprint.

5. Relationship of components by:
   a) exploding upward to illustrate various floors and their vertical relationships.
   b) exploding both upward and to the side to show components and their relationships.

6. Illustrating both the interior and exterior in two segments by splitting the structure into two parts. This split may be a vertical or horizontal section cut.

7. Progression from floor plan to interior spaces to the overall building can be illustrated by constructing a series of paralines at sequential heights. Each drawing successively builds upon the preceding one.

8. Sequential rotational views to illustrate all sides of a building by constructing a series of paralines from various viewpoints.

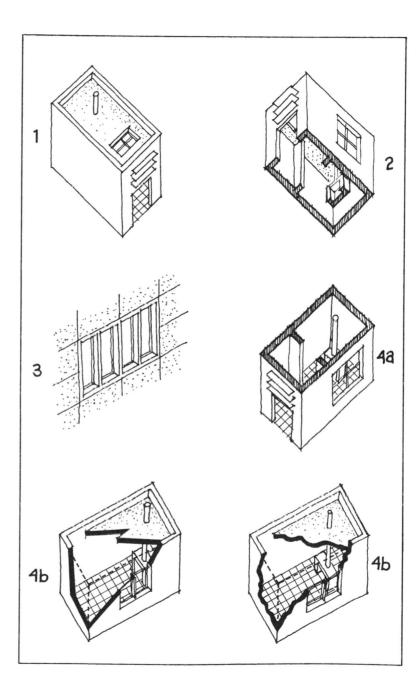

OPTIONS FOR PARALINE CONSTRUCTION

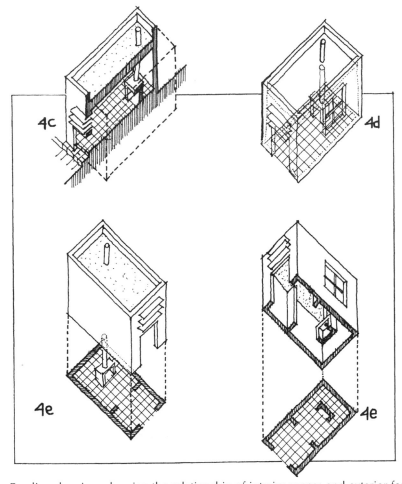

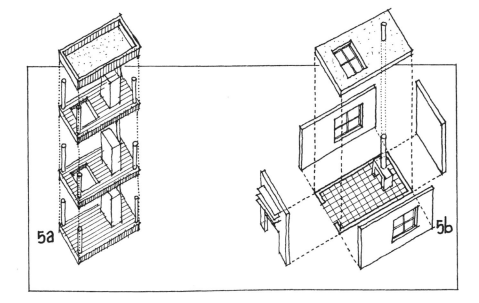

Paraline drawings showing the relationship of interior spaces and exterior form.

Top left: Vertical cut to illustrate building section, interior spaces, and exterior form.

Top right: Transparent exterior walls to illustrate interiors within the total form.

Bottom left: Building shell pulled upward to illustrate plan footprint and exterior form viewed from above.

Bottom right: Building shell pulled upward to illustrate plan footprint and exterior form viewed from below (looking up into the interior spaces).

Exploded paraline drawings showing the relationship of components.

Above left: Exploded upward to illustrate various floors and their vertical relationships.

Above right: Exploded upward and to the side to illustrate the components and their relationships.

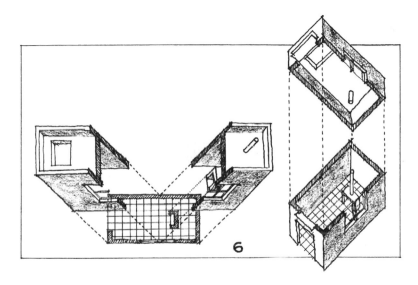

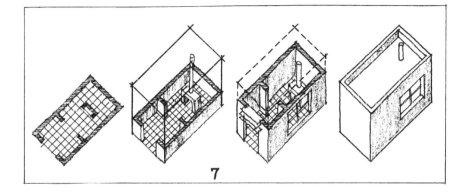

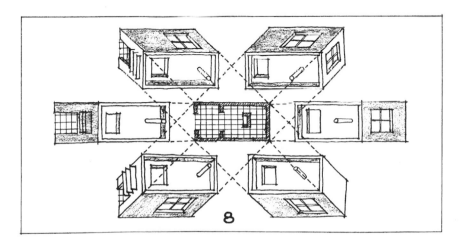

Above: Splitting the building into two halves (with vertical or horizontal cuts) and arranging each half in relationship with the other half to illustrate both interior and exterior.

Right: Progression from floor plan to overall form to illustrate various elements of the structure.

Above right: Sequential rotational views to illustrate various facades of the structure.

2. PARALINE PROJECTION AT VARIOUS ANGLES

The final three-dimensional view of any paraline drawing will mainly depend on the orientation of the plan to the T-square, and angle of receding lines representing the vertical lines of the object. The following sketches show a variety of paraline views that are a result of change of plan orientation, and projection angles of receding lines.

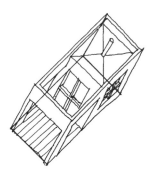
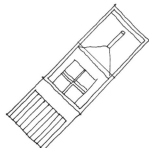
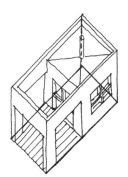
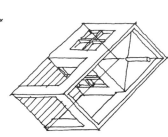

- Plan orientation remains same
- Projection lines for vertical elements at various angles (1 through 4)

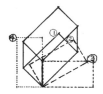

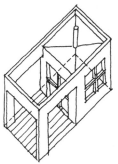

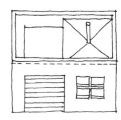

- Plan orientation (1 through 4) at various angles
- All projection lines for vertical elements are drawn vertical

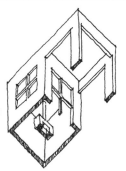
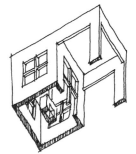
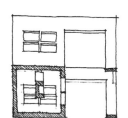
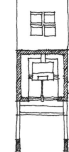

- Plan orientation (1 through 4) at various angles
- All projection lines for vertical elements are drawn vertical
- Creates worm's-eye view when two main vertical planes showing the exterior are constructed at the back corner of the plan

2 . . . Conventions and Construction of Paralines

3. STEP-BY-STEP CONSTRUCTION OF PARALINE DRAWINGS

PLAN OBLIQUE CONSTRUCTION

A basic manual procedure for producing a simple plan oblique drawing is shown in sequence in the left column of the adjacent drawings. In this case a basic rectangular volume can be constructed directly over the true plan, by the method of projecting the plan upward to its finished elevation height.

The plan should be placed on the drawing board and rotated to any desired angle. The plan is taped down, and a fresh sheet of tracing paper is laid over it, orienting its edges to the T-square.

Vertical line (1) is drawn on the new tracing paper at the nearest corner to the observer and the exact height of the object is marked on the vertical line. With an adjustable triangle, starting at the marked point, a line is drawn (2) that runs parallel to the plan edge. A vertical line (3) is drawn at the next corner to reach the line just drawn to construct the side of the object.

The other three sides of the object are constructed, repeating the same procedure to produce the final drawing.

ISOMETRIC CONSTRUCTION

Isometrics cannot be constructed from a true rectangular plan because of the obligatory 30-degree angles with the T-square on both sides, and thus require reconstruction of the plan. A 30-degree/60-degree triangle is essential for such drawings.

First the plan is redrawn (as shown in the adjacent right-hand column, top drawing), making adjacent edges of the front corner 30-degree angles with the T-square. This will make the corner of the object create a 120-degree angle, instead of a true 90-degree corner.

Once the plan is drawn, then the similar steps of a plan oblique construction need to be followed in order to create the final isometric of the object.

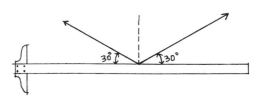
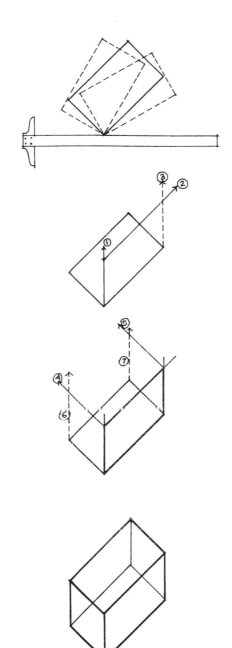
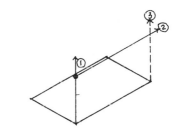
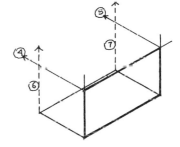
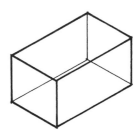

Plan Oblique Construction

Isometric Construction

STEP-BY-STEP CONSTRUCTION OF A PLAN OBLIQUE DRAWING

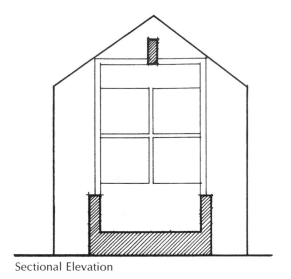

Sectional Elevation

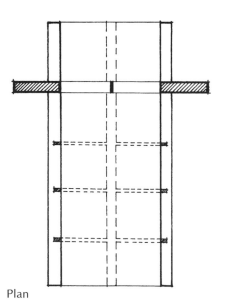

Plan

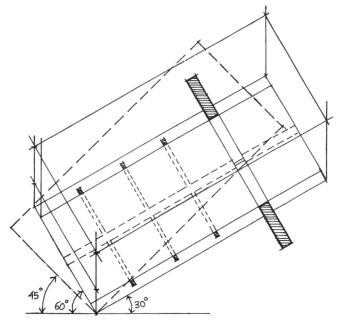

Plan may be placed at any suitable angle. In this case the plan is oriented at 30-degree/60-degree with the T-square. The basic box is constructed using the heights from the given elevation drawing.

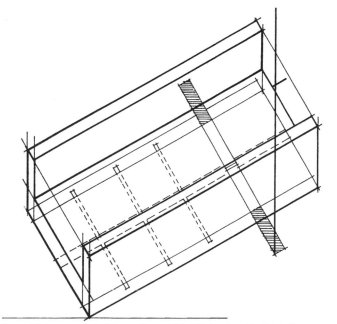

Floor thickness and side walls are highlighted with thick lines.

A plan oblique drawing can easily be constructed from a given floor plan and elevation drawing that are both drawn to a particular scale.

This page and the following two pages illustrate plan oblique construction of an architectural structure composed of several elements; a floor element, a wall plane, an overhead beam, and framework supporting the overhead beam. For such structures it is recommended that elements should be constructed one at a time.

The floor element:
The plan is placed at a suitable angle to the T-square (in this case, 30-degree/60-degree angles).

As shown in the sectional elevation, the floor is a U-shaped element with an expressed thickness of its floor and side walls. The top drawing on the right shows construction of the basic box for the floor and side walls. A vertical line is drawn at the front corner of the plan and the height for the floor and the side walls are marked on the line, measuring from the elevation.

The drawing on the bottom right shows thicknesses of the side walls and floor slab, highlighted with heavier lines.

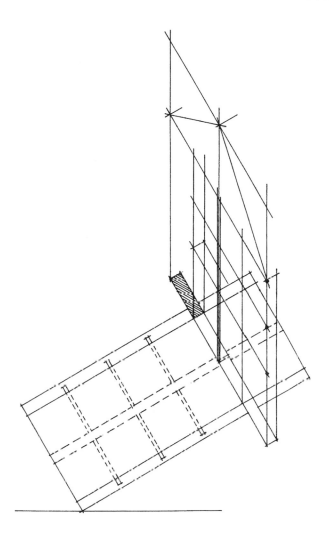

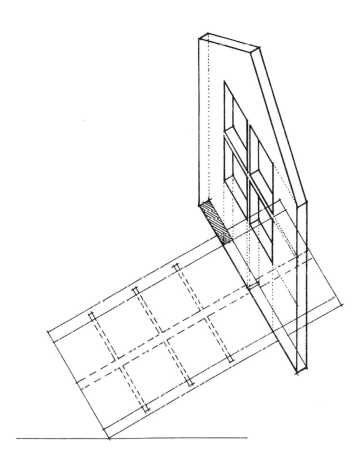

The wall plane:

The wall in the plan is projected vertically upward to its intended heights. As shown in the sectional elevation, the wall plane has a gable top, and four square openings in the middle. A basic rectangle is constructed first for the entire wall. The bottom height of the gable end and the peak at the middle are marked. The window locations are projected from the plan to construct the basic outline.

The depth of the window openings are added, and the wall is drawn with thickened lines. The dotted lines shown in the drawing above are projection lines from plan and height lines from the elevation that are used to determine the final window openings.

STEP-BY-STEP CONSTRUCTION OF A PLAN OBLIQUE DRAWING

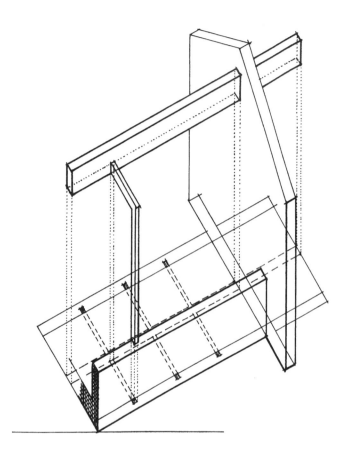

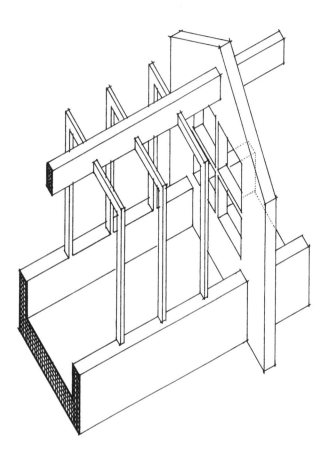

The overhead beam and framework:

For constructing a paraline of the beam, all four corners of the beam in the plan are projected upward to its respective bottom and top portions in space. The intersecting points of the beam and the upright wall plane are found by projecting the intersecting points in the plan upward until they cut the beam. For constructing the framework, points on the plan are projected upward to their intended height, and the portion within the side wall is deducted. The intersecting points of the frame with the beam are projected up from the plan to the horizontal piece of the frame. The same procedure is followed to construct the rest of the framework.

This final drawing shows all the elements of the structure in place that are constructed individually from the same plan. When two elements intersect each other, the intersecting edges in the paraline must be the result of the projection from the intersection points in plan.

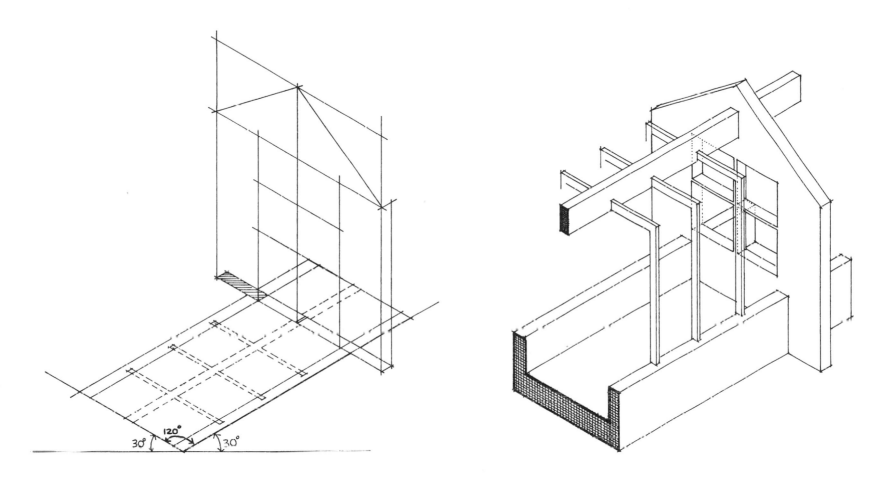

To construct an isometric of the same structure, a similar procedure is followed, except in this case the true plan could not be used. As shown in the above left drawing, the floor plan was reconstructed using 30-degree angles on both sides for the two major axial lines. The inside front corner of the plan creates a 120-degree angle instead of the 90-degree in the true plan. All other components of the plan are added to complete the reconstruction of the plan. Once the plan is redrawn all plan elements are extended vertically upward to their respective heights to construct the three-dimensional isometric drawing. Similar to the plan oblique drawing components of the structure are constructed individually and intersecting lines are found from their respective plan location.

Plans

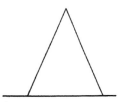

Elevations

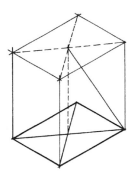

Isometric
Pyramid

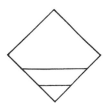

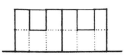

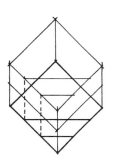

Plan oblique
Cubic solid with recession

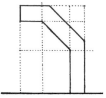

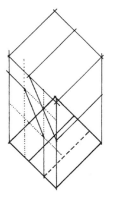

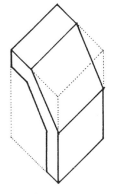

Plan oblique
Solid with inclined surfaces

4. CONSTRUCTION OF SOLIDS

Solid objects can be constructed from a true plan or from a reconstructed plan, when the elevation is given or the height is known.

Pyramid in isometric:

The plan was redrawn using 30-degree angles on both sides of the front corner. An enclosing box was made and the peak of the pyramid was found. Connecting the peak to all four corners of the base created the final isometric of the pyramid.

Cubic solid with recession in plan oblique:

The true plan was projected and the box was drawn. Lines for the recessed portion of the cube in the plan was projected upward to get the vertical slices of the recession. The depth of the recession was measured in elevation and transferred in the plan oblique drawing. Dashed lines in the elevation and in the final plan oblique are a reference to the vertical and horizontal limits of the recession.

Solid with inclined surfaces in plan oblique:

The true plan was projected and the enclosing box was drawn. Points where the vertical and horizontal plane change direction were marked in the elevation and transferred to the plan oblique box. Drawings show dotted lines to mark surface changes. Connecting end points where the surface becomes inclined and turns back to the horizontal or vertical sides, created the inclined planes in the plan oblique drawing.

2 ... Conventions and Construction of Paralines

Solid objects with intersections can be constructed from a true plan or from a reconstructed plan, when the location of intersection in the plan and the height in the elevation are known.

Two intersecting walls in plan oblique:

The true plan at 30-degree/60-degree with T-square was projected upward to construct the plan oblique drawing. The dotted lines 1, 2, 3, and 4 were marked on the larger wall (A) to demark the rectangular opening. Line 4 also is the intersecting line where planes A and B pass through each other. The plane B was projected upward from the ground plan using the bottom and top heights from the elevation. Thickness of plane B was added to complete the drawing.

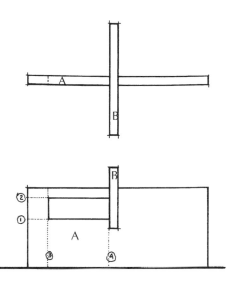

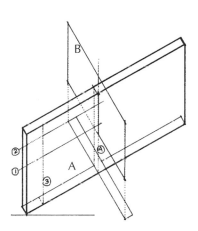

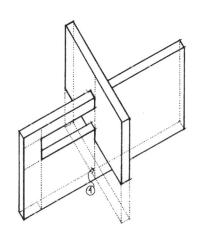

Intersection of a plane with an inclined solid in plan oblique:

The true plan at 30-degree/60-degree was projected and the enclosing box was drawn for the solid with the inclined surface. The inclined plane was found by connecting the beginning point at the ground and the end point on the roof. 'A' is the point on the ground where the wall plane intersected the inclined surface. Drawing a line (AB) parallel to the inclined edges through the point 'A' created the edge where the intersection occurred. The wall plane was projected upward from the plan to its respective height. Line AB was cut at B, C, and D by the height lines of the wall with the opening. Lines 4 and 5 indicate the location of the opening that was projected from the plan to find the vertical edges of the opening on the wall.

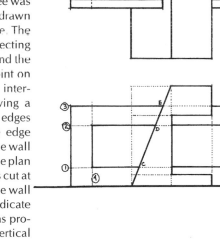

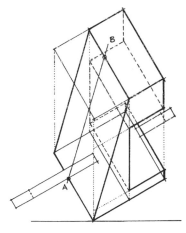

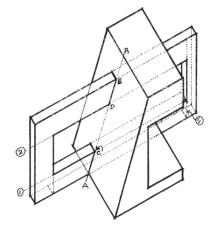

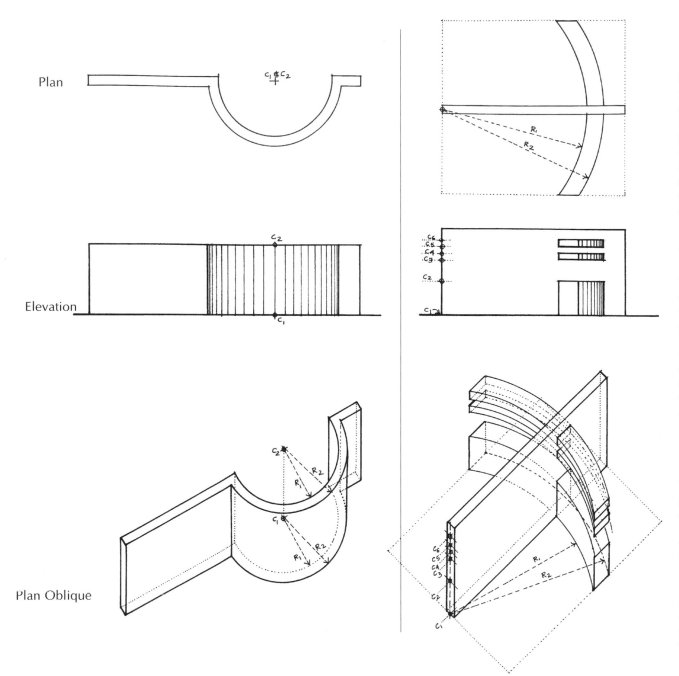

Plan

Elevation

Plan Oblique

6. CONSTRUCTION OF CURVILINEAR PLANES

Planes with curves can be constructed from a true plan by projecting the true shape of the curve upward to its known height. It is recommended that the complex shapes and curvilinear forms remain in their true shape in an oblique drawing. For instance, if a complex shape occurs in elevation, it is convenient to construct an elevation oblique so that the shape may retain its true form.

Wall with circular curve in plan oblique:

The true plan of the wall with the half circular curve was placed at 30-degree/60-degree with T-square. The plan was projected upward to its elevation height. Point C1, center of the circular curve on the ground (with R1 and R2 being the radii of inner and outer arc), was projected upward to point C2 as the new center with which to draw the top surface of the inner and outer curve.

Intersection of flat and curvilinear planes:

The true plan at 45-degree/45-degree was projected upward for both the flat and curved planes to construct the plan oblique drawing. The flat wall was drawn first, and the centers for the curves (C1 through C6) were marked on the height line of the wall. Using the radii R1(inner radius) and R2 (outer radius) from the plan, arcs were drawn to construct the curvilinear planes. The intersecting points of flat wall and curved planes in the plan were projected upward to locate intersecting edges in the plan oblique drawing.

PLANS

ELEVATIONS

Lines that are not parallel to any of the three major paraline axes will not have true length. Such nonaxial lines cannot be measured at their true scale. Rectangular forms or enclosing boxes following axes directions need to be constructed to offset the dimensions of the inclined lines. Inclined lines can be found by plotting the beginning and end points on the constructed form (or box) and by connecting respective points.

A grided rectangle was created on the elevation to block in the primary horizontal, vertical, and inclined lines. The same grid was drawn in paraline to construct the final shape of the object.

An enclosing box was created for this wedge-shaped block. Dimensions were transferred from plan and elevation to the enclosing box to construct the final shape.

An enclosing box was created and dimensions were transferred from plan and elevation to construct the larger volume. The intersecting wall plane was drawn to its elevation height from the floor plan.

An enclosing box with guide lines (parallel to axes) running through the beginning and end of inclined lines were created. Dimensions were transferred to the paraline construction to create the final drawing.

7. INCLINED SURFACES IN PARALINES

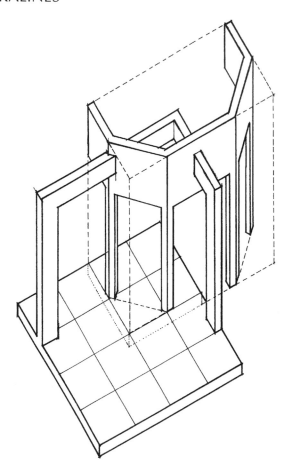

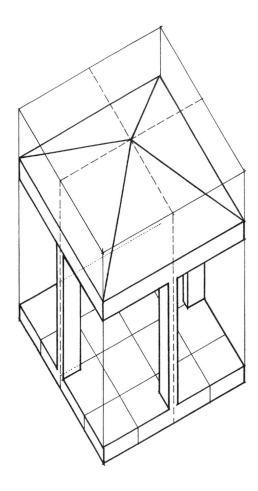

The drawing on the above left locates angular planes by constructing a rectangular block, and connecting the end points of true-shaped planes along the sides of the constructed block. In a plan oblique drawing the angular lines in paraline remain unchanged in dimension from its plan. In an isometric drawing the change of dimension will occur, since the shape of the plan does not remain in its true shape.

The drawing on the above right shows construction of inclined surfaces for a roof structure in plan oblique drawing. The peak of the roof was found by extending the base of the roof to its peak height to form a cubical form. Connecting the center of the cube (peak of the roof) to all four corners of the roof base creates the final form of the inclined roof planes.

8. CIRCLES AND ELLIPSES IN PARALINES

Circles in paraline drawing appear as circles only when they are in true shape planes. This usually occurs in oblique drawings, where one of the front surfaces is parallel to the picture plane. In all other visible planes in an oblique drawing circles will appear as true ellipses. Circles will always appear as ellipses in all isometric and dimetric drawings.

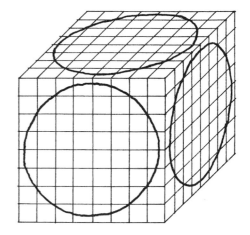

Offset Method
Circles, circular arcs, and other free-form shapes may be drawn by offset measurements as shown for a cube. The offsets are first drawn on the plane which is in true shape and scale. Then these lines are transferred to the oblique sides. In this drawing the sides are drawn at a reduced scale. In such a drawing the offset measurements must be drawn to the same reduced scale as the sides. The final shape is drawn by plotting all offsets on the sides.

Four-Center Method

Using a compass or circle template, the four-center method may be employed to construct an ellipse close enough to suit most purposes.

The circumscribing square is drawn first in paraline.

At the midpoints of each side of the oblique square, perpendiculars are drawn and extended until they intersect at C1, C2, C3, and C4.

With C1, C2, C3, and C4 as centers and with R1, R3, R2, and R4 being their respective radii (R1=R3 and R2=R4), four segments of arcs (two sets) are drawn to form the final ellipse.

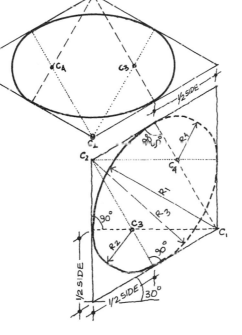

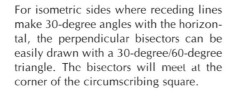

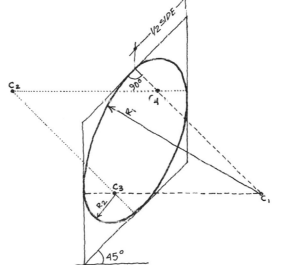

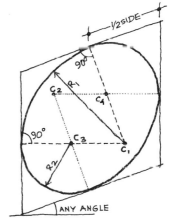

For isometric sides where receding lines make 30-degree angles with the horizontal, the perpendicular bisectors can be easily drawn with a 30-degree/60-degree triangle. The bisectors will meet at the corner of the circumscribing square.

The bisectors meet farther away when the receding lines make a greater than 30-degree angle with the horizontal line. The perpendicular bisectors can be easily drawn with a 45-degree/45-degree triangle if the receding lines are at a 45-degree with the horizontal.

The bisectors meet within the circumscribing square when the receding lines make a less than 30-degree angle with the horizontal line.

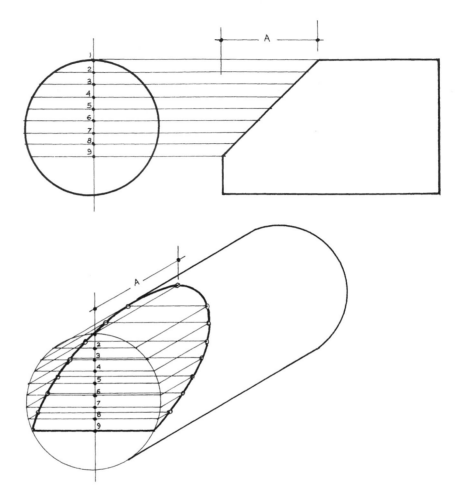

INCLINED ELLIPSE IN PARALINES

Drawing an ellipse in a plane inclined to the plane of projection is shown in the illustration above using offset dimensions. A number of parallel lines are drawn on the front elevation and extended to cut the sloped plane of the side elevation to represent imaginary cutting planes that run horizontally between the front face of the cylinder and the inclined surface.

Using the given orthographic front and side elevation, the object is drawn as a full cylinder without the inclined plane. Since the front is a true circle, all cutting planes 2 through 9 can be drawn in true scale at the front face of the cylinder. These cutting planes are extended in oblique to the back of their respective dimensions to form the shape of the elliptical plane.

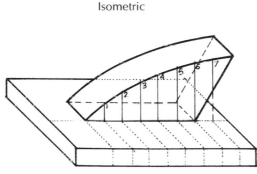

9. IRREGULAR OBJECTS IN PARALINES

Plan

Isometric

Elevation

Elevation Oblique

CURVES IN ISOMETRIC AND ELEVATION OBLIQUE

For ease of construction, complex shapes may be drawn on the plane of the paraline that is parallel to the picture plane. Plan oblique and elevation oblique drawings often can be drawn that way. In an isometric or other type of axonometric drawing the curve or an irregular shape will not retain its true shape.

ISOMETRIC
An irregular object may be drawn by creating a series of sections as shown in the isometric drawing. The drawing (top right) shows a total of seven cutting planes that created a wireframe shape of the curved form on its platform. Imaginary planes are constructed in the isometric drawing by means of offset dimensions from the plan and elevation drawing. The shape is completed by drawing lines connecting corners of all imaginary sections.

ELEVATION OBLIQUE
Since the irregular curved shape appears in its true configuration only in elevation, it is fairly simple to construct the elevation oblique drawing. The curved shape is drawn first in true elevation. Depth is added along the receding lines to create the shape of the curved form. Base is added by means of measuring offset dimensions. The illustrated drawing (bottom right) does not show foreshortening along the receding lines.

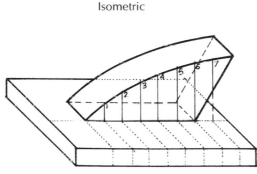

10. STRAIGHT-RUN AND DOUBLE-FLIGHT STAIRCASES

11TH STEP HEIGHT

LANDING

INTERMEDIATE PLATFORM

TOP LANDING HEIGHT

LANDING HEIGHT

20 19 18 17 16 15 14 13 12 11

10 9 8 7 6 5 4 3 2 1

FIRST STEP HEIGHT

60° 30°

Constructing plan oblique paralines for straight-run and double-flight staircases are fairly simple, and may be easier to construct than they appear.

Instead of finding each of the steps, constructing ghost ramps using the peak of the first step and consecutive landings will minimize the construction time and inaccuracy involved in a staircase where a number of steps are involved.

The paraline should begin with placing the plan at an angle (illustrations show 30-degree/60-degree) and projecting the heights upward. Connecting the first step height to the first landing height (10th step) will create the sloped plane where all the step peaks will meet.

The elevation of the 11th step is higher than the intermediate landing. Steps 11 through 20 will create the second sloped plane where steps of the second run will rise and meet. Step 20 and the top landing have the same height.

STRAIGHT-RUN AND DOUBLE-FLIGHT STAIRCASES

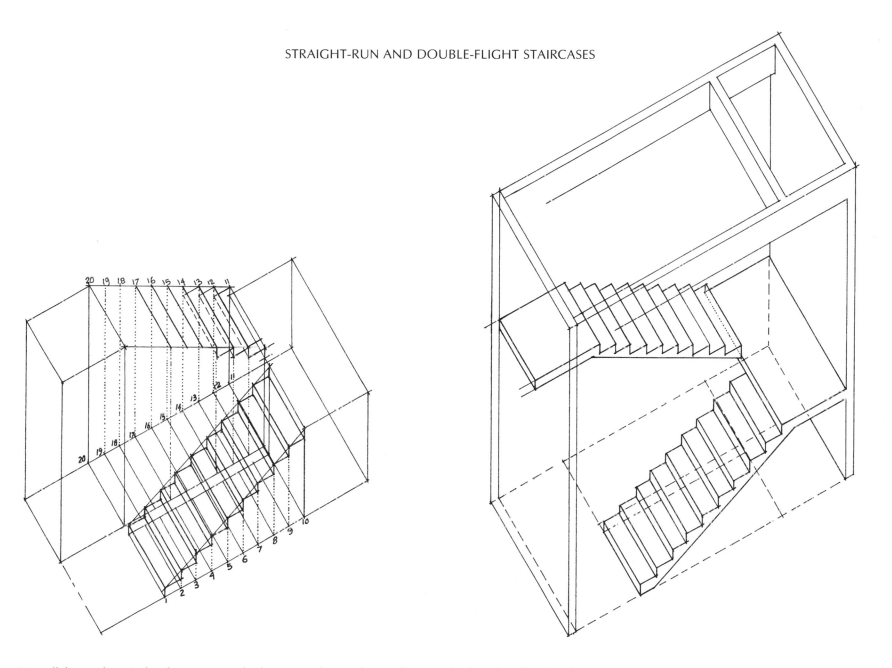

Now all the step lines in the plan (risers) need to be projected upward vertically to cut the sloped profile of the flight. The points where these projection lines meet the sloped line will demark the peaks of the steps in the axonometric. Using the peaks as the riser heights the steps in plan need to be moved up to their new locations.

11. SPIRAL STAIRCASES

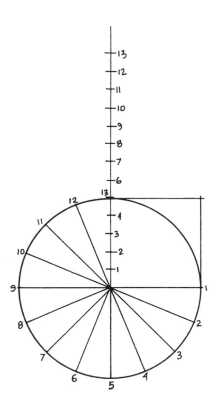

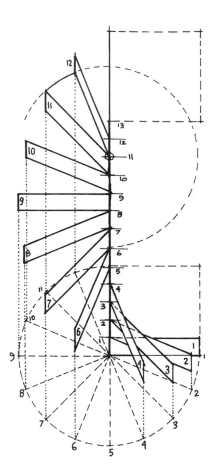

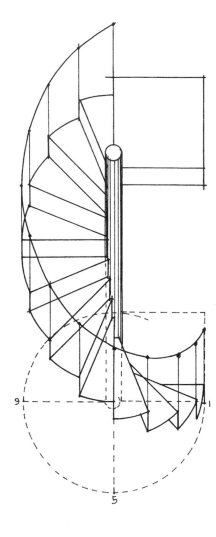

Spiral stairs in plan oblique may easily be constructed by projecting the risers in plan to their respective heights upward or downward from the plan level. The construction of the drawing should start with the floor plan containing all required steps and landings. In this drawing the center of the circle is projected upward and the heights marked for each of the respective risers.

Like any other plan oblique drawing, each riser will move up from its plan location to its appropriate height. The bottom for each of these risers also needs to be marked. The drawing shows vertical planes for all risers projected from the plan and marked by their numbers taken in sequence. To draw the treads of the steps, arcs should be drawn using the marked height lines as the centers for the circles. The tread for step number 11 is shown in the drawing.

Drawing all treads for the risers will complete the construction of the spiral staircase in plan oblique. To add a handrail to this staircase, heights were plotted at each step and connected to form the shape of the sculptural handrail. Thicknesses and other details may be added to the drawing to take the drawing to its presentation level.

SAMPLE EXERCISE 01

Draw a 45-degree/45-degree plan oblique of the objects shown below in roof plans and in corresponding south elevations. Use a scale of 1/4" = 1'-0". Place plans at a 45-degree oblique to the horizontal axis of the drawing page. The drawn paralines should show roof (top), south elevation, and west elevation.

(Draw plan initially with very thin but clear construction lines. Project all height lines upward with light lines. Darken all object lines after construction of each object to emphasize elements of form. Try to develop a habit of not using an eraser.)

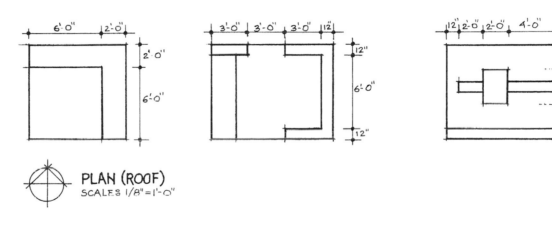

PLAN (ROOF)
SCALE: 1/8"=1'-0"

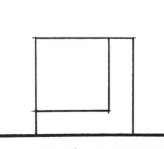
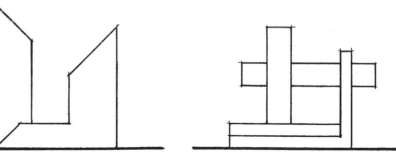

SOUTH ELEVATION
SCALE: 1/8"=1'-0"

SAMPLE EXERCISE 02

Draw a 45-degree/45-degree plan oblique of the objects shown below in plans cut at certain heights and in corresponding south elevations. Use a scale of 1/4" = 1'-0". Place plans at 45 degree oblique to the horizontal axis of the drawing page. The drawn paralines should show roof, south elevation, and west elevation.

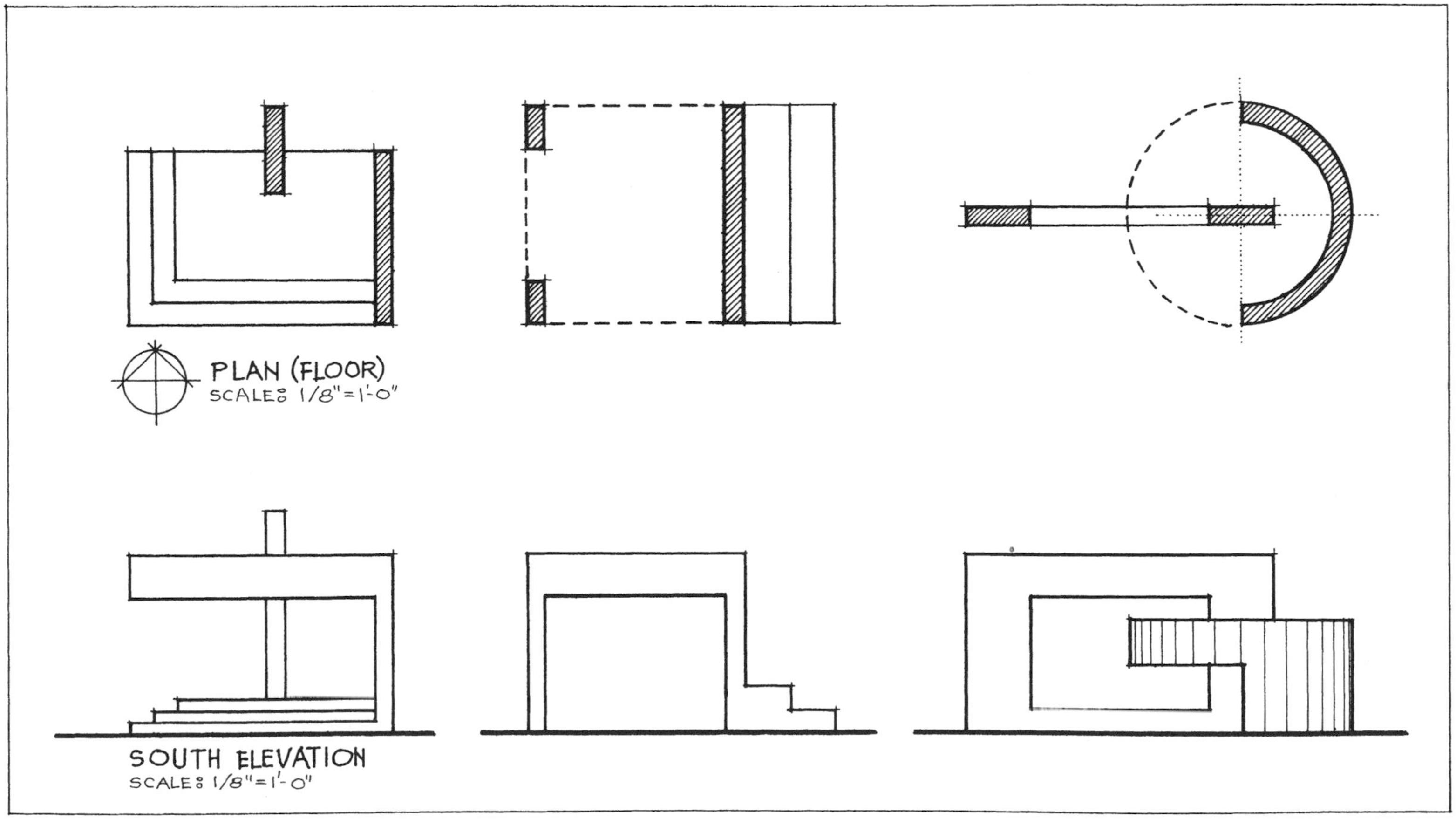

PLAN (FLOOR)
SCALE: 1/8"=1'-0"

SOUTH ELEVATION
SCALE: 1/8"=1'-0"

SAMPLE EXERCISE 03

Draw a plan oblique of the structure viewing the south-west side. Rotate the plan to a suitable angle for your desired view.

Draw your plan first (light but clear). Leave all projection/construction lines light. Use dark lines for the object.

SAMPLE EXERCISE 04A and 04B

A. Draw a 45-degree/45-degree or 30-degree/60-degree plan oblique of the structure shown below in plan and corresponding south elevations. Use a scale of 1/4" = 1'-0". The drawn paralines should show roof, south elevation, and west elevation.

B. Draw a 30-degree/30-degree isometric of the structure at 1/4" = 1'-0" scale. This time draw the view showing the south and east sides of the structure.

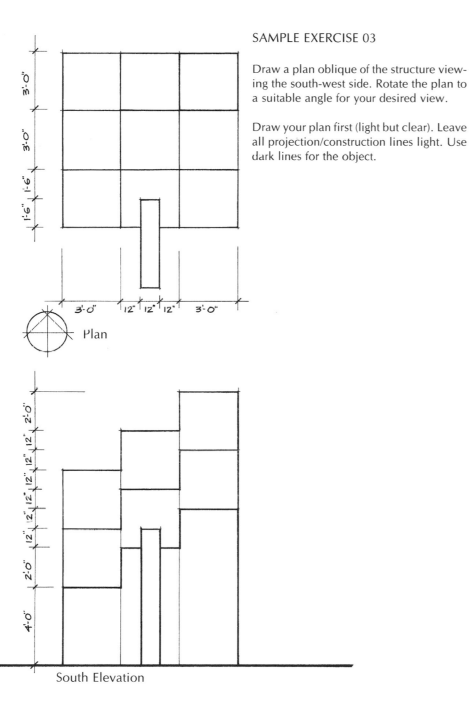

Plan

South Elevation

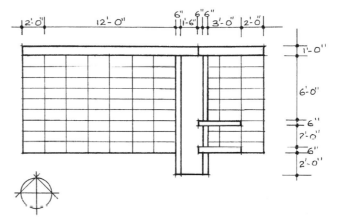

Roof Plan
Scale: 1/8"=1'-0"

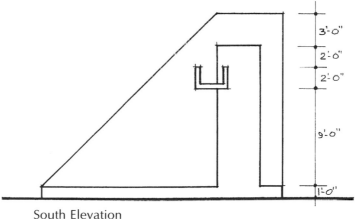

South Elevation
Scale: 1/8"=1'-0"

Conventions and Construction of Paralines . . . 2

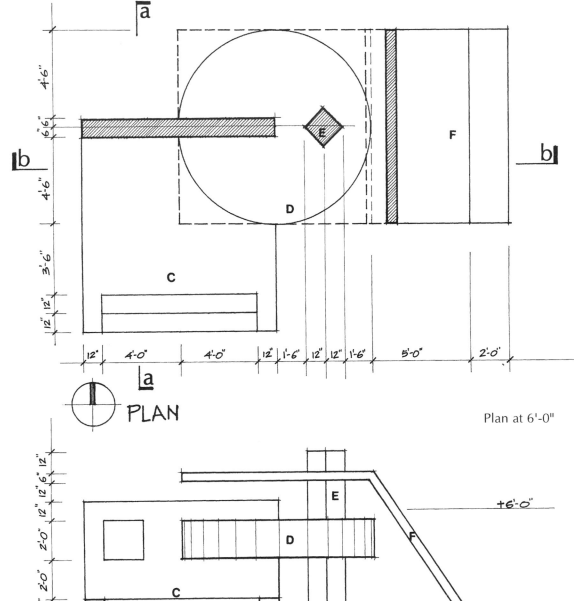

05A. The structure illustrated on this page is composed of four individual elements C, D, E, and F (see both plan and elevation drawing). Given to you is a plan (taken at 6'-0" from the ground) and the south elevation. Draw a 45-degree/45-degree plan oblique for the structure showing the south-west corner. The paraline may be drawn at a scale of 1/4" = 1'-0" or 1/2" =1'-0".

NOTE: The circle in the plan will remain a circle in the plan oblique.

05B. Draw a sectional 45-degree/45-degree plan oblique considering the section cut at "aa" and removing the western section of the cut.

05C. Draw a sectional 45-degree/45-degree plan oblique considering the section cut at "bb" and removing the southern section of the cut.

PLAN

Plan at 6'-0"

SOUTH ELEVATION

South Elevation

SAMPLE EXERCISE 06

Given to you is a plan (taken at 12'-0" from the ground) and the south elevation. Draw a 30-degree/60-degree plan oblique (south edge should align with the 30-degree line) for the structure showing the south-west corner. The paraline is to be drawn at a scale of 1/4" = 1'-0".

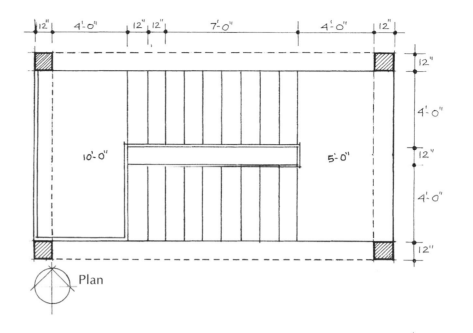

Plan

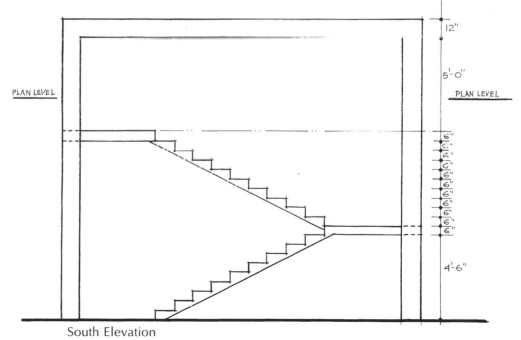

South Elevation

A. Given to you is a plan (a horizontal section taken at 7'-6" from the ground plane) and the south elevation. Draw a 30-degree/60-degree plan oblique (south edge should align with the 30-degree line) for the structure showing the south-west corner. The paraline is to be drawn at a scale of 1/4" = 1'-0".

B. Draw a frontal 0-degree/90-degree elevation oblique for the structure showing south elevation and top view. You must use the given plan to construct your frontal paraline by projecting heights from the plan.

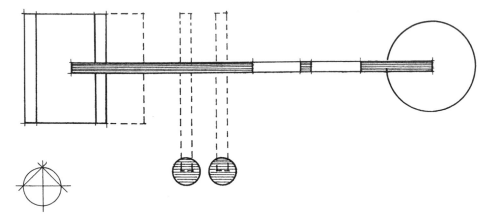

Plan
Scale: 1/8" = 1'-0"

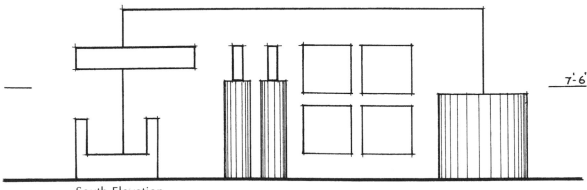

South Elevation
Scale: 1/8" = 1'-0"

7'-6"

2... Conventions and Construction of Paralines

Shades and Shadows

How to plot shadows in paralines

SHADES AND SHADOWS

How to plot shadows in paralines

Any part of an object not reached by light rays from an established source is said to be in the shade.

A shadow is caused by the interruption of light rays that results from the presence of a body between the source of light and the surface on which the shadow falls. The outline of a shadow is dependent upon the shade lines of an object.

Shades and shadows help clarify an object's shape and form.

1. BASIC CONCEPTS OF SHADOW CASTING

Shades and shadows are used in architectural presentation drawings to clarify the visual perception of depth. While shadows in plan and site plan illustrate upright elements and relative height differences between them, shadows in elevation drawing illustrate projected elements and relative depth differences between surface planes that are recessed or projected. Shades and shadows are also effective in expressing the three-dimensional quality of an object by emphasizing the roundness, slantness, flatness, openness, and other qualities of that object's form.

Constructing shadow configuration and rendering surfaces in shade and shadow with paraline drawings provide clarity and distinction between different surface planes (with respect to vertical, horizontal, inclined, and the three-dimensional nature of individual elements) of an object.

Even though shades and shadows are not often seen in finished paraline drawings, they can effectively enhance the design intent of the drawing. Compared to a perspective drawing, a rendered paraline drawing with shades and shadows takes much less time to draw and creates a more believable environment without going overboard with the rendering of trees and other environmental features (as may be the expectation of most perspective presentations).

SUN ANGLE IN PLAN AND ELEVATION

To cast shades and shadows in the axonometrics it is important to understand the concepts of shadows both in plan and elevation.

The sun angle on a three-dimensional object needs to be seen both in plan and elevation and then cross referenced to cast the correct shadow profile.

The sun angle in plan may be referred to as either a BEARING or an AZIMUTH. For our convenience, we shall use the term bearing.

In elevation the same sun angle is called ALTITUDE.

It is also important to understand the following:
• Sun angles and parallel light rays in plan and elevation
• Shade and shadow
• Body shadow and cast shadow

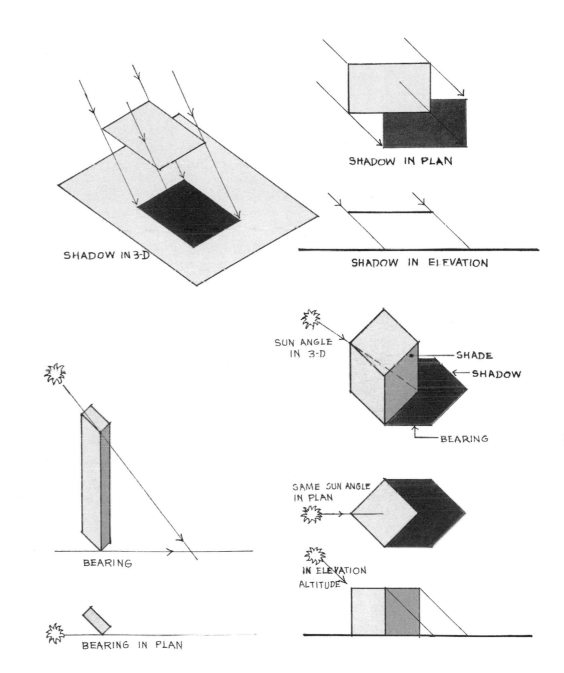

SHADOW IN 3-D

SHADOW IN PLAN

SHADOW IN ELEVATION

SUN ANGLE IN 3-D

SHADE

SHADOW

BEARING

SAME SUN ANGLE IN PLAN

IN ELEVATION ALTITUDE

BEARING

BEARING IN PLAN

VARYING THE BEARING DIRECTION

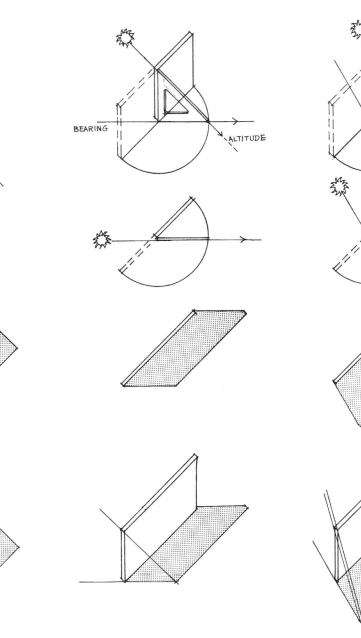

Bearing
and altitude

Bearing
in plan

Shadow
in plan

Shadow
in paraline

Changing the bearing direction of the sun's ray in a paraline drawing will affect the profile of the shadow.

Specific bearing direction should be determined by looking at the character of the axonometric or oblique drawing. Usually an appropriate direction is chosen so that the projected shadow does not obscure the detail of the design drawing.

For simplicity and to save time, horizontal bearing direction (middle column example) is the most preferred direction. The edge of the T-square or the parallel rule is used to get the bearing lines. A 45-degree triangle gives an altitude angle which cuts the bearing line to get the shadow length. No ruler is necessary to get the dimension of the shadow length.

These illustrations show a changing pattern of the shadow for the same wall as affected by three different bearing directions.

Sun rays are always assumed to be parallel in orthographic drawings, because of the virtually infinite distance of the light source from the object.

Vertical lines or upright elements cast shadows in the direction of the light ray on the ground or base plane (line BA').

Horizontal lines or elements parallel to the ground or base plane cast shadows parallel to and identical in length to the element (line A'D').

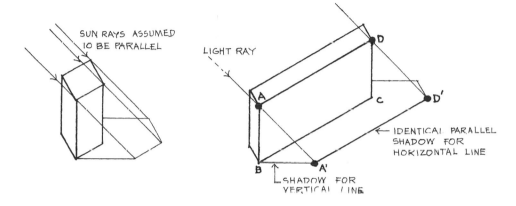

SHADOW CASTING EDGES

It is important to identify all the edges that will block the sun's rays and cast shadows on other planes before constructing the total shadow profile (BA, AD, DE, and EF for top right figure).

The two diagrams (right) show the number of total surfaces (planes) and their casting edges for a rectangular volume both on the ground and above ground. If these two conditions are understood, one can be assured of casting shadows correctly.

A rectangular volumetric object has six sides, four vertical and two horizontal. The same object sitting on the ground will have five sides, one being coinsiding with the ground plane. When it is placed angularly with the bearing of the sun (angle in plan), the sun will shine on three sides, two vertical sides and one top. The other two sides will be in the shade. BA, AD, DE, and EF are the edge lines that will cast the shadow profile. Plotting these four edges will construct the final shadow on the ground.

Casting edges are highlighted with thicker lines for both conditions; on ground and above ground. These are the edges that separate exposed sides from shaded sides. When above ground two additional edges need to be considered for the bottom side. Notice that the edges are the same except the above ground case has two additional edges (BG and GF) for the bottom plane to complete the shape.

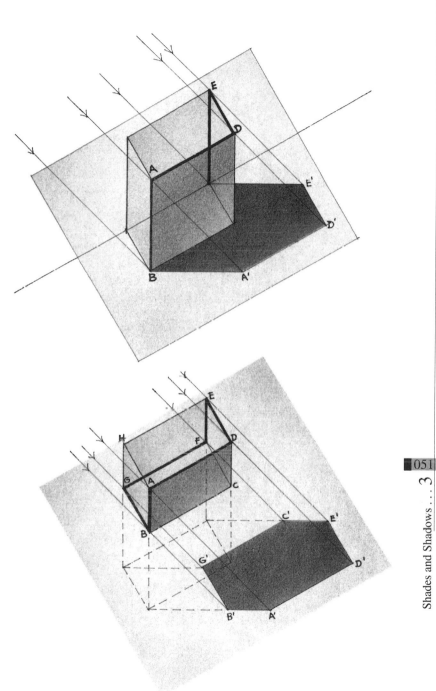

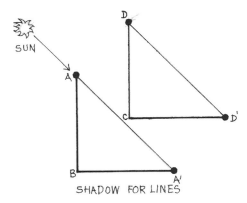

SHADOW FOR LINES

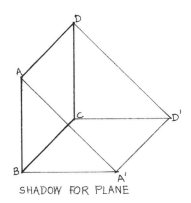

SHADOW FOR PLANE

Line AB will cast a shadow of equal length to line BA' if the sun is at 45 degrees both in plan and elevation. Similarly line DC will cast a shadow of equal length to line CD'.

Connecting points A and D, and points B and C will create a new plane ABCD. The shadow of this new plane can be formed easily by connecting points A' and D', and then again B and C. A'BCD' is the shadow for the plane ABCD.

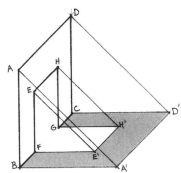

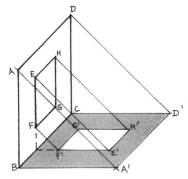

SHADOW OF PLANE WITH OPENNING

Shadow for the plane ABCD with an openning EFGH can be constructed as shown (left) by first casting the shadow of the larger plane ABCD. The opening EFGH will cast the outline E'FGH'. All shadows for the vertical lines need to start from the base or the ground plane.

Extend the vertical lines EF and HG to the base plane if they do not meet the base. This will create the starting point of the shadow line. Specific points along the vertical line can be determined (point E) by drawing the sun angle from that point to where it cuts the shadow line (bearing) on the ground.

3. SHADOW OF BASIC PLANE AND VOLUME

SHADOW OF TWO PLANES AND A SOLID VOLUME

ABCD and EFGH are two individual vertical planes, both rectangles and both parallel to each other. Their combined shadow in this case would be simply two individual shadows slightly overlapped on top of each other on the ground plane. The overlapping shadow area will have the same shadow intensity as the individual shadow areas.

Connecting all corresponding points (AE, BF, CG, and DH) of the two planes ABCD and EFGH will transform them into a volumetric "solid."

The shadow of this new volume can be formed easily by connecting shadow points D' and H' (as connected to create the plane FE'H'D'C). This configuration is the shadow for the new mass created by the original two planes.

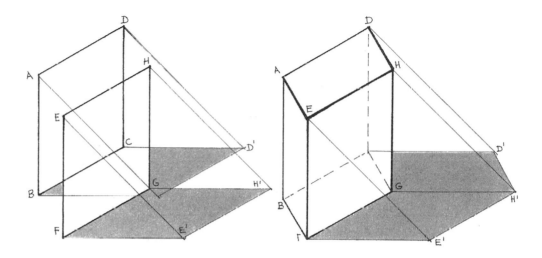

SHADOW OF VOLUME WITH OPENING

For volumes with openings, the shadow casting edges need to be identified first (refer back to the section on Shadow Casting Edges). In the drawing to the right all hidden edges are drawn with dashed lines.

All vertical elements with volumes will have two vertical casting edges. Lines FE and LM are two such vertical casting edges in both drawings. Horizontal elements having volumes will have one casting edge if the element sits on the ground (see bottom element on the right drawing). Line HK is the casting edge for the right drawing. Elements above ground will have two casting edges, one on the top plane and one at the bottom plane. Line EP is the top edge and MN is the bottom edge for both drawings.

Once shadow edges are found, casting their heights on the ground will construct the shadow profile. Lines FE' and LM' are examples of shadow lines for vertical edges for the left drawing. Similarly lines E'P' and M'N' are shadow lines for horizontal elements for the same drawing.

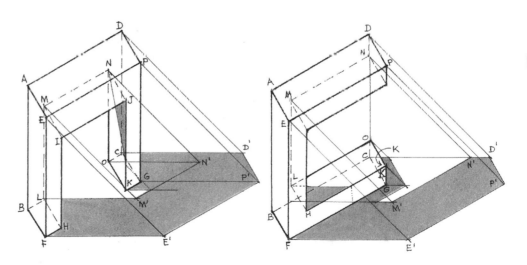

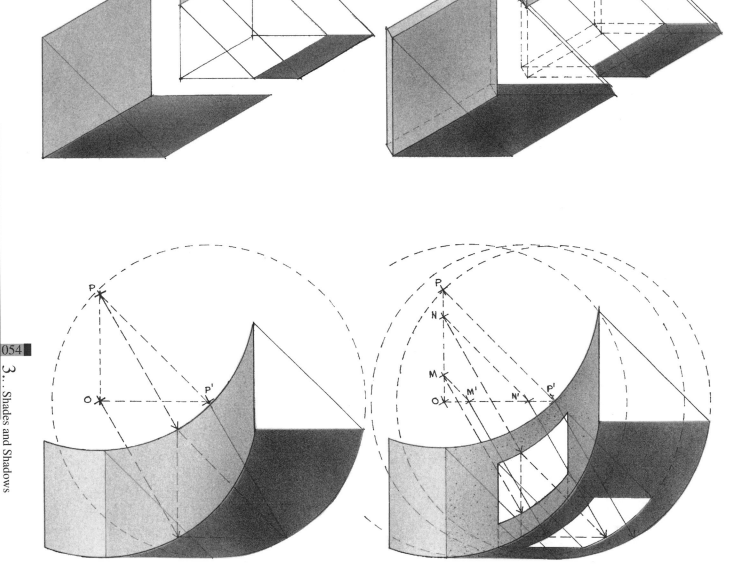

4. SHADOW OF VERTICAL PLANES

Consider two different conditions: one vertical plane with its base line on the ground, and the other with its base line raised above the ground. The drawings to the left cast a shadow of a vertical flat plane on the ground. When a plane is raised above the ground, the height of the top and bottom edge needs to be found. Simply extending vertical edges to the ground will show that height.

Planes with thickness will show additional shadow edges. Shadows may be constructed by projecting lines from both front and back planes and connecting all corners, or by projecting casting edges to their respective heights. The drawings show hidden casting edges in dashed lines.

For curvilinear forms the geometry must be known first. The drawings on the bottom show shadows of curvilinear planes that are segments of circles. The height of the plane should be found first. Line OP is the total height for both planes. The second plane has an opening at the height of M and N from the ground.

Projecting the heights along the bearing direction will give the centers for the shadow circles. Drawing circles using these new centers (P' for the top and M' and N' for the opening) will create the shadow lines.

5. SHADOW OF VERTICAL PLANES WITH OPENINGS

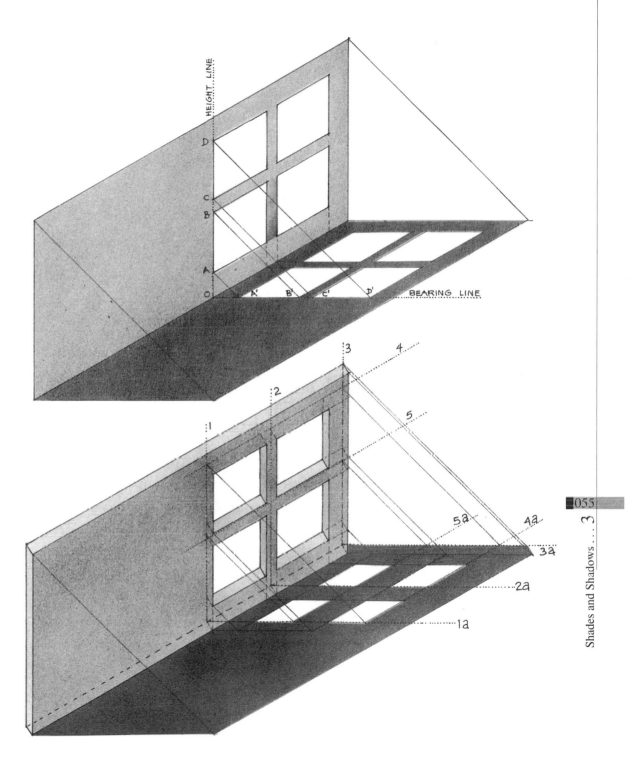

To find the shadows of openings above ground, the shadow of the height line and points along the height line need to be found. Point O is the extension of the height line to the ground plane where the bearing line will pass through for the heights A, B, C, and D. Intersection of the bearing line and the actual rays from A, B, C, and D will create respective shadow points A', B', C', and D' on the bearing line. All horizontal edges of the plane will cast parallel shadows on the ground. Shadows for all horizontal and vertical edges need to be constructed in order to complete the shadows.

For planes with thicknesses, as in vertical wall, there will be hidden casting edges for the back surface plane. All actual rays (in this case, 45-degree projection lines) coming from the back plane must be projected to meet the bearing line for that back plane only.

Lines marked 1, 2, and 3 are the three hidden vertical casting edges for the back plane (facing the sun). Lines 1a, 2a, and 3a are their respective bearing and shadow lines. Similarly 4a and 5a are the shadow lines for the bottom casting edges (back plane) 4 and 5.

6. SHADOW OF COMPLEX MULTIPLE PLANES

SHADOW OF A BOX WITH VERTICAL, HORIZONTAL, AND INCLINED PLANES

The shadow of a box with complex multiple planes can be constructed, simply by calculating the shadow of each individual plane. Heights of all corner points for each plane (whether vertical, horizontal, or inclined) are required to construct the shadow profile.

In the illustration to the left, the box is pulled apart in four pieces to show how the shadow was constructed for each segment. Each segment contains one vertical plane and one inclined or horizontal plane.

The first segment (top left) has a vertical plane (AEHD) and an inclined plane (ADOP). Point A and point D of the vertical plane will cast a shadow at point A' and point D'. Since points E and H of the plane are on the ground, the shadow for this vertical plane will be EA'D'H.

The inclined plane (ADOP) floats above the ground plane. Point E and point O need to be brought down to the ground plane to find out their heights. Lines GP and GO are the respective heights for points P and O. Point P will cast a shadow at point P' on the ground. Similarly, point O will cast a shadow at point O'. Line P'O' is the shadow line for the PO edge of the inclined plane ADOP. Since point A and point D (common to both planes) have shadow points A' and D', connecting shadow points P' and O' will construct the A'D'O'P' shadow profile for the inclined plane ADOP.

Constructing shadows for the rest of the three segments and combining their shadow profile will create the final composite shadow of the box.

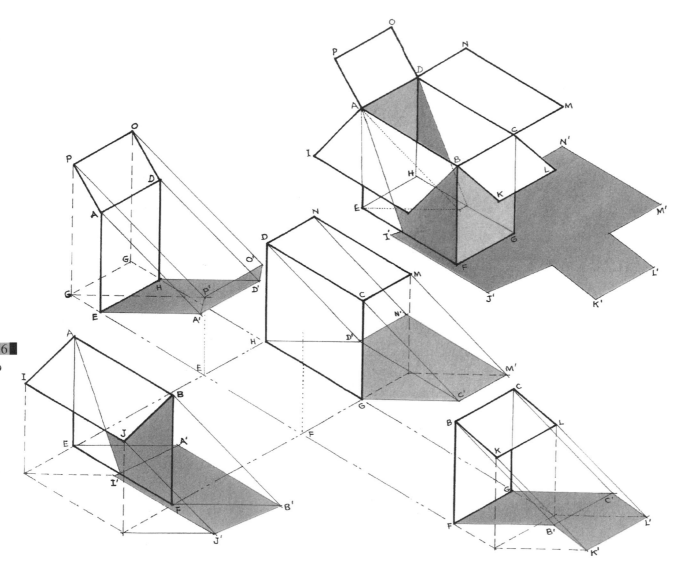

7. SHADOW OF HORIZONTAL AND VERTICAL PLANES

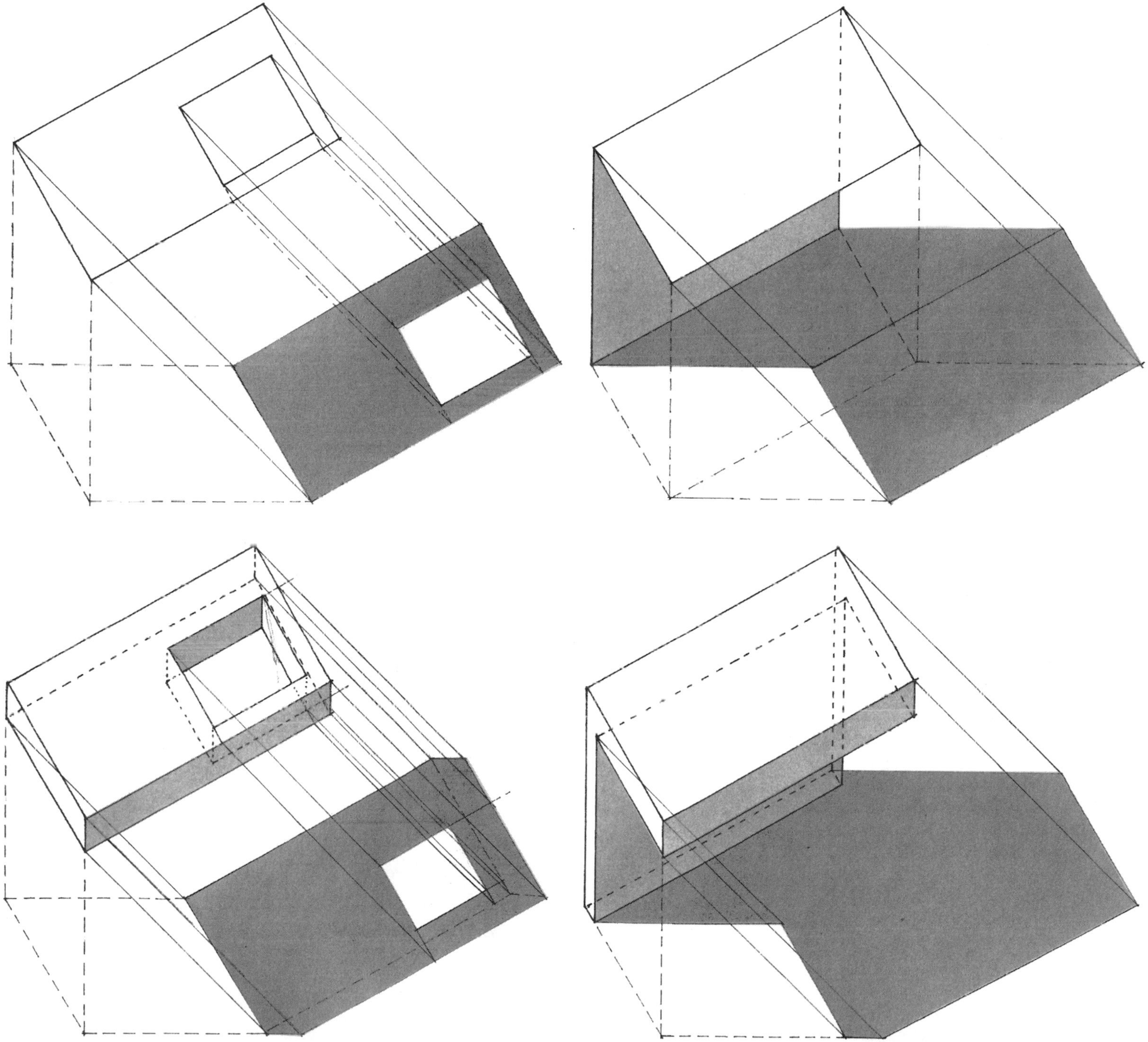

8. SHADOW OF
INTERSECTING PLANES

For intersecting vertical and horizontal planes, shadows need to be cast for each plane individually. Horizontal planes (ABCD) above ground (AH being the height) will cast identical shadows (A'B'C'D') on the ground. In the drawing to the right the horizontal shadow cuts the vertical plane at points E and F. Points E and F need to be connected to points G and H to construct the shadow on the vertical plane. The raised portion (HP) of the vertical plane will cast a shadow (HP') on the horizontal plane.

For two intersecting vertical planes shadows need to be cast for each plane individually on the ground. BA' is the shadow for the vertical edge BA. The BA' shadow line cuts the other vertical plane at point O. From point O the shadow line will rise vertically on the wall and cut the sun ray at E. BO and OE are the shadow lines for the edge BA. Point E needs to be connected to point F to get the shadow line for AF.

For planes with thicknesses, as in a slab, hidden shadow casting edges (shown in dashed lines) need to be found.

Planes that are raised above ground with thickness need to be brought down to the ground to project the bearing and sun angle lines. Hidden shadow casting edges (shown in dashed lines) need to be found for both top and bottom surfaces of the plane.

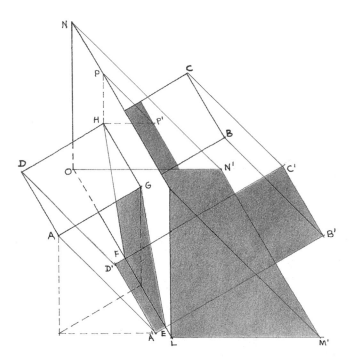

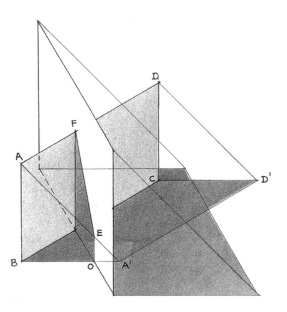

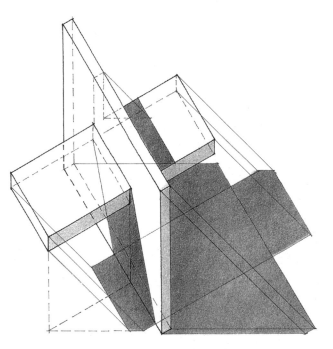

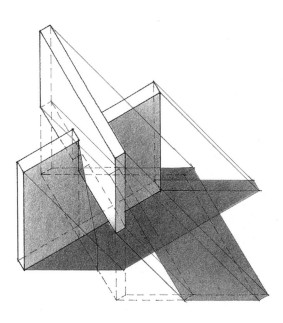

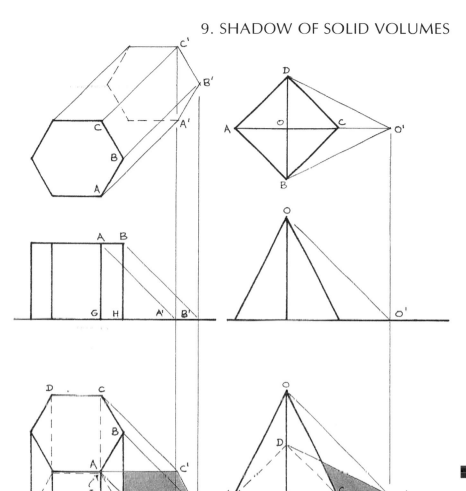

WEDGE

This wedge-shaped volume has no height on the AB side. There will be no shadows for the points A and B. Lines EC and FD will cast shadows EC' and FD', respectively. Connecting BC' will construct the shadow of the object line BC. BC'D'F is the shadow outline for this wedge-shaped volume.

CYLINDER

The shadow for this cylindrical volume can be found by slipping the top disc of the cylinder along the shadow direction to a length equal to the height of the object. In the drawing above the center of the top disc A will cast a shadow point A' on the ground. Drawing the same circle at A' and interconnecting tangents from the bottom circle B will outline the shadow for this cylinder.

HEXAGON

This volume with its hexagonal top will cast identical hexagonal shadows similar to the cylinder. Connecting tangents to the shadow of the top disc will outline the shadow. The fastest way to cast shadows for such volumes would be to project the shadow length for each hexagonal corner for the top disc and to connect those to the base on the ground.

PYRAMID

First, the height needs to be determined in order to project the shadow of the peak. As shown in the drawing above the peak height EO will cast an equal shadow EO' on the ground. This volume has no height at the base. Connecting point O to the base points (B, C, and D) will create the shadow profile BO'D for this pyramid.

10. SHADOW OF VARIATION OF SOLID VOLUMES

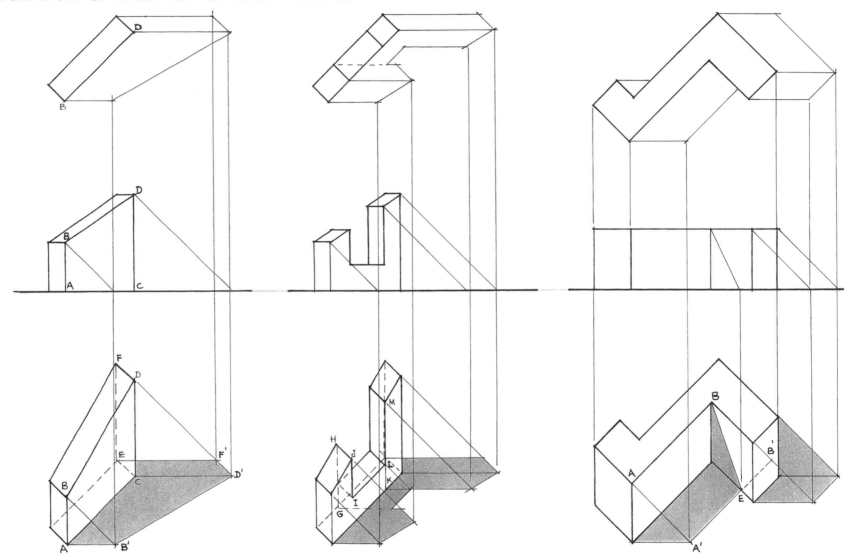

This wedge-shaped volume has two different heights at two ends. Line AB will cast a shadow AB' (lower end) and line CD will cast a shadow CD' (higher end). Connecting B'D' will construct the shadow of the inclined object edge BD. Line EF' is the shadow of the hidden casting edge EF. AB'D'F'E is the final shadow outline for this wedge-shaped volume.

For the open portion of this wedge-shaped volume there will be additional shadow casting edges. GH and LM are the two new vertical shadow casting edges. Lines HJ and IL are two other edges that will cast a shadow.

Line A'B' would have been the shadow of the edge AB if there was no interruption by any other object. Since shadow line A'B' is stopped at (E), it will change its direction and climb up until it connects the corner B to complete the shadow outline.

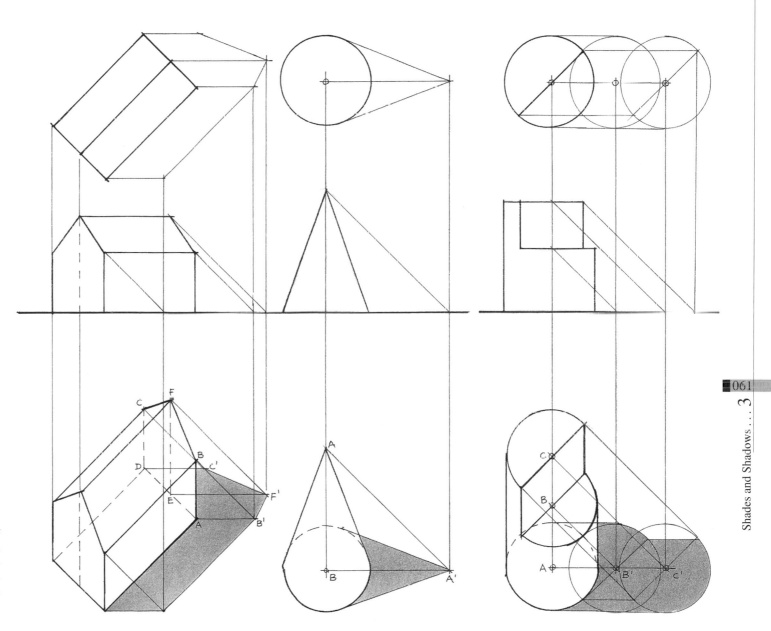

For a rectangular volume with a wedge-shaped top, the peak of the wedge needs to be projected along the bearing direction. F' is the shadow point for the peak F. AB'F'C'D is the shadow profile for the side ABFCD.

For conical objects the height of the tip needs to be found. AB is the height, B is the center of the circular base. A' is the shadow point for the tip A. Drawing tangents to the edges of the base from A' will outline the shadow.

A, B, and C are the center heights of this cylindrical volume. Slipped centers (B' for B and C' for C) to respective heights along the bearing direction will construct the shadow profile on the ground.

11. SHADOW CAST BY INTERSECTING BLOCKS AND PLANES

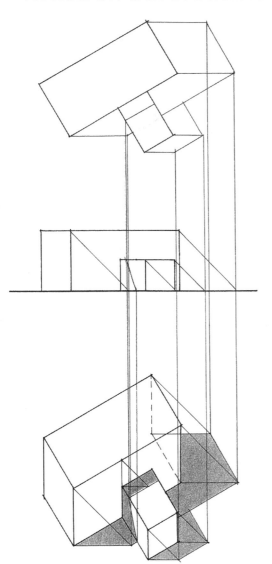

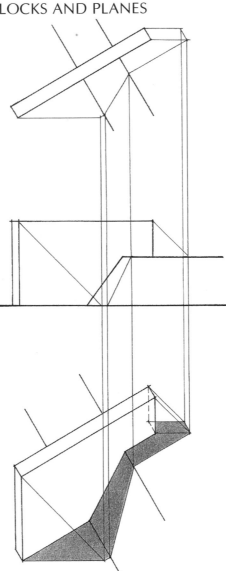

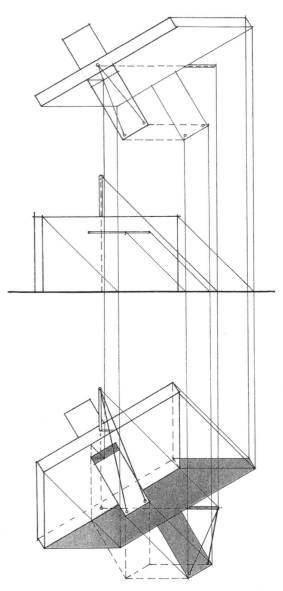

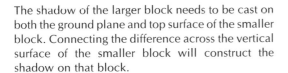
3... Shades and Shadows

The shadow of the larger block needs to be cast on both the ground plane and top surface of the smaller block. Connecting the difference across the vertical surface of the smaller block will construct the shadow on that block.

The shadow of the wall needs to be cast on both the lower and upper planes. Connecting the difference across the inclined surface will construct the shadow on the incline.

The shadows for all three elements need to be cast separately on the ground. Because of the height difference the vertical wall will cast a shadow on the horizontal intersecting plane.

12. SHADOW OF STAIRS

The shadows of stairs can be located by finding the shadow outline for each step.

Stairs with railings or a wall will have shadows on the steps from that rail or wall. Shadows need to be projected from the rail to all the steps individually. Tread planes need to be extended sometimes to find shadow wedges.

A set of steps rising above the ground will cast an apparently complex shadow outline which needs to be found by casting the shadow for each step. Hidden casting edges need to be located for the side which is exposed to the sun.

Steps comprised of individual slabs that each float above the ground will show shadows for each step. The condition of shadow casting will be similar to a beam running horizontally above the ground. Hidden casting edges need to be located for each step.

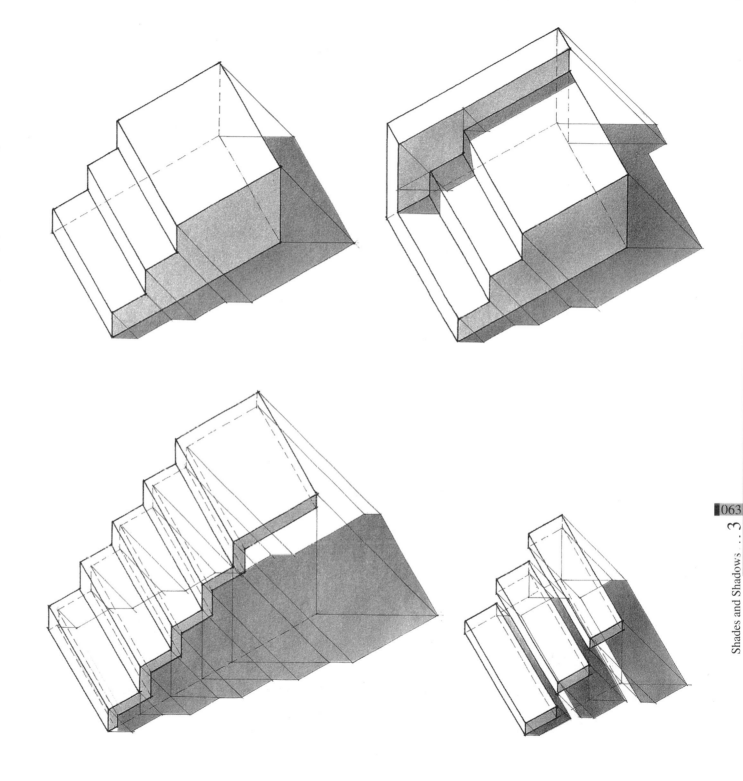

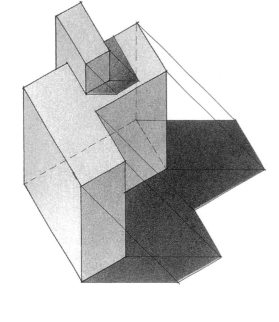

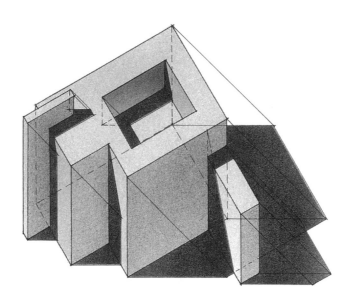

13. SHADOW OF IRREGULAR VOLUMES

LEFT DRAWING:
When a form projects upward above another form, the upper form will cast a shadow on the top plane of the lower form. The lower form will cast a shadow on the ground plane.

RIGHT DRAWING:
For irregular volumes with recessed surface planes and intersecting elements, shadows may be cast by constructing individual shadows for each element.

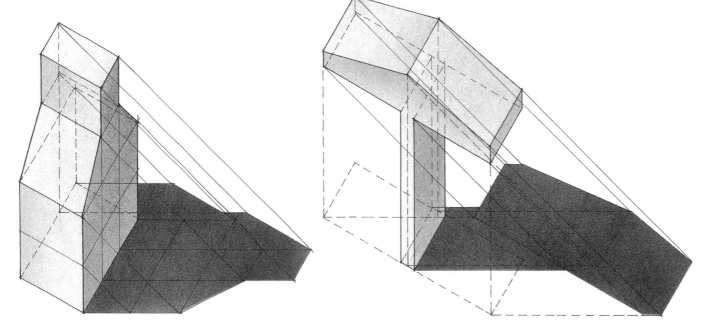

LEFT DRAWING:
Shadows for inclined surfaces of a volume can be found by projecting shadows for major vertical lines and connecting appropriate points on those lines that constitute the sloped surfaces.

RIGHT DRAWING:
To cast shadows of volumes comprised of horizontal extensions above the ground, a footprint of the floating element may be constructed to draw bearing lines. For the gabled top the peak points need to be brought down to the ground for shadow length. Hidden casting edges need to be located for both vertical and horizontal elements.

3... Shades and Shadows

14. SHADOW CAST BY EXTENDED BLOCKS ON VERTICAL AND INCLINED PLANE

SHADOW OF EXTENDED BLOCKS ON A VERTICAL PLANE

Extended objects on a vertical plane above the ground need to be brought down to the ground plane to draw the bearing lines. If the bearing line (which is the shadow line for the vertical edge) is stopped by the vertical wall (point O) before it intersects the actual sun ray (45-degree line), the shadow line will rise vertically on the wall until it intersects the same sun ray (point P'). Then the shadow line will be drawn back to point Q. P'Q is the shadow for the edge PQ. P'R' is the shadow for the edge PR.

SHADOW OF A BLOCK ON A WEDGE

To cast the shadow of a block on an inclined plane it needs to be determined where the block's actual rays strike the inclined surface. In order to do that the shadow plane along the vertical casting edge that slices through the wedge in the bearing direction needs to be constructed. Actual rays strike the surface of the inclined plane where they meet these slices.

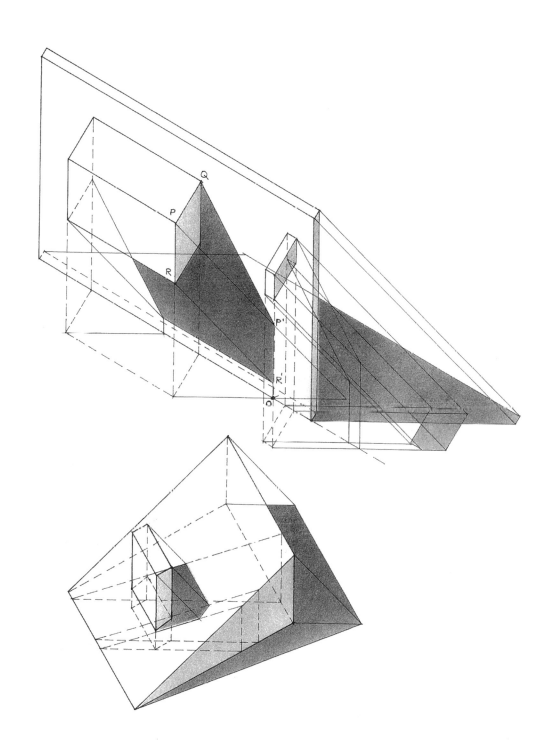

15. SHADOW CAST BY AN OBJECT ON ANOTHER WALL OR BLOCK

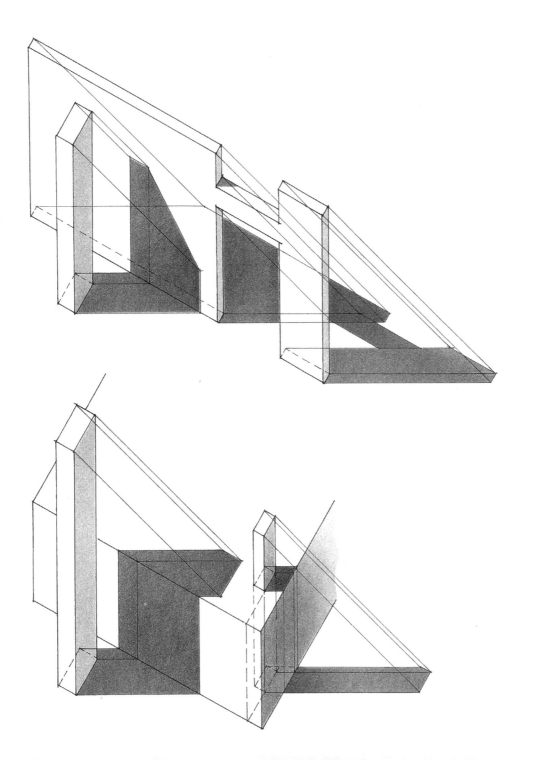

SHADOW OF AN OBJECT ON A WALL

If the shadow receiving wall is parallel to the shadow casting edge of the other object, the shadow will be parallel to the edge on the wall. The shadow on the ground will be along the bearing direction until it meets the vertical wall. At the wall the shadow will change direction and climb vertically up until cut by the actual ray.

SHADOW OF AN OBJECT ON ANOTHER BLOCK

To cast the shadow of a block on another block, the shadow line for the vertical edge (bearing ray) should be drawn until it meets the vertical wall. At the intersection points the lines will rise vertically up on the wall and change direction again on the roof. It should be noted that the shadow on the vertical wall will be perpendicular to the ground on a vertical plane and will change direction again on the roof to follow the bearing direction.

16. SHADOW OF
A BUILDING BLOCK

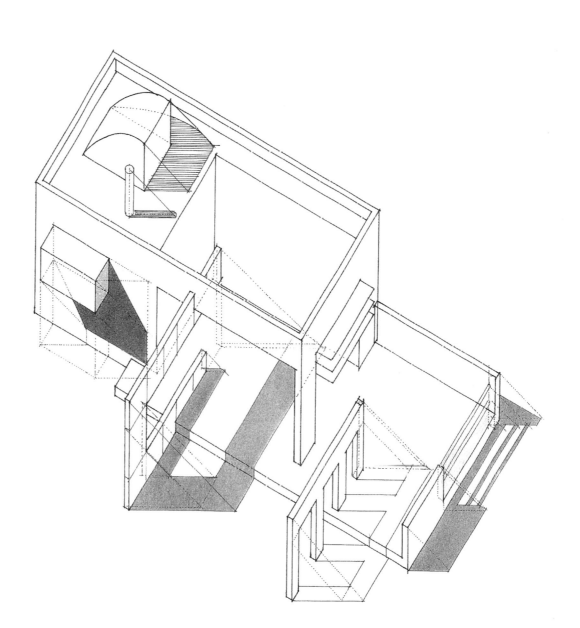

For complex objects like a building, the building should be broken down into simple planes, shapes, and volumes. The shadow of each simple shape should be cast. The overall shadow configuration will be the composite of all simple shadows.

When casting shadows for complex objects the intersection of the actual ray and the bearing line may not be immediately evident. Other elements of the object may create an obstruction and some confusion in visualizing these intersections. It will be appropriate to construct imaginary lines and planes as extensions of given lines and planes, or to simplify the drawing consider leaving some of the surfaces out of the drawing (as needed). All elements of the drawing will be taken into account as the drawing is understood.

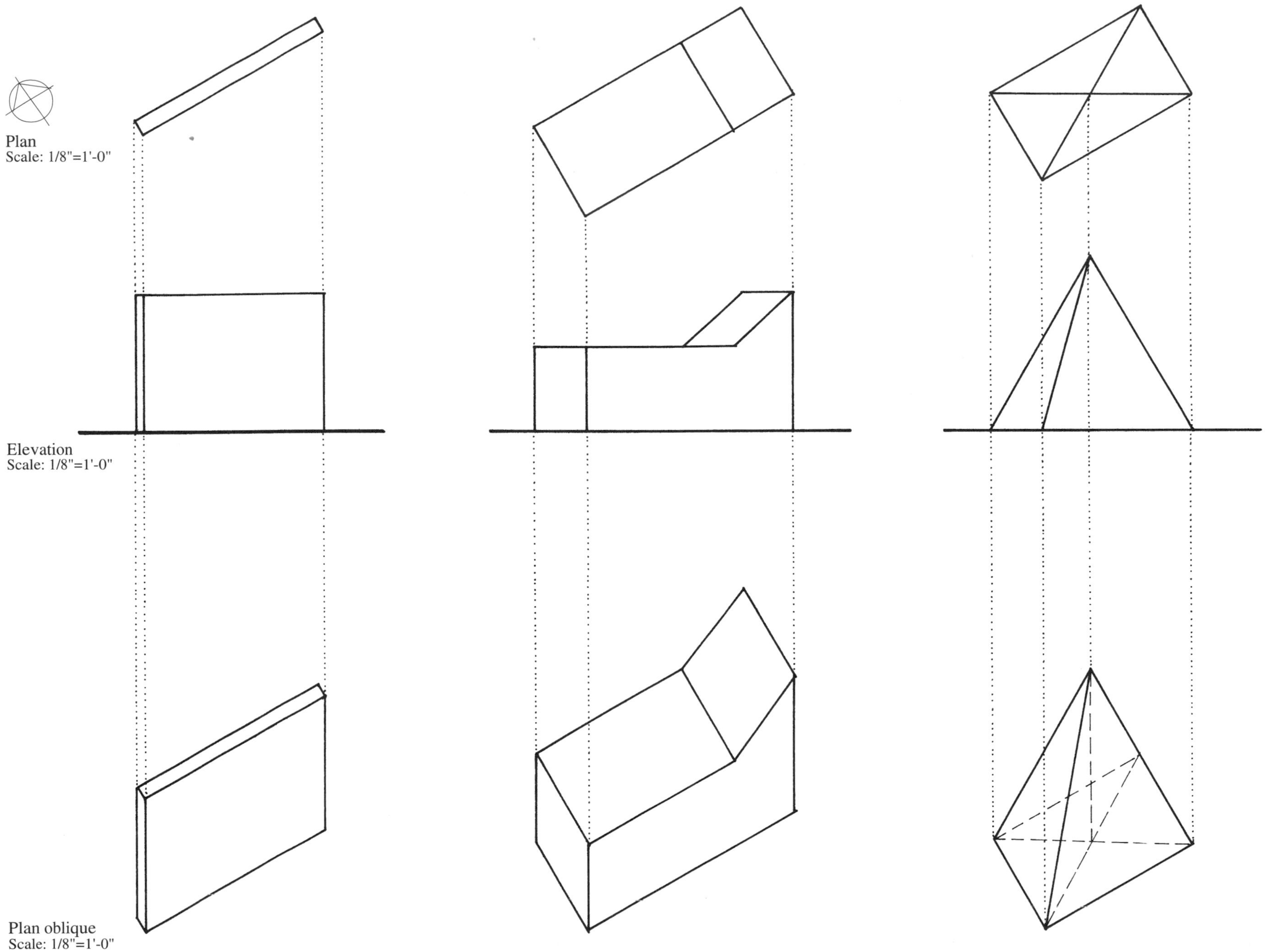

3... Shades and Shadows

Plan oblique
Scale: 1/8"=1'-0"

SAMPLE EXERCISE 01: Cast a shadow of the above objects both in plan and plan oblique. The actual sun angle is 45 degrees in all drawings (plan, elevation, and paraline). Considering the bearing direction to be horizontal (i.e., parallel to the bottom edge of the paper) going to the right from the front corner edge, cast shades and shadows of the objects illustrated here. Elevations will have shades but not any shadows.

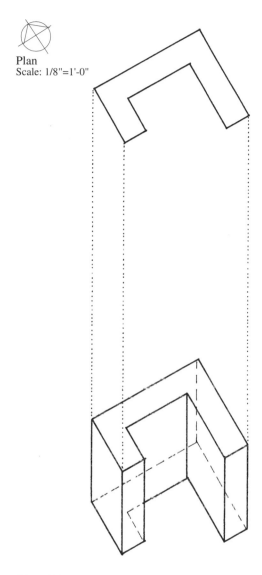

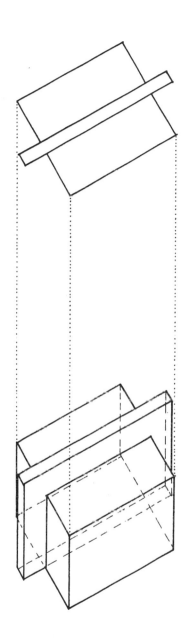

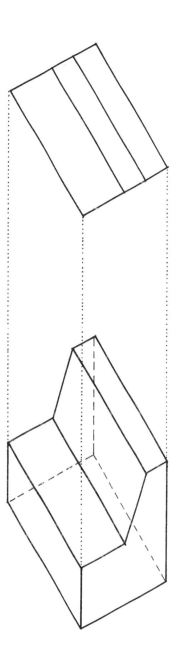

Shades and Shadows . . . 3

SAMPLE EXERCISE 02: Given to you are plans and corresponding 30-degree/60-degree plan obliques. Considering the bearing direction to be horizontal (i.e., parallel to the bottom edge of the paper) going toward the right from the front corner edge and the actual sun ray at 45 degrees. Cast shades and shadows of the objects illustrated here.

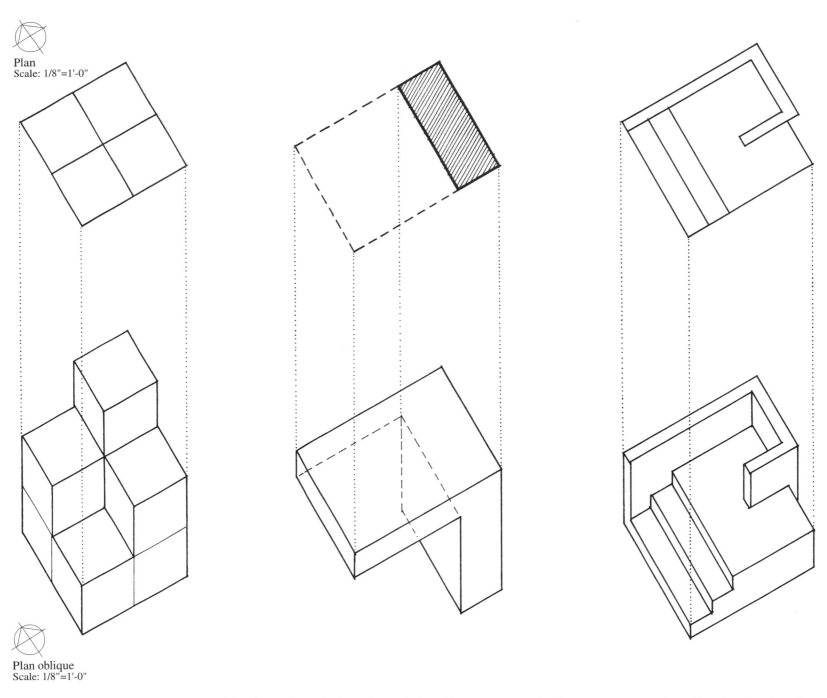

Plan oblique
Scale: 1/8"=1'-0"

SAMPLE EXERCISE 03: Cast a shadow of the above objects both in plan and plan oblique. You may decide your own sun angle and bearing direction. If necessary redraw these drawings at a larger scale.

070

3... Shades and Shadows

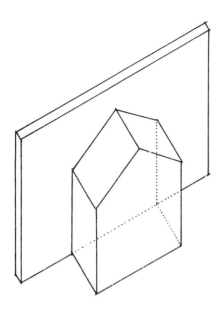

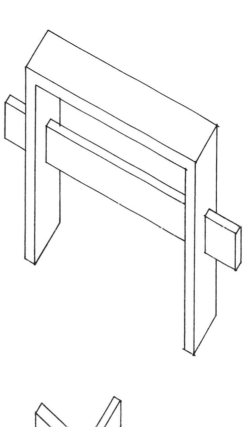

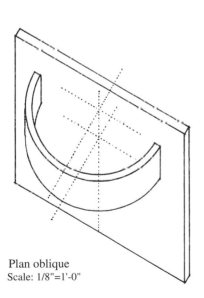

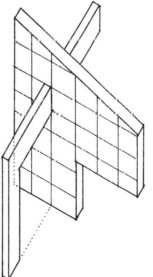

Plan oblique
Scale: 1/8"=1'-0"

SAMPLE EXERCISE 04: Given to you are four plan oblique drawings. Cast shadows of these objects using different sets of actual sun angle and bearing direction for each drawing. If necessary redraw these drawings at a larger scale.

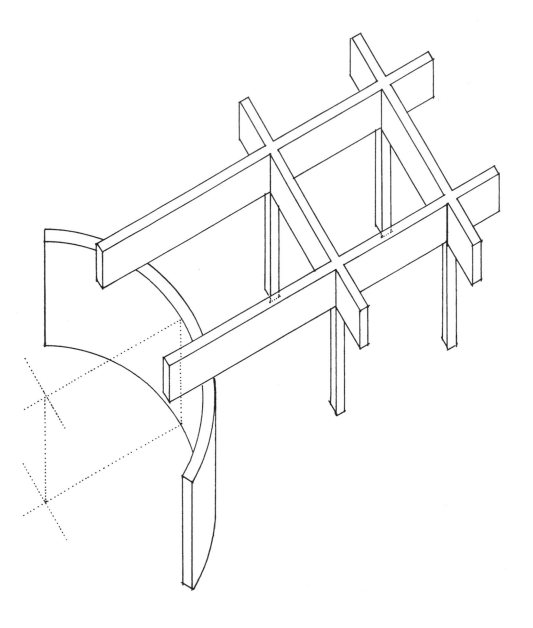

Given to you is a composite object comprised of beams and columns and a curvilinear wall plane. Centers of the wall plane at ground level and at the top are shown in dashed lines. Cast shadows of each element and construct the composite shadow of the total object.

3...Shades and Shadows

SAMPLE EXERCISE 06:

A floor plan and its corresponding plan oblique are illustrated on this page. Using these
as your base drawing recreate a modified
design and draw the following:

1. Floor plan
2. South and west elevation
3. Two plan obliques (from opposite corners).

Cast shades and shadows on all of your
drawings.

Enlarge all drawings to a scale of 1/4"=1'-0".
Modify the dimensions as necessary.

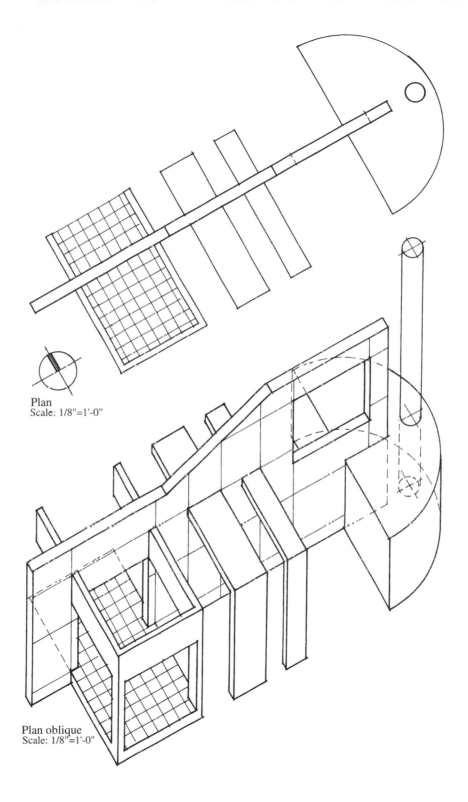

Plan
Scale: 1/8"=1'-0"

Plan oblique
Scale: 1/8"=1'-0"

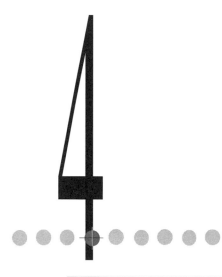

Rendering Techniques

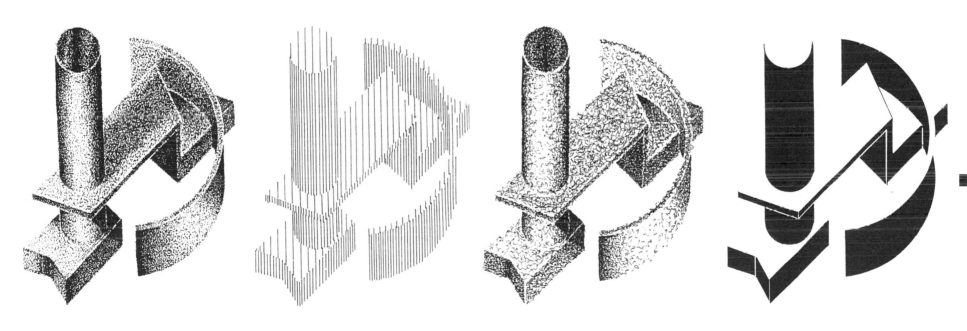

Axonometric rendering in black and white. Base drawing is produced on 8.5 x 11-in tracing paper with a lead pencil and then traced over on vellum to create these four individual renderings using .18, .25, and .7 technical pens. Techniques used from left to right are: dots, vertical lines, scribbles, and high contrast black and white.

Courtesy: Southern University, Baton Rouge, Louisiana. Student: Ron Mathis. Studio Critic: M. Saleh Uddin. Course: Graphic Presentation.

Rendering Techniques

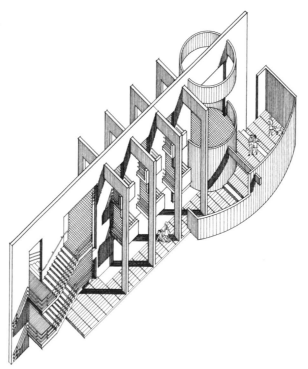

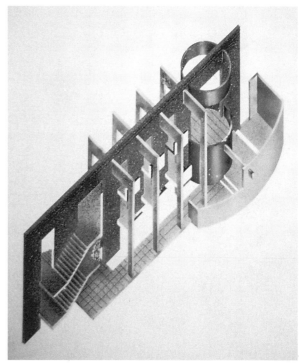

Original pencil-drawn axonometric with a touch of prisma-color. Construction of the axonometric from the floor plan was the primary intention of this drawing. Quick color pencil shades were used to identify and differentiate individual elements. This base drawing was used to produce other finished drawings. Not intended for final presentation.

Pen-and-ink line drawing traced from the original pencil drawing on the left. A 4x0 rapidograph pen was used for the floor texture, curved surfaces, and shade and shadow.

Airbrush technique with acrylic color. The pencil drawing was transferred to a masking film and applied to the drawing surface. The drawing surfaces were exposed by cutting out the masking film to apply color with a Badger airbrush.

Courtesy: M. Saleh Uddin, Associate Professor, Southern University. The Urban Wall.

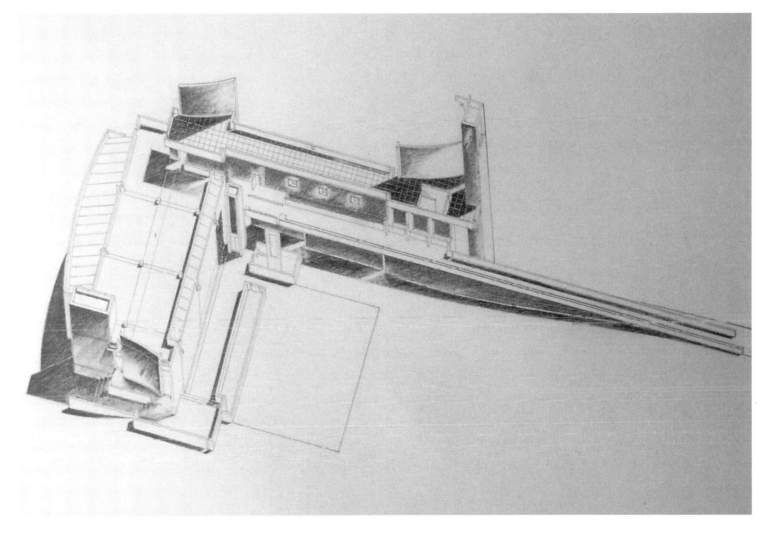

A pencil-drawn plan oblique generated on yellow tracing paper from constructed floor plans. The drawing was then transferred to a smooth watercolor board with a hard pencil. Shades and shadows were cast first and rendered with 6B and 8B pencils. Lighter pencil tones were applied with a 2B pencil.

Courtesy: University of Southwestern Louisiana.
Student: Liao Kok Chuan. Studio Critic: George Loli.
Urban Zen Center.

Rendering Techniques

Graphite pencil on tracing vellum.

Courtesy: Richard B. Ferrier, FAIA
Professor, University of Texas Arlington.
HGMV

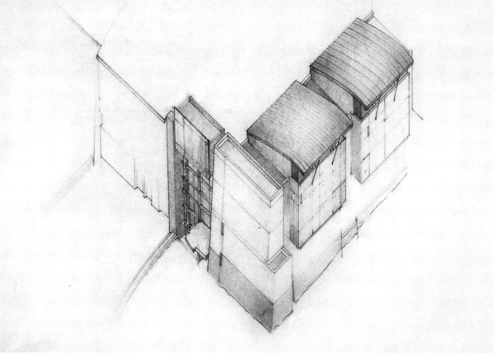

Color pencil on tracing vellum.

Courtesy: Richard B. Ferrier, FAIA
Professor, University of Texas Arlington.
National Cowboy Hall of Fame
Oklahoma City, Oklahoma.

Rendering Techniques

Exterior 90-degree/0-degree frontal axonometric. Pencil on Kent paper. Expressed the composition of the regional landscape and three solid buildings with achromatic and different shades of lead pencil technique.

The drawing was first drawn with a hard lead pencil on Kent paper and then with three softer pencils to highlight the brighter-to-darker area. The depth of the building was emphasized by the clear edges between the darker and lighter areas. The accurate grids of the pavements were achieved by scoring on the paper with a cutter and then applying soft lead over the scored area.

Courtesy: Shin Takamatsu Architects & Associates.
Drawing: Norihiro Banba.
Gotsu Community Center, Gotsu-shi, Japan.

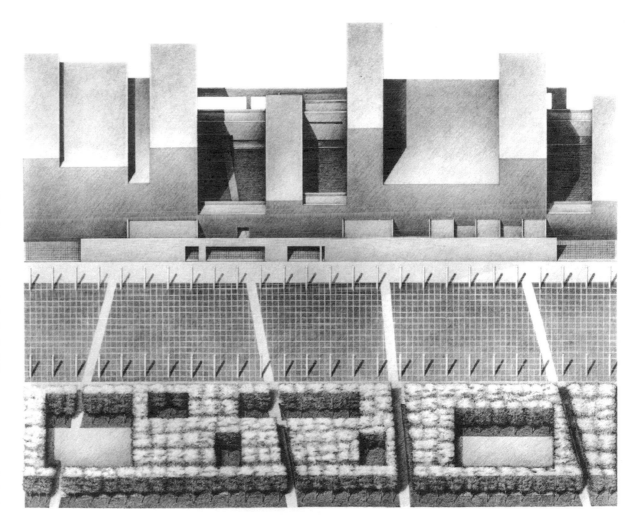

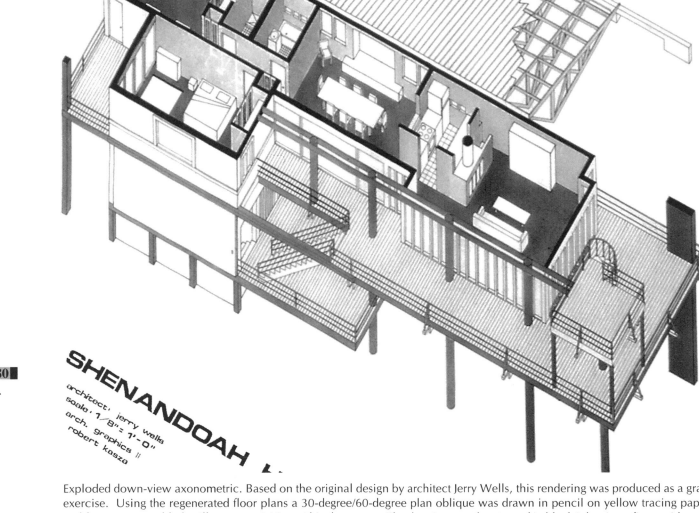

SHENANDOAH

architect: jerry wells
scale: 1/8": 1'-0"
arch. graphics ii
robert kasza

Exploded down-view axonometric. Based on the original design by architect Jerry Wells, this rendering was produced as a graphics studio exercise. Using the regenerated floor plans a 30-degree/60-degree plan oblique was drawn in pencil on yellow tracing paper. Furniture and fixtures were added to illustrate activities within the spaces. The drawing was then traced in black ink using a fine rapidograph pen onto a white vellum. Interior walls and floors were shaded in different tones of adhesive dot screens. Roof top and floor decks were hatched with a 4x0 rapidograph pen. Yellow prismacolor pencil was used to render exposed portions of the roof trusses. Adhesive Pantone color films were used to render support columns and beams connecting those columns.

Courtesy: Savannah College of Art and Design. Student: Robert Kasza. Studio Critic: M. Saleh Uddin.

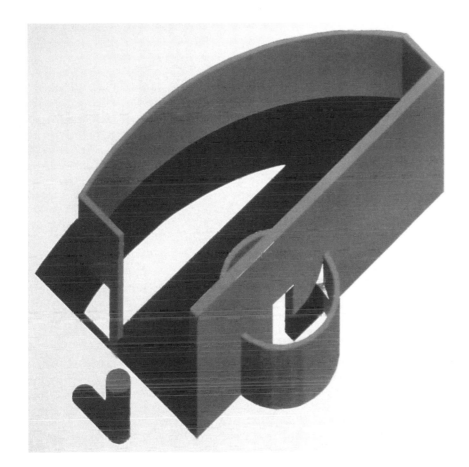
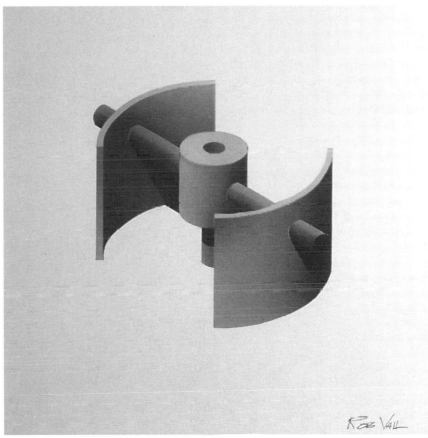

Axonometric rendering of forms that are variations of cylindrical volumes. These renderings were executed with one color with an additional tone of black to accentuate surface variation and highlight shades and shadows.

Each drawing was produced on 12 x 12-in illustration board with a lead pencil. Masking film was placed on the drawing surface to cover the areas that would not receive color. The painted areas were cut and exposed for spraying. Opaque red acrylic color on the left drawing and opaque flesh color on the right drawing were applied on the forms with a Badger double-action airbrush, without any shade variation. The drawings were then remasked and exposed to receive black tone gradation for the purpose of illustrating surface variation.

Courtesy: Savannah College of Art and Design. Savannah, Georgia.

Students: Christopher Smith and Robert Vail. Studio Critic: M. Saleh Uddin. Begining studio exercises for an advanced graphic presentation course.

Rendering Techniques

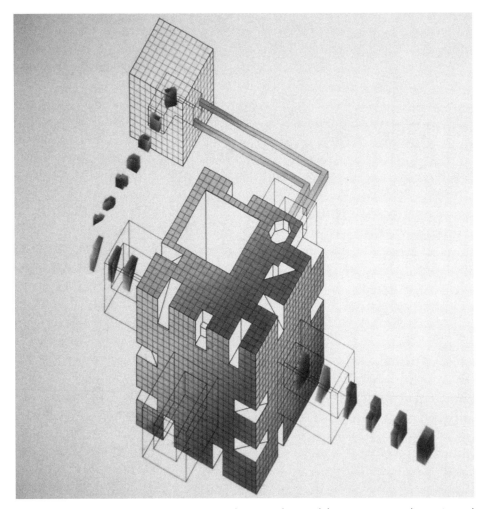

Exploration of a cube in axonometric rendering to be used for generating schematic and design ideas for a studio project. Exploded cube drawn in black ink line and rendered with airbrush technique. Two colors were used; one for the object, and the other for the shade gradations. Use of an airbrush accentuates the sterile and formal quality of the cube.

Courtesy: University of Southwestern Louisiana.
Studio Critic: George Loli. Student project from Graphic Communication course.

Schematic axonometric rendering generated from a balsa wood model. Entry element of a house design pulled out and enlarged to explore the mood, scale, and environmental context. The sketchy effect of the rendering was created by using quick strokes of oil pastels on an illustration board.

Courtesy: University of Southwestern Louisiana.
Studio critic: George Loli. Student project from Graphic Communication course.

Rendering Techniques

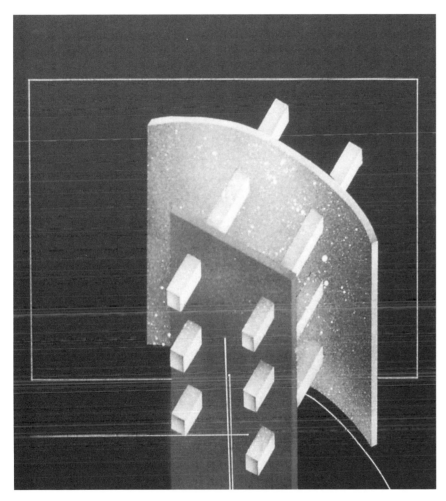

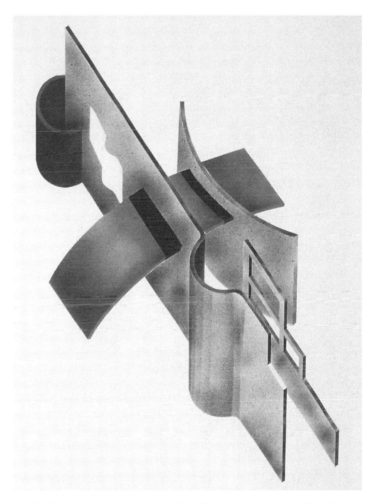

Opaque white-and-red paint on black mount board. The drawing was produced on a transparent masking film and placed on the black drawing surface. Painted areas were cut and exposed for spraying. Red paint was sprayed with an airbrush. White paint was sprayed straight from a spray paint can. White lines were drawn with a technical pen using white-colored Rotring ink.

Courtesy: M. Saleh Uddin.
National Laboratories Ltd, Dhaka, Bangladesh. Study of a shading device.

Opaque black-and-red paint on white illustration board. The drawing was produced on a transparent masking film and placed on the drawing surface. Painted areas were cut and exposed for airbrush spraying.

Courtesy: M. Saleh Uddin.
Study of planar elements.

Rendering Techniques

Rendering in prismacolor pencil and airbrush. Ink line drawing traced from original pencil drawing to produce both drawings. The drawing shows shades of prismacolor pencil applied on the ink line drawing.

Courtesy: M. Saleh Uddin, Associate Professor, Southern University. The Cube House.

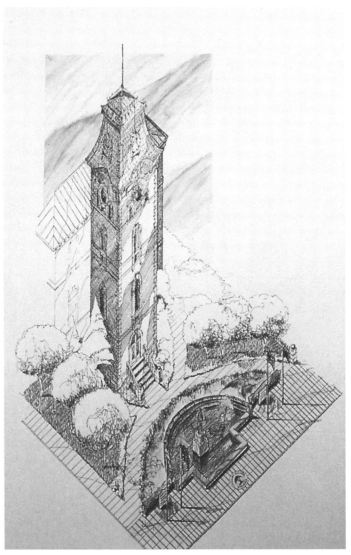

India ink on vellum with color marker and pencil. This technique combines both freehand and ruled line work.

Courtesy: Harry A. Eggink, Professor of Architecture.
Ball State University, Muncie, Indiana.
Henry Cikinty Courthouse, Entry Plaza and Fountain.

Rendering Techniques

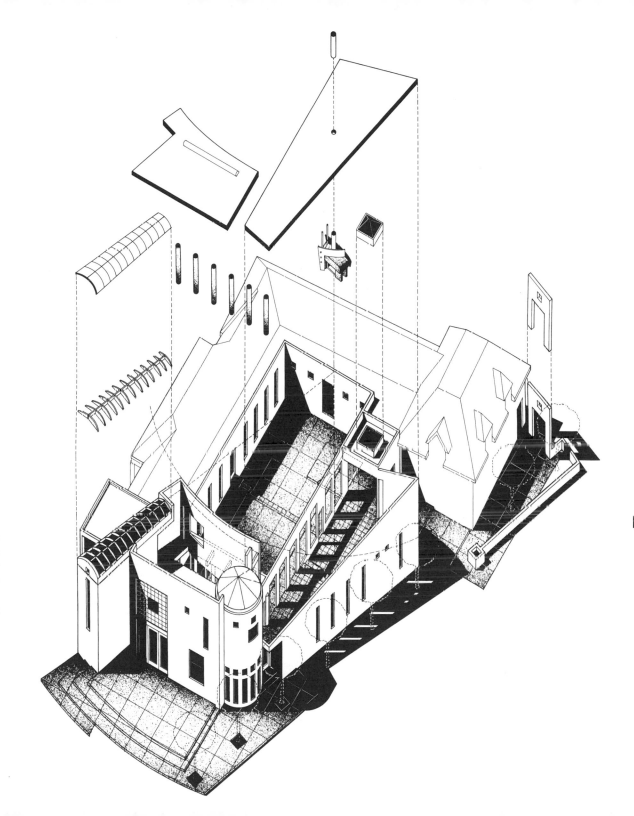

Exploded axonometric. Pen and India ink with airbrush on 24 x 32-in mylar. The drawing was used to emphasize the new addition and its relationship to the original house with the creation of an interior courtyard. Roofs and other architectural elements are pulled up to clarify their shapes and allow the view to the interior. Shading was used as a graphic element to add contrast and texture to the drawing.

(This new addition is composed of a series of architypical building forms arranged around the courtyard by a ridged geometry which also controls proportions and openings.)

Courtesy: House + House Architects, California.
Drawing: David Thompson and Steven House.
Shamash Residence, Hillsborough, California.

Rendering Techniques

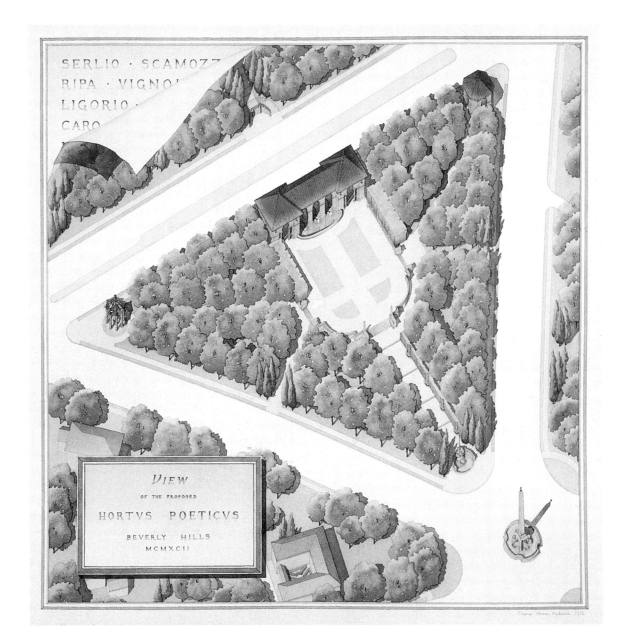

SERLIO · SCAMOZZ

RIPA · VIGNO

LIGORIO ·

CARO

VIEW

OF THE PROPOSED

HORTVS POETICVS

BEVERLY HILLS

MCMXCII

Watercolor and ink wash over pencil line work. An axonometric drawing is used to describe the physical relationship of a series of freestanding architectural elements which together comprise a design for a new public park in Beverly Hills, California. The roles of these elements within the iconographic schema of this unified composition of architecture and landscape are thus rendered legible. The drawing reveals the names of those whose lives and work began this intellectual tradition.

The drawing is composed to allow the central axis of the architectural design to establish a primary compositional diagonal through the drawing from lower right to upper left. The position of the *trompe-l'oeil* "scroll," and the names of the great architects and iconographers it reveals, provide a counterbalance to the figural isolation of the obelisk fountain, creating a taut polarity along the diagonal axis. The title plate, together with the central terrace in the park, suggest a more subtle, opposing diagonal which serves as a counterpoint.

Courtesy: Thomas Norman Rajkovich, Architect.
Drawing: Thomas Norman Rajkovich.
Hortus Poeticus.
Beverly Hills, California.

Rendering Techniques

Isometric projection. Original ink on polyester film. Copy of ink line drawing colored with Faber Castell Polychomos pencils. The building surfaces are hatched and cross-hatched for tonal variation. The rendering with its background creates almost a three-dimensional model-like quality in its illustration techniques.

To visualize this urban renewal project, some specific buildings were added to show more detail with relation to the surrounding cityscape. This was achieved through the use of an isometric projection (30 degree/30 degree). The existing fabric is shown in an abstract blue color. The proposed structures are cut and hatched and the specifically designed building is shown in its interior layout. The overall image is floating on a blue background underlining the importance of the river which crosses both site and city alike.

Courtesy: Alexis Pontvik.
Alexis Pontvik Arkitekt, Sweden.
Holmens Bruk urban renewal
competition, Norrkoping, Sweden.

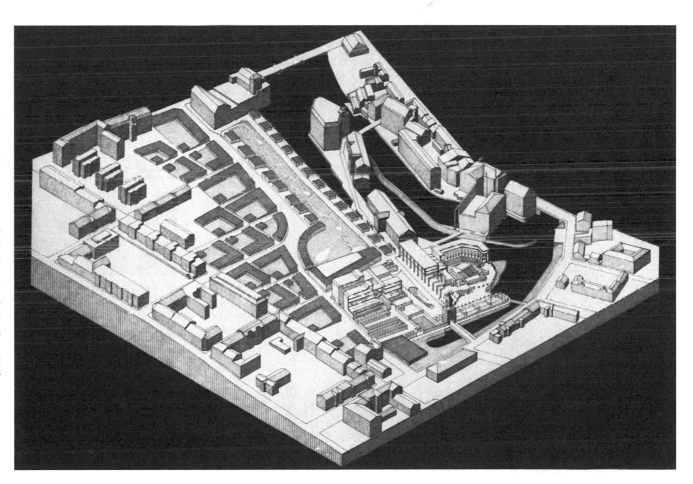

Rendering Techniques

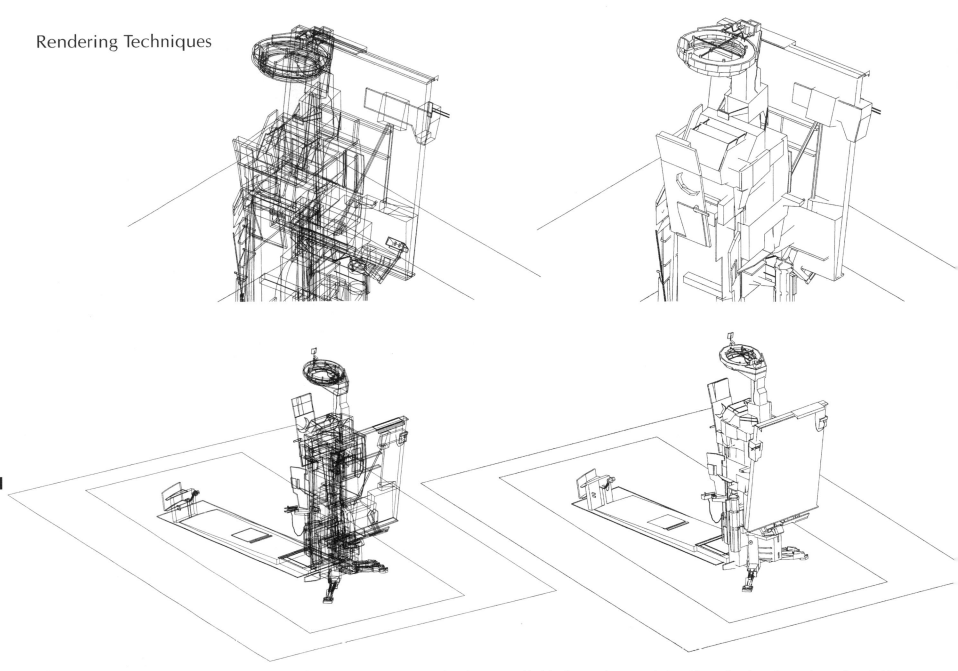

4... Rendering Techniques

Computer sequence axonometric views. Progression from: construction wire mesh to dimensional hidden line to phong rendering. Above drawings show wire mesh and hidden line views. The next page shows phong rendering views and a cardboard model photograph.
Courtesy: Bryan Cantley + Kevin O'Donnell. Outhouse Prototype no. 93.7.

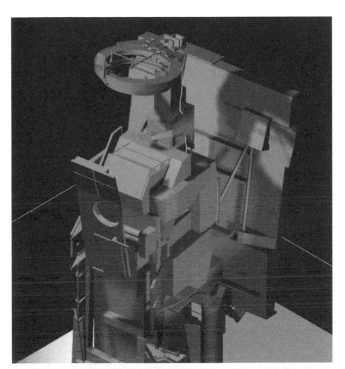

Computer sequence axonometric views. Progression from: construction wire mesh to dimensional hidden line to final phong rendering. Views show solids development as an overall system and detailed components. Drawn on Microstation 5.1. Computer renderings were executed on an Intergraph InterPro 120 and Macintosh Power PC. Final image output are hard-copy Fiery Prints.

Orthographic sketches were used from the onset of the concept to facilitate the proper investigation of the three-dimensional form. Most of the concept sketches were developed as isometric drawings that explored the integral relationships between the machine components. Drawings were made from a variety of angles to understand formal juxtapositions prior to solid modeling. After design development in traditional graphic media and models, an orthographic computer model was designed to understand possible daylighting and rendered lighting effects. The computer model also facilitated rapid visualization of the three-dimensional relationships in alternate situations from different viewpoints.

(These axonometric views are part of a study for an urban variant prototype of a public restroom. The project responds to a dense context of urban flux. The project stands as an urban sculpture until users interactivate the architecture from folding wall panels within the core and sidewalk. Facilities are a self-sustainable architecture, and include two user-interactive information/ entertainment screens with a communications port for going "on line." It is designed to be completely self-cleaning and thwart graffiti and vandalism. Considered to be an *architextural* experiment of information distribution.)

Courtesy: Bryan Cantley + Kevin O'Donnell.
Design: Bryan Cantley + Kevin O'Donnell.
Computer Rendering: Lori Cantley. Computer Coordination: James Choi, Bob Holmes, and Gary Hunt.
Outhouse Prototype no 93.7.

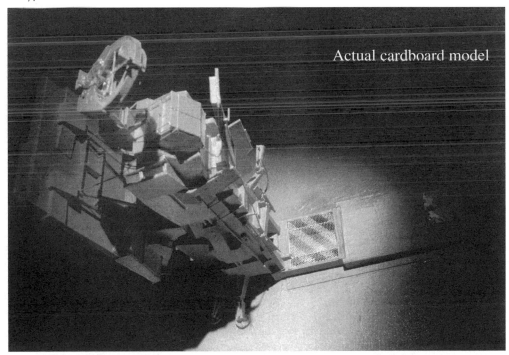

Actual cardboard model

Rendering Techniques . . . 4

Rendering Techniques

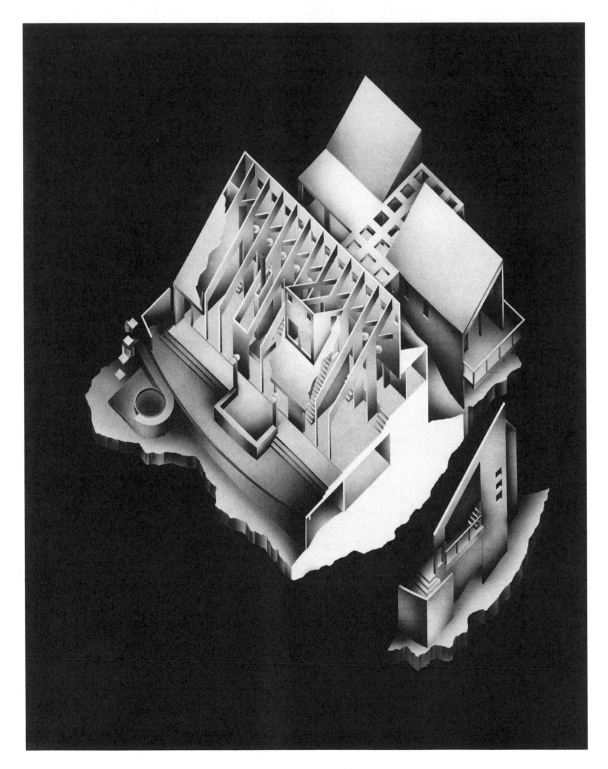

Exploded/eroded axonometric. Airbrush using India ink and acrylic inks on 30 x 30-in cold press illustration board. The drawing composition dramatically presents the main spatial ordering system of the shed-roofed volumes of the building by presenting the roof as a see-through membrane. The slope of the land is shown on the partial section of the main image. The color palette is metaphorical; green for natural surfaces, pink for artificial interior surfaces, gray for artificial exterior surfaces, and black as the universal background.

Courtesy: House + House Architects.
Renderer: Mark English.
Abott-Elpers Residence, Woodside, California.

Free-Hand •
View from Above (Bird's-Eye) •
View from Below (Worm's-Eye) •
Cut-Away •
Frontal •
Transparent •
Exploded •
Assembled-Disassembled •
Split-segmented •
Simultaneous Views •
Hybrid •

Exploration and Point-of-View

5 . . . Exploration and Point-of-View

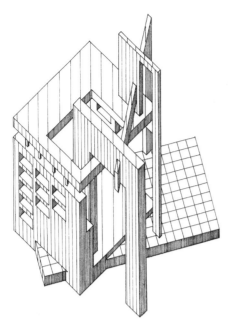

View from Above (Bird's Eye)

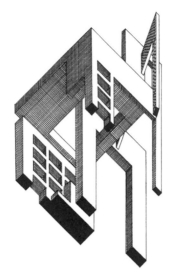

View from Below (Worm's Eye)

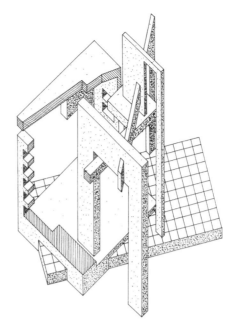

Cut-Away

Frontal/Elevation Oblique

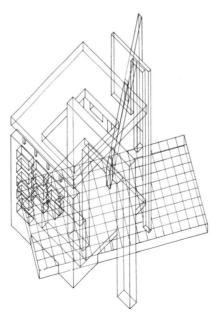

Transparent

Inspired by Hiromi Fujii's original design of T-29 and T-39, the drawings on these two pages, show the student-designed structure visualized from various points of view explored through eight different axonometric types.

Student project from:
Graphic Communication course.
Student: Gardenier Ware.
Studio Critic: M. Saleh Uddin.
Southern University, Baton Rouge, Louisiana.

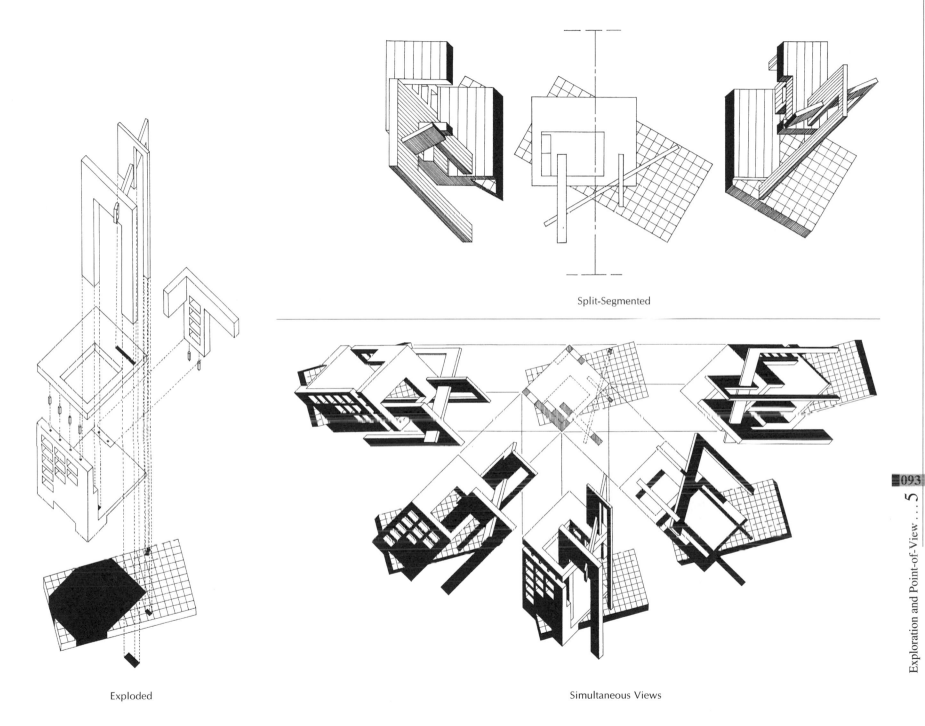

Split-Segmented

Exploded

Simultaneous Views

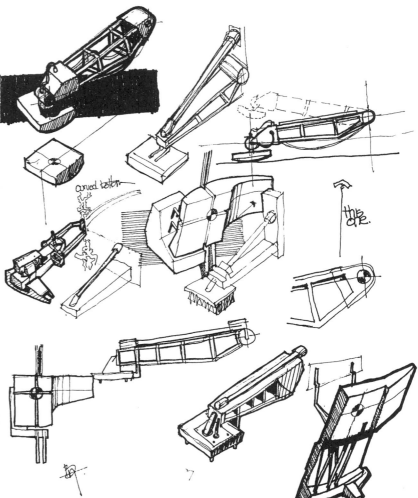

Free-Hand Axonometric

Free-hand sketchbook studies of the major lateral support arm, attempting to abstract hydraulic arms found on construction equipment. These studies also show early suggestions of front public gate assembly of the project Outhouse Prototype no. 93.7. Ink on paper.

Courtesy: Bryan Cantley + Kevin O'Donnell.
Sketches: Bryan Cantley.
Outhouse Prototype no. 93.7.

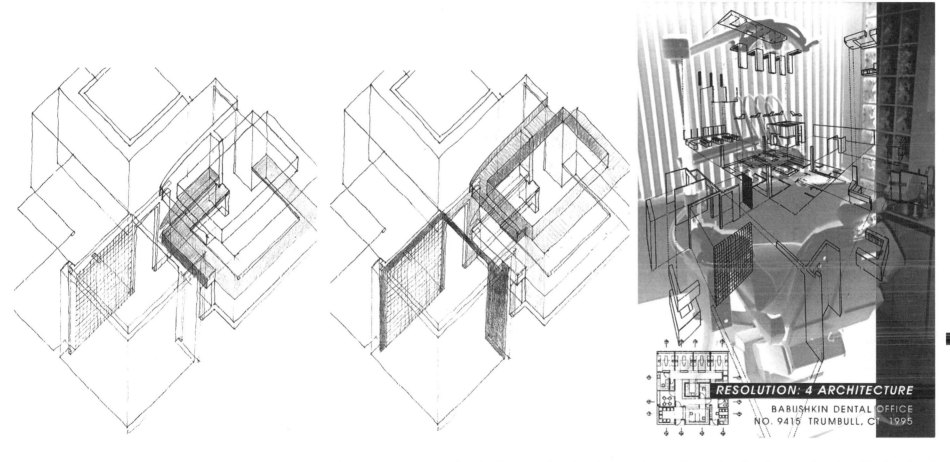

RESOLUTION: 4 ARCHITECTURE

BABUSHKIN DENTAL OFFICE
NO. 9415 TRUMBULL, CT 1995

This conceptual free-hand axonometric explores design studies and composite graphics by showing a line drawing superimposed on an interior photographic view. The free-hand sketches illustrate shifting volumes and spacial sequences at entry. The sketches highlight the reception area, soffit, and entry.

Courtesy:Resolution: 4 Architecture. Joseph Tanney, Gary Shoemaker, and Robert Luntz.
Dentist Office, Trumbull, Connecticut.

Freehand Axonometric

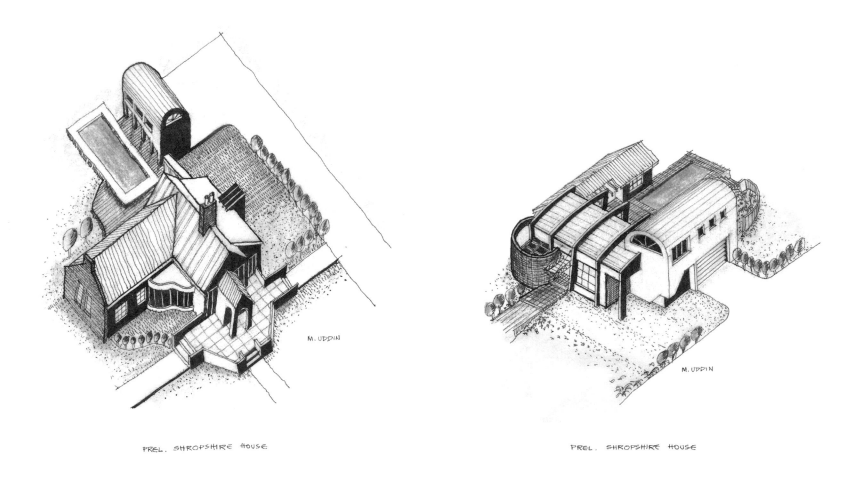

PREL. SHROPSHIRE HOUSE

PREL. SHROPSHIRE HOUSE

M. UDDIN

M. UDDIN

Free-hand axonometric drawing. Black ink line drawing and prismacolor pencil on yellow tracing paper. Conforming with the floor plans these two axonometrics were drawn freehand using a .25 technical pen. Prismacolor was added to accentuate form and material of the designed structure. These sketches were part of the preliminary design study to examine the forms and their connections for a house.

Courtesy: M. Saleh Uddin, Associate Professor, Southern University. Shropshire Residence, Baton Rouge, Louisiana.

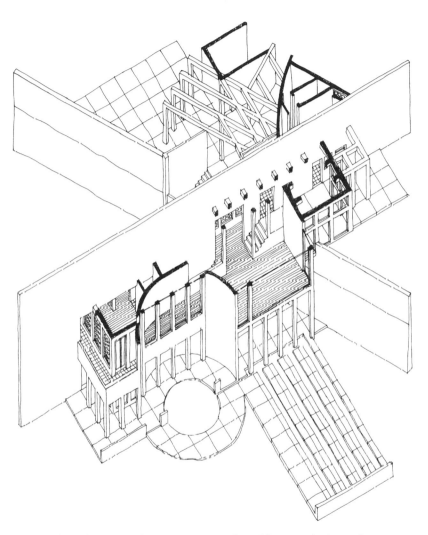

Free-hand sketch study of basic forms in marker and lead pencil. Line sketch drawn with a lead pencil. A darker tone of color marker was applied for the ground and settings of the elements. A lighter marker tone was applied to identify the horizon and to create a contrast with the ground plane. Additional pencil tones were applied over the marker to highlight surface shades.

Courtesy: George Loli, Associate Professor.
University of Southwestern Louisiana.

Free-hand 60-degree/30-degree cut-away plan oblique. The base drawing was constructed on yellow tracing paper using pencil. The pencil-drawn axonometric was traced over in freehand using a rapidograph pen to save time.

Courtesy: Savannah College of Art and Design.
Student: Jonathan Biron. Studio Critic: M. Saleh Uddin.
House Chang(ed).

Freehand Axonometric

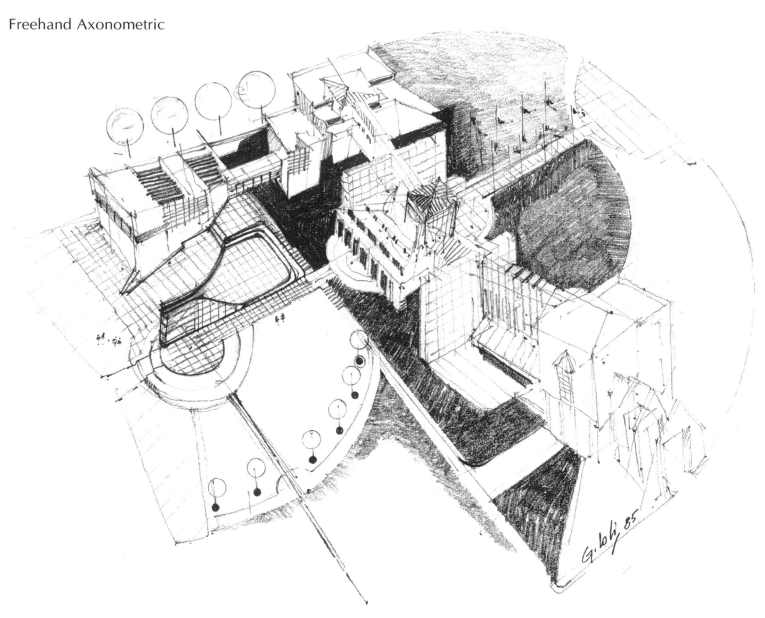

This free-hand lead-pencil axonometric was drawn on an 8-1/2 x 8-1/2-in sketchbook page. The drawing illustrates the schematic design of a multifunctional cultural center. Drawn with B and 6B pencils, the sketch study emphasizes the relationship of the basic building forms to the adjacent open spaces, both paved and green. The primary emphasis of the sketch was to highlight the approach sequence from both sides.

Courtesy: George Loli, Associate Professor. University of Southwestern Louisiana. Schematic of a cultural center.

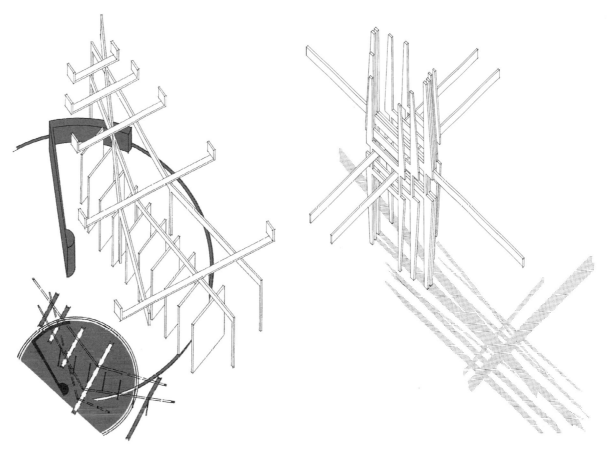

Ink line drawing with adhesive dot screen and color Pantone film.
Courtesy: Thomas Sofranko, Assistant Professor, Louisiana State University.

Bird's-Eye or Down-View Axonometric

• Full down view
• Down view segmented
• Down view disassembled

Bird's-Eye or Down-View Axonometric

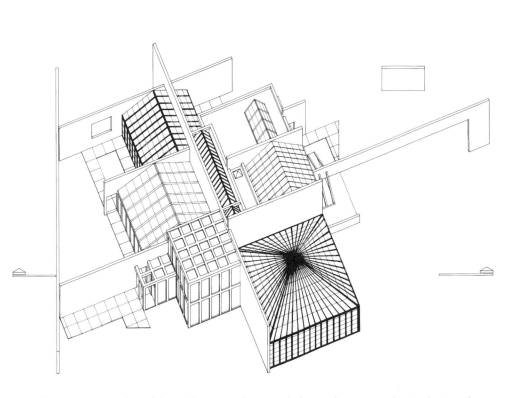

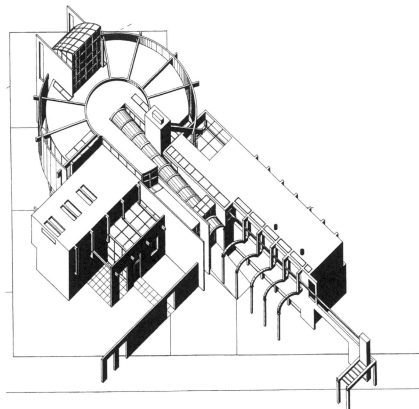

This down-view plan oblique illustrates the use of planar elements and articulation of space enclosures. Pen-and-ink line drawing on vellum.

Courtesy: Savannah College of Art and Design, Savannah, Georgia.
Student: Johnathan Biron. Studio Critic: M. Saleh Uddin.
Florist Shop and Green House.

This 45-degree/45-degree down-view plan oblique illustrates the design elements and articulation of the massing of form volumes. Pen-and-ink line drawing on vellum.

Courtesy: Savannah College of Art and Design, Savannah, Georgia.
Student: Kevin Schellenbach. Studio Critic: M. Saleh Uddin.
Reprographic Facilities.

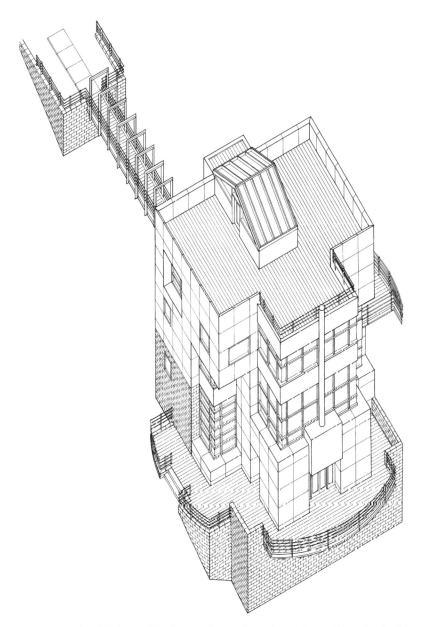

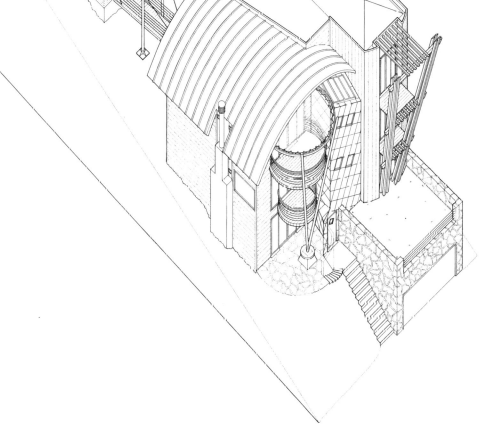

This 30-degree/60-degree down-view plan oblique illustrates building form, fenestration, and surface texture. Pen-and-ink line drawing on vellum.

Courtesy: Dean Nota Architect.
Robertson Residence, Flathead Lake, Montana.

The 45-degree/45-degree down-view plan oblique above illustrates the manipulation of various forms and their interrelationships. Pen-and-ink line drawing on vellum.

Courtesy: David Baker.
Schuh Project.

Bird's-Eye or Down-View Axonometric

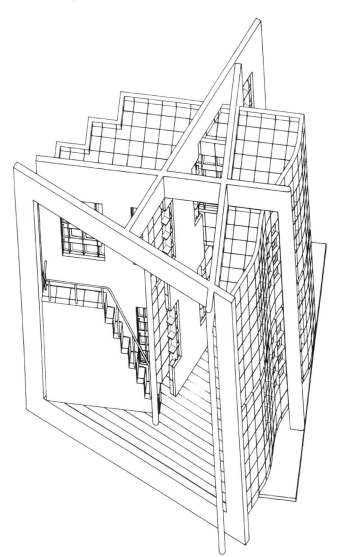
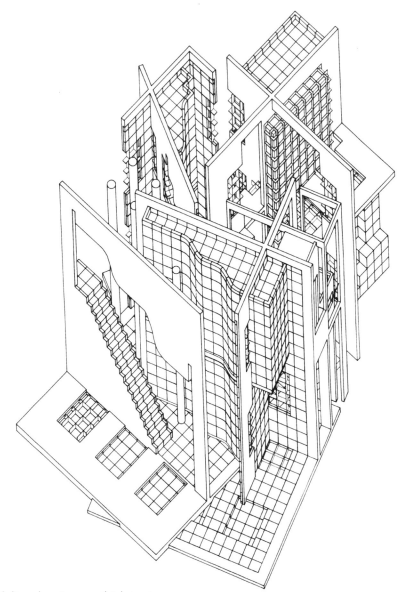

The two illustrations above are down-view plan obliques. Both are pen-and-ink black line drawings on thick tracing paper.

Courtesy: Hiromi Fujii, Tokyo, Japan.
Project T-29 (left drawing). Project T-39 (right drawing).

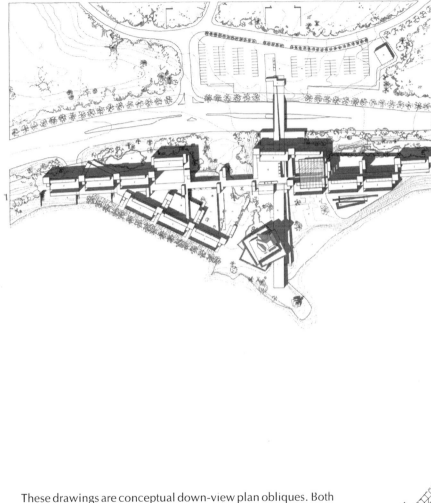

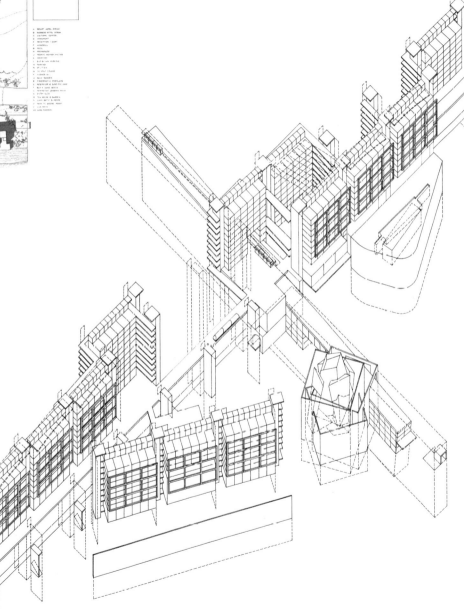

These drawings are conceptual down-view plan obliques. Both the drawings illustrate clear relationships and linkages between all linear volumetric elements. The site plan above emphasizes contextual references. Pen-and-ink line drawing on vellum. An adhesive dot screen overlay was used on the line drawing for the site plan.

Courtesy: Resolution: 4 Architecture.
Joseph Tanney, Gary Shoemaker, and Robert Luntz.
Wainaku Mill Hotel, Hilo, Hawaii

Bird's-Eye or Down-View Axonometric

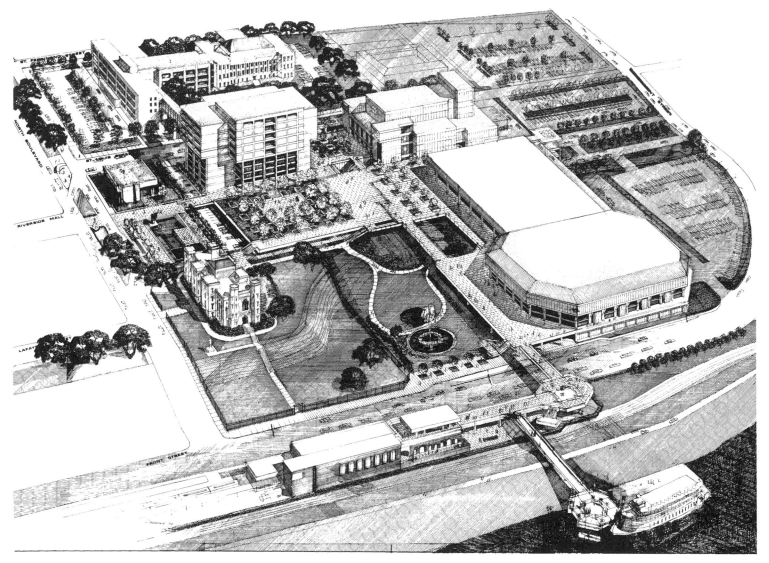

Down-view perspective with vanishing points at the far distance. The drawing creates a quasi-axonometric effect by having lines running almost parallel instead of converging to a visible vanishing point. The drawing illustrates a large portion of the downtown area encompassing several city blocks. Pen-and-ink line drawing on vellum.

Courtesy: John Desmond, FAIA. Governmental and Cultural Centroplex, Baton Rouge, Louisiana.

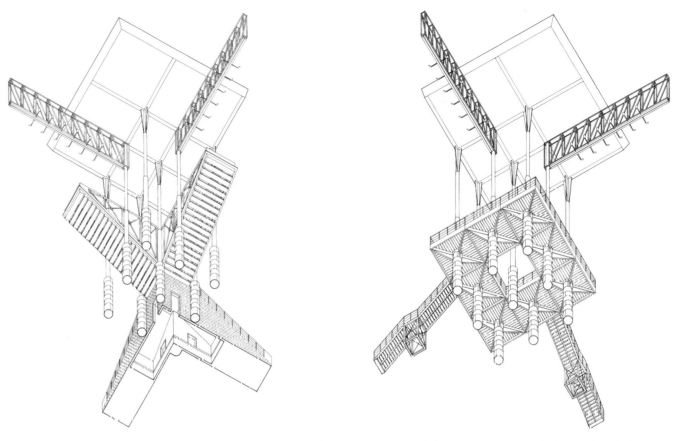

Plan oblique views looking up to illustrate the structural support systems and their connections with the overhead planes.
Pen-and-ink line drawing.
Courtesy: Machado and Silvetti Associates. Pershing Square, Los Angeles, California

Worm's-Eye or Up-View Axonometric

- Full up view
- Up view segmented
- Up view exploded/disassembled

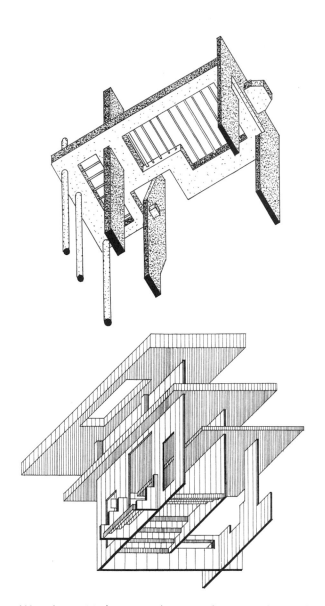

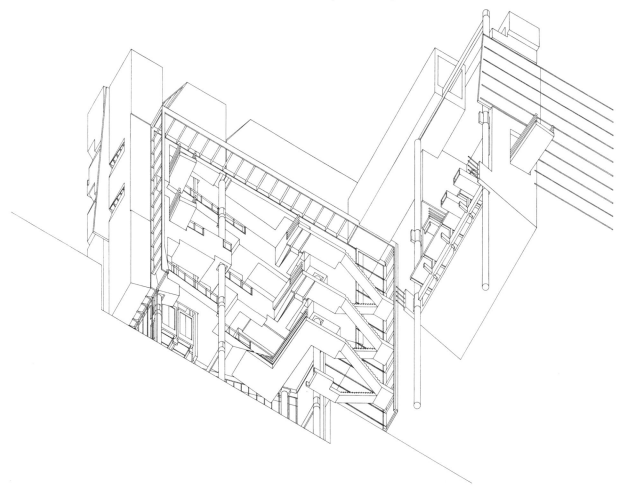

Worm's-eye 30-degree/60-degree, 0-degree/45-degree elevation oblique, and 45-degree/45-degree axonometrics. Cuts taken at the floor level and raised up to view the ceiling. Ink line drawings on vellum. Dots, vertical lines, and cross hatching used for surface tones.

Courtesy: Southern University, Baton Rouge, Louisiana.
Students: Karlton McMeans and Aaron Johnson.
Studio Critic: M. Saleh Uddin.

Worm's-eye cut-away axonometric. Ink line drawing on 24 x 24-in mylar. The drawing shows a good overview of interior space articulation and the vertical circulation system that connects different floor levels by removing the front walls.

Courtesy: Carnegie Mellon University.
Student: Jason Alden. Studio Critic: Agus Rusli.
Mixed-Use Theatre/Art School in Montreal (Competition).

5 . . . Exploration and Point-of-View

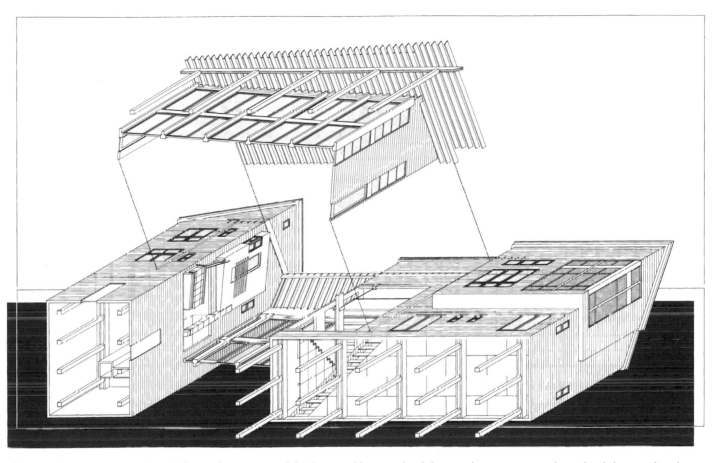

This worm's-eye axonometric reinforces the concept of the fractured bar as a backdrop to the great covered porch while revealing how structure and materiality contribute to those forms. The composition of form, structure, and material are expressed in the drawing as component parts contributing to the whole. (This simple bar also serves as a sheltering backdrop for the double-height public area, conceived of as a great covered porch. Materials and shed-roofed massing elements are similar to the gulf coast cottages found throughout the region; deviations from the vernacular occur in scale relationships and in the arrangement of the parts to the whole. The fracture of the bar acts as a portal which directs the entry sequence toward the sweeping views of the bay.) Ink on mylar with color and shading film.

Courtesy: Natalye Appel Architects.
Drawing: Natalye Appel and Kevin Stevens.
Susman Bay House, Galveston, Texas.

Worm's-Eye or Up-View Axonometric

The up-view axonometric was favored in the nineteenth century by Auguste Choisy for its ability to facilitate a comprehensive understanding of the tectonic order of a design and its inherent ability to regulate proportion and define space. This image, executed in watercolor and ink wash over pencil line work, acknowledges the critical role of drawings as "re-presentations" of architectural ideas. The logical and essential gravitas of all great architecture is perceptually amplified, not diminished, when the axonometric depicts the structure seemingly suspended in the air. This delightful paradox is reinforced by the depiction of a bird in flight in the distance. Here, through the art of representation, the nature of simple things becomes explicit, clear, and poetic.

Courtesy: Thomas Norman Rajkovich, Architect.
Drawing: Thomas Norman Rajkovich.
Tuscan Market Loggia, Evanston, Illinois.

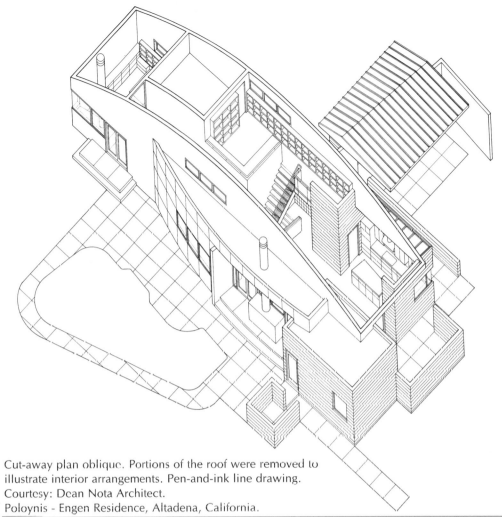

Cut-away plan oblique. Portions of the roof were removed to illustrate interior arrangements. Pen-and-ink line drawing.
Courtesy: Dean Nota Architect.
Poloynis - Engen Residence, Altadena, California.

Cut-Away Axonometric

- Roof removed (full or portion)
- Wall removed (full or portion)
- Portions of both roof and wall removed
- Full roof and wall removed

Cut-Away Axonometric

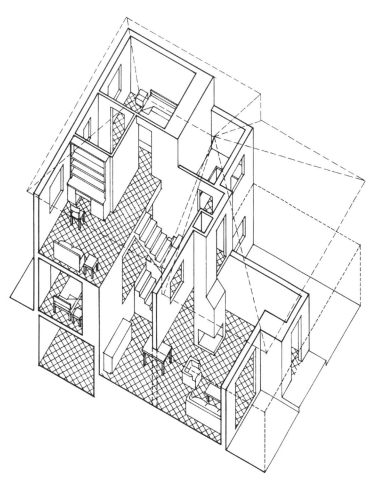

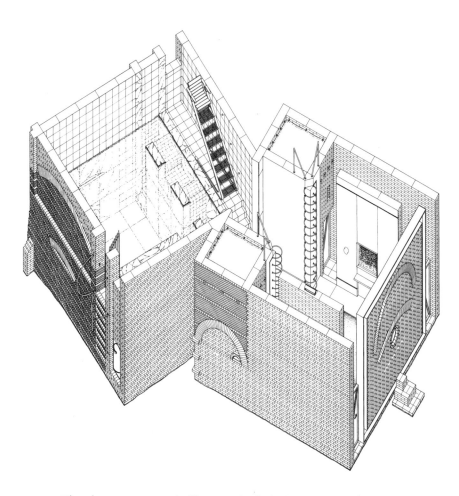

By removing the roof and one face, the relationship of various levels in the house, the central core, and its architectural elements are made visible as they would be experienced in the house. The representation provides an excellent opportunity for volumetric and spatial analysis. Ink line drawing on 11 x 17-in transparent mylar.

Courtesy: Jawaid Haider, Associate Professor, and Talat Azhar.
The Pennsylvania State University.
International Small Home Design Competition.

The above axonometric illustrates both the interior spatial arrangement and the exterior volumetric relationship. Adding informative details on the wall planes describes the material, texture, and execution of planes. Hand-drawn pen-and-ink line drawing.

Courtesy: Machado and Silvetti Associates.
Taberna Ancipities Formae, Natchez, Mississippi

Cut-Away Axonometric

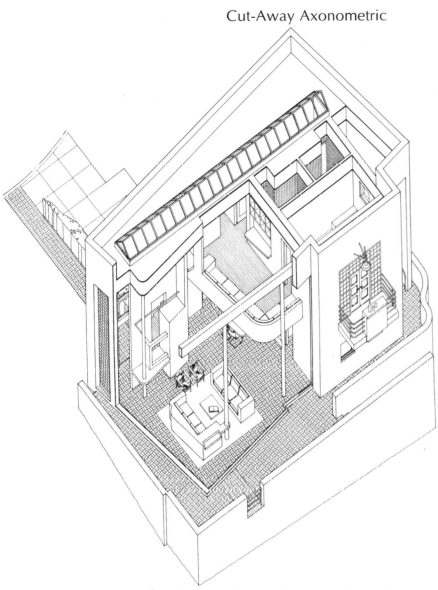

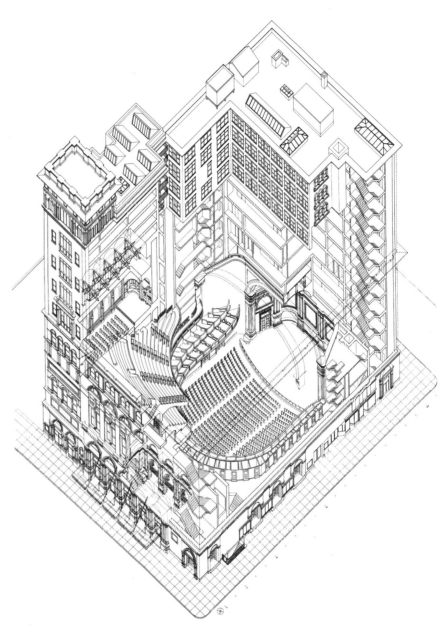

Cut-away axonometric. Portions of the roof and two side walls were removed to show the double-height living space. Pen-and-ink line drawing.

Courtesy: Anthony Ames Architect.
House in Mississippi, Laurel, Mississippi.

Cut-away axonometric. Portions of the roof and side walls were removed to show the details of the main auditorium space. Pen-and-ink line drawing on 42 x 48-in mylar.

Courtesy: Polshek and Partners Architects.
Carnegie Hall Restoration and Renovation, New York, New York.

Cut-Away Axonometric

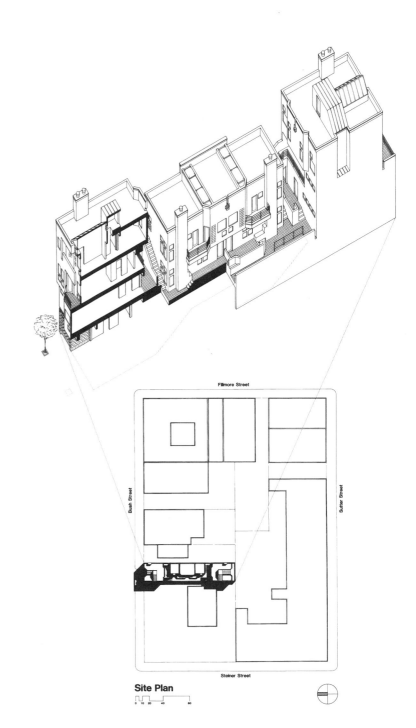

Site Plan

Above Drawing:
Cut-away axonometric illustrates the structural framework as well as the interior spaces by removing the exterior walls and the roof system of the front half of the building. Pen-and-ink line drawing on vellum.

Courtesy: John Desmond, FAIA.
National Competition for Mobile County Governmental Building.

Right Drawing (Top & Bottom):
Cut-away axonometric and site plan composite. India Ink on 30 x 54-in mylar. The drawing illustrates the relationship of a six-unit housing complex to its site and provides a cross-sectional view of the interior. The upper portion of the drawing consists of an axonometric cut-away with half of the front building removed to expose the interiors of the units. The site plan with shadows illustrates the building's relationship to its urban context.

Courtesy: House + House Architects. Bush Street Condominiums.

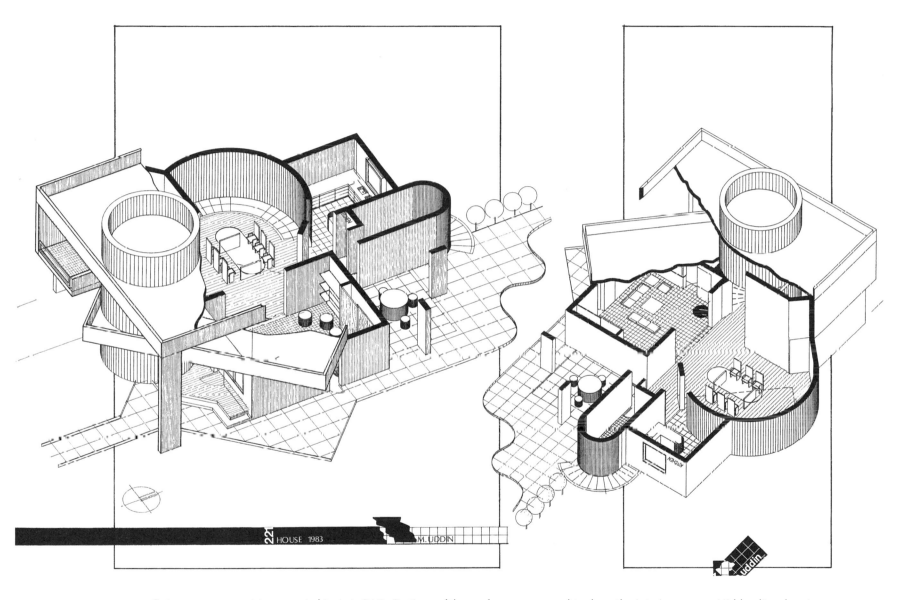

HOUSE 1983   M. UDDIN

Cut-away axonometric generated in AutoCAD. Portions of the roofs were removed to show the interior spaces. Hidden line drawings were plotted on 20x30-in white bond paper.

Courtesy: M. Saleh Uddin. Preliminary design for Rahman Residence, Dhaka, Bangladesh.

Elevation oblique provides a precise scaled representation of the side elevation which is most critical to the thematic characteristics. A limited number of site features were added in order to visually balance the drawing and provide clues to the immediate context. Varied line weight is intended to enhance the kinetic characteristics of several rooftop components. Ink on 32x 40-in transparent mylar.

Courtesy: Robert J. Fakelmann, Associate Professor. Louisiana Tech University.
The His-And-Her House.
Open rural landscape near the town of Calhoun, Louisiana.

Frontal Axonometric

- Frontal with side walls vertical: 90-degree/0-degree
- Frontal with side walls in oblique: 90-degree/other angles

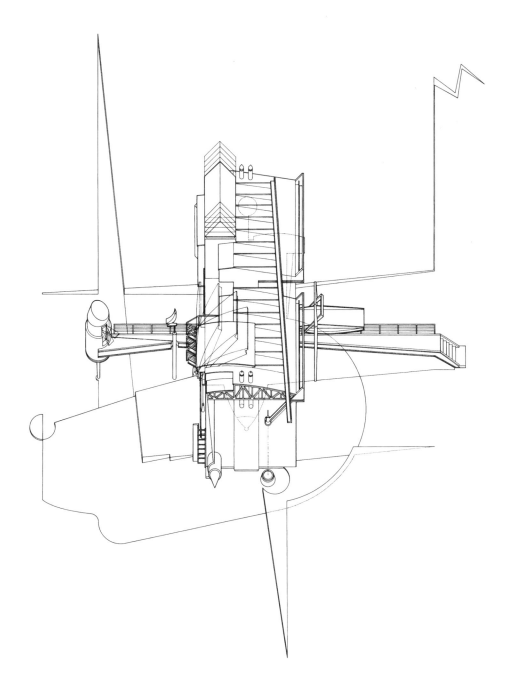

AXONOMETRIC
EXTERIOR ———— SOUTHWEST

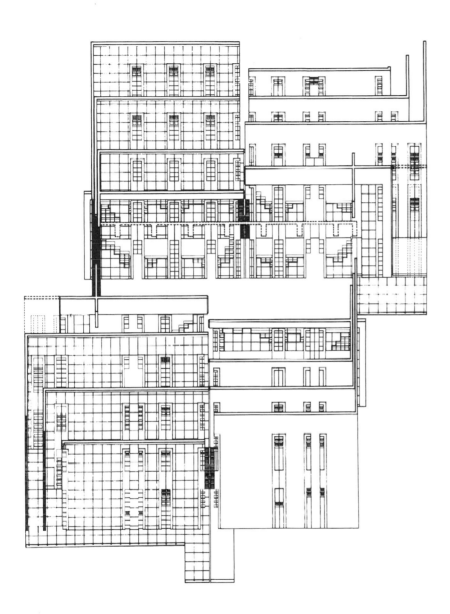

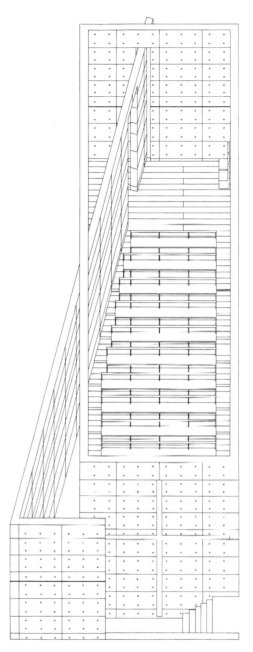

Axonometric in vertical projection. Pen-and-ink line drawing on heavy-weight tracing paper.

Courtesy: Hiromi Fujii.
Second Gymnasium at the Shibaura Institute of Technology, Japan

90-degree/0-degree plan oblique. The roof was removed to show the interiors. Pen-and-ink line drawing.

Courtesy: Tadao Ando Architects & Associates.
Church of the Light, Osaka, Japan.

Frontal Axonometric or Elevation Oblique

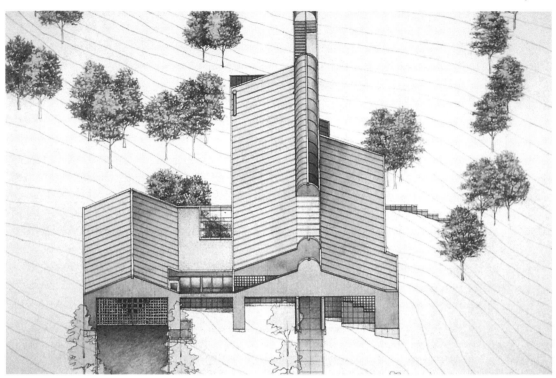

Above:
Frontal 0-degree/90-degree elevation oblique illustrates building forms and the surrounding site context. Graphite and watercolor on board.

Courtesy: Richard B. Farrier.
Stroud House

Left:
Pen-and-ink line drawing. A 0-degree/90-degree frontal axonometry was employed as a means of emphasizing the thematic (iconographic) and formal importance of the design's axial organization, in the tradition of the Italian Renaissance ville etchings executed by Giovanni Battista Falda in the 18th century. The spatial layering of the design along the primary axis is reinforced by the ability of the axonometric to establish and communicate foreground, middleground, and background. The existing tower's ruinous state is revealed in true perspective behind the *trompe-l'oeil* "scroll." The image is thus a celebration of the rich interdependence of the arts in the Renaissance, in which the visual laws of perspective, so integral to the theater, influenced the design of public spaces from the piazza to the formal gardens of the great ville.

Courtesy: Thomas Norman Rajkovich, Architect. Drawing: Thomas Norman Rajkovich.
Project for the Reconstruction of the Chicago Water Works Tower and
Adjacent Gardens, Chicago, Illinois.

Frontal Axonometric or Elevation Oblique

A very large (36 x 72-in) pencil on vellum, elevation oblique drawing at one-quarter scale was projected from the plans of the building. A light #4H lead layout was then drawn over with a heavy #2 Mongol pencil by Eberhard Faber. The drawing was then Diazo-printed onto heavy-weight, presentation, black line paper. The drawing was colored with a combination of washes of Magic Marker with colored pencil touch-ups and a "ghetto airbrush" sky using different blue commercial spray paint canisters. Subtle shading and shadows, by using repeated washes of the Magic Marker, creates depth and three-dimensional modeling of the building assemblage. The drawings accurately rendered the materials and colors of the building in order to convince the local urban design board of their appropriateness in terms of materials, form, color, and siting in the park.

(Piedmont Park, reportedly designed by Olmstead, is bordered by major thoroughfares in the rapidly developing midtown area of Atlanta. A sense of harmony is achieved between the old clubhouse (1930s) and the new construction through combinations of elements that are contrasting or analogous in their material, form, and symbolism. Parkside restores and embellishes the American, and especially Southern, tradition of a gracious, civic life centering on the park and on the representative values of verdant nature. Parkside seeks to reestablish the importance of Piedmont Park in Atlanta's resurgent architectural and cultural tradition.)

Courtesy: Anderson/Schwartz Architects.
Design:Frederic Schwartz.
Rendering: Frederic Schwartz and M. J. Sagan.
Parkside at Piedmont Park, Atlanta, Georgia.

Frontal Axonometric or Elevation Oblique

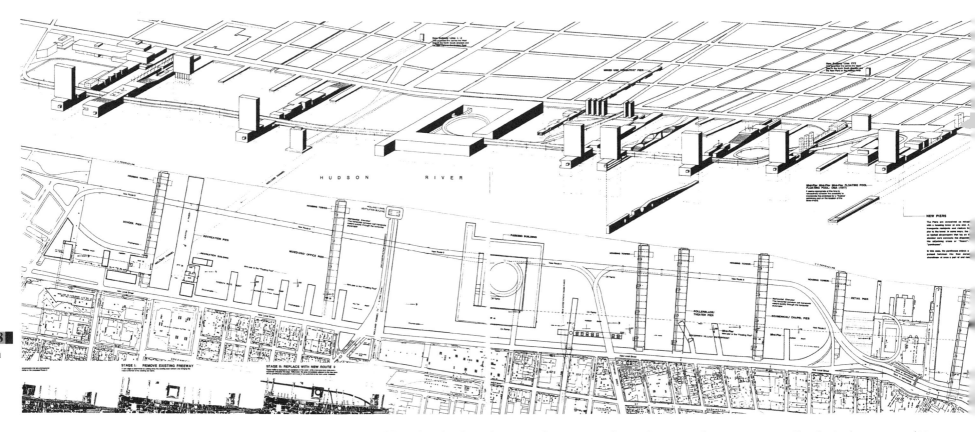

This frontal axonometric for an urban design project was projected from the plan from the point of view across the Hudson River from New Jersey. Clearly, in the context of New York City, an aerial drawing made from the other direction would be obscured by city fabric. The frontal axonometric was chosen over the plan projection or plan axonometric because of its lower point of view, i.e., the elevation is emphasized over the roof plan. In this case, the vertical surface of the housing towers located at the end of each pier was highlighted. The original drawing was a composite, consisting of a few different techniques. The frontal axonometric drawing was ink on mylar; the plan was photocopied onto the mylar and subsequently altered; the smaller diagrams were photocopies of aerial photographs that were also later altered. A photographic print was made from the original composite drawing.

Courtesy: Stephen K. Chung. Drawing: Stephen K. Chung.
NYC Waterfront Competition-Proposals for the Westside Highway, New York, New York.

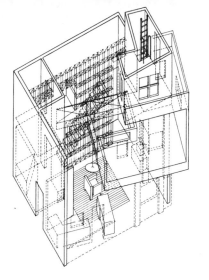

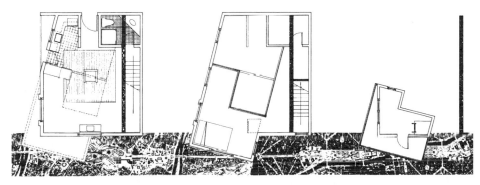

See-through axonometric with floor plans. Courtesy: Savannah College of Art and Design.

Transparent Axonometric

- Transparency with solid lines of same intensity
- Transparency with variation of dashed and solid lines
- Transparency with hierarchy of line thicknesses
- Transparency with implied lines and shapes

Transparent Axonometric

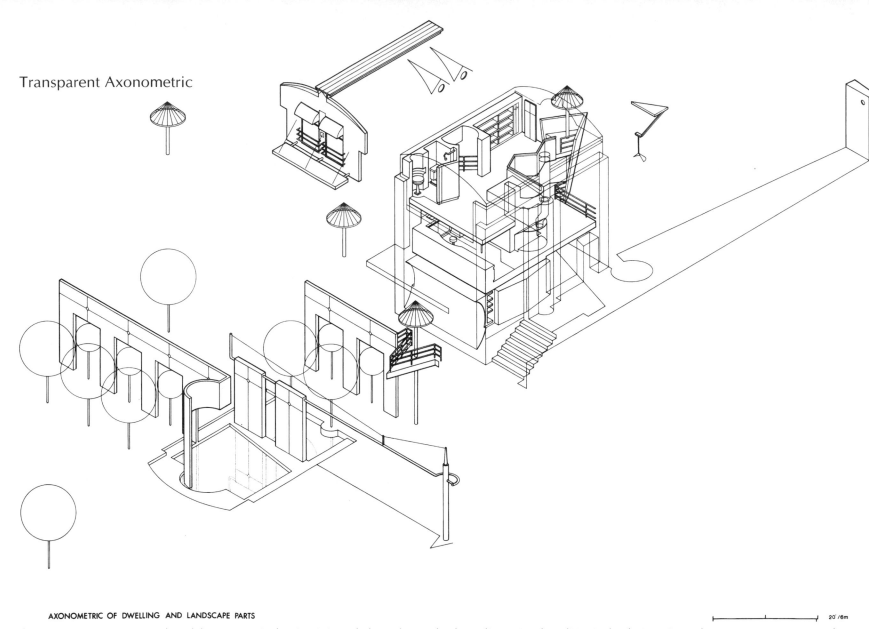

AXONOMETRIC OF DWELLING AND LANDSCAPE PARTS

20'/6m

This 30x40-in transparent mylar ink line isometric drawing is intended to enhance the three-dimensional qualities in the design. Several components are removed to reveal the interior spatial configuration. The lines of the exterior shell are left intact illustrating the relationship of the interior volume to the exterior form while rendering the surface transparent. Executed at angles of 30 degrees by 30 degrees with an interior angle of 120 degrees, as opposed to the customary 90 degrees typical in axonometiic drawing, it creates an illusion of perspective and visually settles the building to the ground.

Courtesy: Robert J. Fakelmann, Associate Professor. Louisiana Tech University.
A Residential Complex for Visiting Faculty and University Dignitaries. Louisiana Tech University Campus, Ruston, Louisiana.

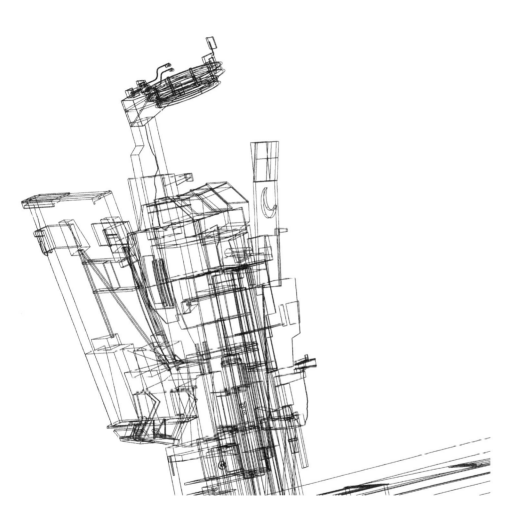

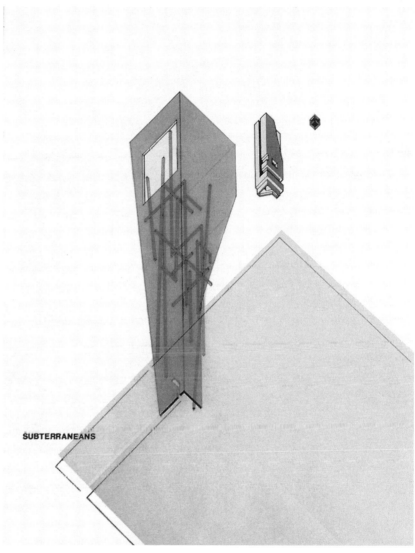

SUBTERRANEANS

Computer-constructed transparent wire mesh drawing. Drawn on Microstation 5.1. Computer drawings executed on an Intergraph InterPro 120 and Macintosh Power PC.

Courtesy: Bryan Cantley + Kevin O'Donell.
Design: Bryan Cantley + Kevin O'Donell. Computer Rendering: Lori Cantley. Outhouse Prototype no. 93.7.

Ink on vellum and colored film. Translucent worm's-eye axonometric provides a study of structure/skin relationship. The drawing represents an analytical study of a detail of a larger design to consider the relationship of the composite pieces.

Courtesy: Thomas Sofranko, Assistant Professor. Louisiana State University. Subterraneans.

Transparent Axonometric

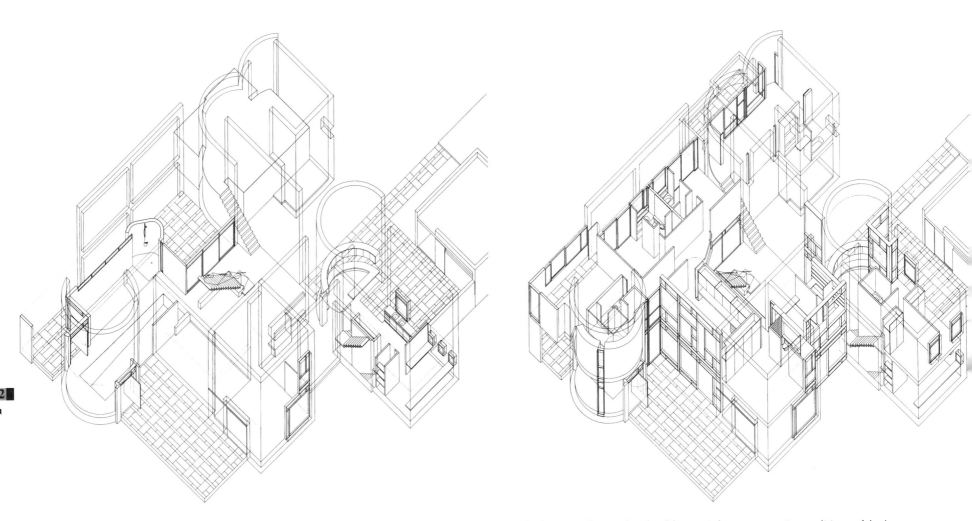

This sequence of drawings, part of a larger set which documents a private residence, illustrates the lower and upper levels of the spatial/programmatic conditions of the house. Varying degrees of transparency and opacity are strategically deployed to hierarchically differentiate preselected conditions important to the development of the work, in this case spatial/internal and enclosure elements. The wire-frame nature of the drawings favors issues of spatiality over formal ones. Hand-drawn ink line drawing on mylar.

Courtesy: Studio Concepcion. Drawing: Carlos E. Concepcion.
House in Madrid, Spain.

5 . . . Exploration and Point-of-View

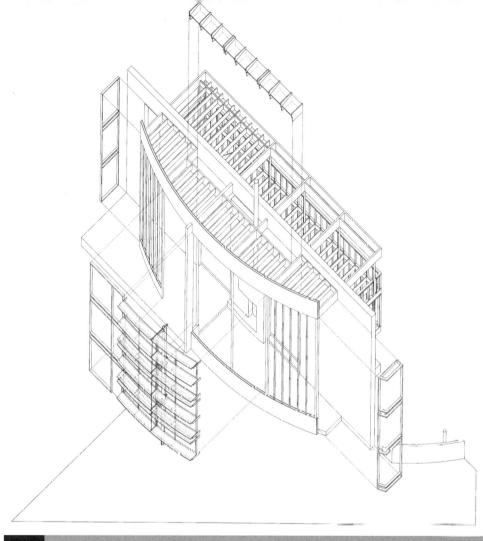

Exploded Axonometric

This exploded axonometric drawing uses a technique of selective editing to focus on a particular [critical] topic of inquiry, in this case the [wood] framing and glazing systems, and their relationships. Critical elements are highlighted by pulling them upward as well as sidewise in relation to the main structure. Ink line drawing on mylar.

Courtesy: Studio Concepcion.
Drawing: Carlos E. Concepcion.
House in Port Townsend, Washington.

- Exploding upward
- Exploding sidewise
- Exploding upward as well as sidewise
- Exploding envelope from main structure
- Exploding roof-shell from main body
- Exploding individual components
- Exploding various layers

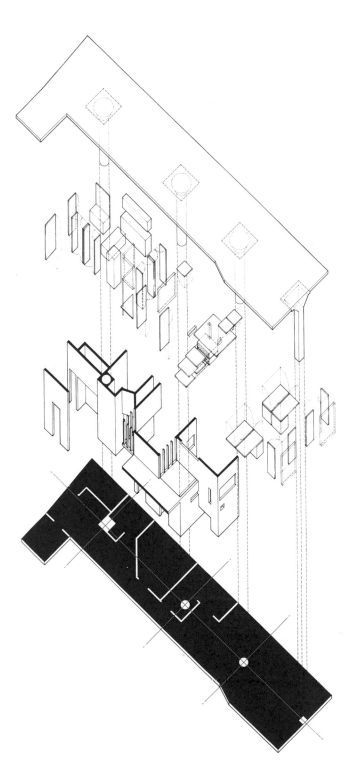

Exploded Axonometric

Far Left Drawing:
This exploded 45-degree/45-degree plan oblique illustrates both exterior forms and spaces enclosed by these forms. The building envelope was pulled up to highlight exterior volumes and basement spaces below the entry level as well as the vehicular circulation and parking layers above. Line drawing in ink.

Courtesy: David Baker Associates Architects. Clock Tower Building, San Francisco, California.

Left Drawing:
Exploded 45-degree/45-degree plan oblique illustrating several layers of information in one drawing. Elements pulled up to show the footprint of the floor plan, arrangement of interior spaces, furniture layout, structural supprt systems, and the roof plane. Line drawing in ink.

Courtesy: Resolution: 4 Architecture Joseph Tanney, Gary Shoemaker, Robert Luntz. A design/build collaboration between Jon Frishman, Gregory Epstein, and Resolution: 4 Architecture. Resolution: 4 Office, New York City, New York.

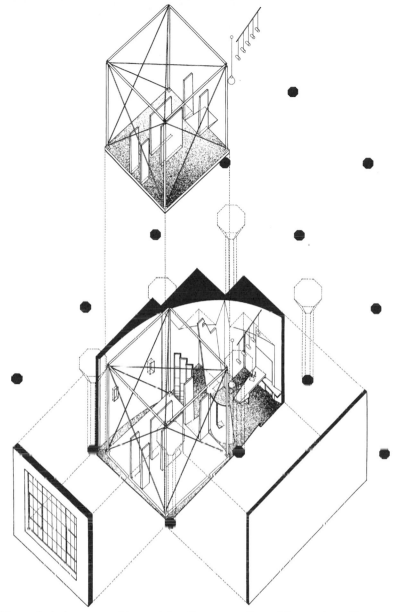

Exploded Axonometric

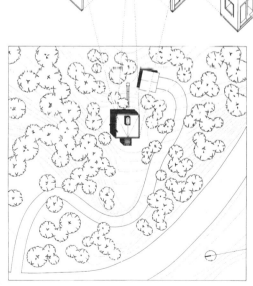

This exploded axonometric explains the conception of the project. The internal pieces such as the steel framework, the feature walls, the steel furniture elements, and the screen and platform all float out of a solid "container" of concrete and plaster walls and soffit. The project "container" itself is only one of many found in an existing manufacturing building and this characteristic is explained by the matrix of black column base locations indicated. Pen and ink with india-ink airbrush tone on 24 x 36-in mylar.

Courtesy: House + House Architects. Drawing: Mark English. Sirius Office & Gallery.

The site Plan (bottom) shows the building in its natural context while the exploded axonometric (top) allows the plan, elevations, and spatial characteristics of the house to be shown in a single drawing. Additional building elements are pulled up from the axonometric to clarify their shapes and interrelationships. Pen and ink was used to enhance the simplicity of the house. India ink on 24 x 48-in mylar.

Courtesy: House + House Architects. Drawing: David Haun & Michael Baushke. Stine Residence, La Honda, California.

SITE PLAN

Exploration and Point-of-View . . . 5

Exploded Axonometric

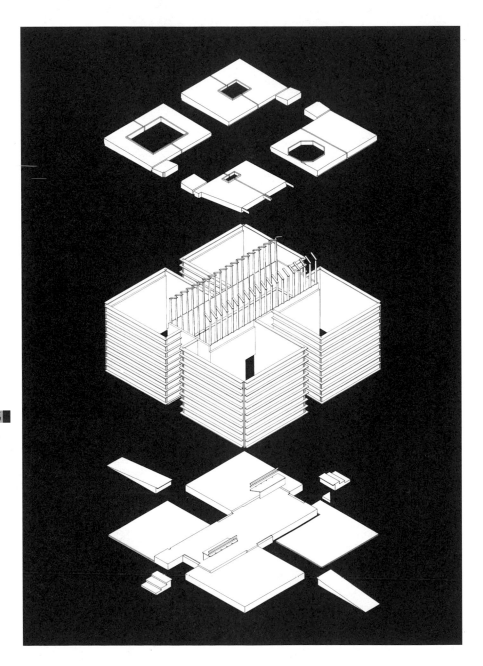

5 ... Exploration and Point-of-View

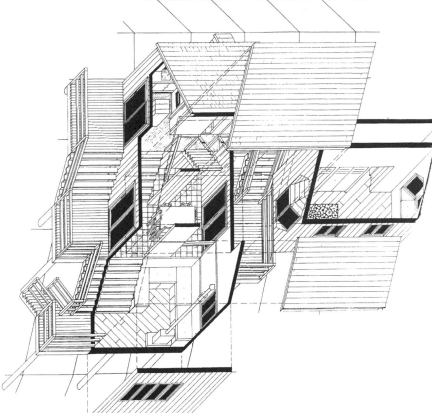

Above:
Axonometric exploded upward and sidewise. Dashed lines show the original position of the pulled-away wall and roof planes. The illustration exposes the interior of the dining and kitchen spaces. Portions of the vertical walls and roof were cut away to show the interiors. Pen-and-ink line drawing on vellum.

Courtesy: Savannah College of Art and Design.
Student: Shannon Stillwagon.
Studio Critic: M. Saleh Uddin.

Left:
Exploded isometric projection of a temporary exhibition pavilion. Ink drawing on 297 x 420-mm polyester film. The background was painted black to highlight various components of the structure. The Arts and Crafts Pavilion is a temporary structure to house the exhibition of four young artists. It is composed of floor, wall, and roof elements that are easily assembled. Each of the equal-sized rooms receives totally different lighting conditions to create different environments for artists' involvement. The rooms are reached by a central atrium.

Courtesy: Alexis Pontvik.
Alexis Pontvik Arkitekt, Sweden.
Exhibition Pavilion for the Arts and Crafts School in Stockholm.

Exploded Axonometric

Sequential exploded axonometric. Pen-and-ink line work with india-ink airbrush tone and black film on 36 x 60-in mylar, 35 mm black-and-white negatives spliced into a negative.

The intent of the drawing is to explain the nested arrangement of various building systems within a very precious small-scale building. The building is conceived as a very simple square pavilion with pyramidal roof structure overlapping a circular ordering system. The square is the building "proper" while the circle encloses an outdoor ritualized garden. The overlap zone of the two systems defines the wet and "natural" bath area. A cedar wood Japanese soaking tub stands at the center point of the circle.

A "bird's-eye" axonometric view at the bottom of the page shows the overall form of the building, while the "worm's-eye" view directly above expresses some basic plan and volume characteristics. The sequential views above focus on the individual building system elements contained within the shell of the building.

Production of the finished drawing was accomplished using the Archicad CADD program to manipulate, compose, and sequentially eliminate drawing elements. The drawing was then enhanced with ink linework where required for clarity or material differentiation. Airbrush india-ink tone was used to distinguish planes and black film was used to fill in large areas at the drawing base. High-contrast model photo negatives were spliced into the drawing negative to show aspects of the project not visible in the drawn form.

Courtesy: Mark English Inglese Architecture.
Drawing: Mark English & Jeff Gard.
The Hausch/Chen Residence, Los Altos, California.

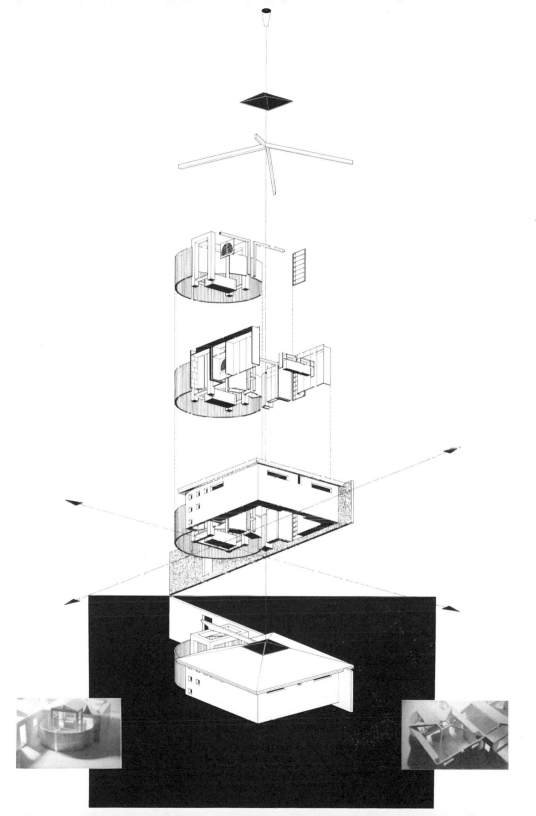

Exploded Axonometric

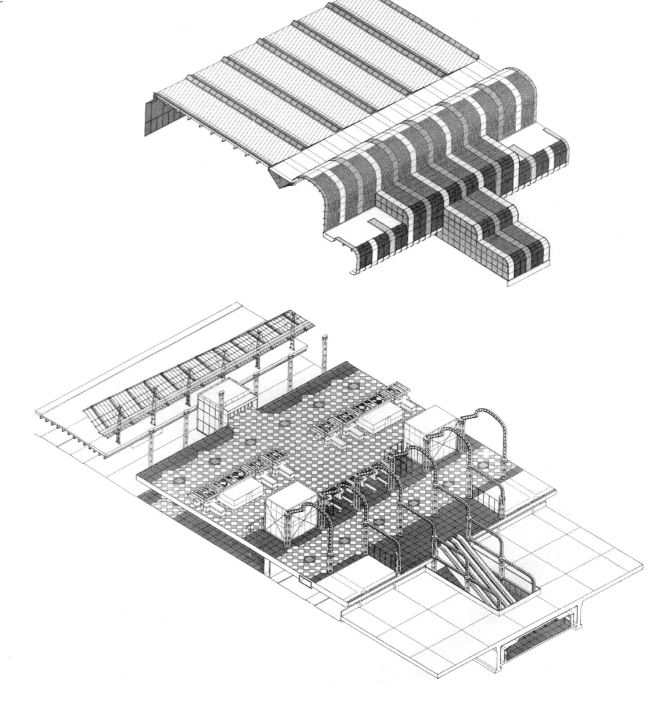

Exploded isometric projection showing structural framework and roof shell. The drawing emphasizes the openness of the structure by pulling the roof membrane upward in reference to the structural framework of the building. Line drawing in ink.

Courtesy: Murphy/Jahn Architects.
United Airlines Terminal 1 Complex,
O'Hare International Airport, Chicago, Illinois.

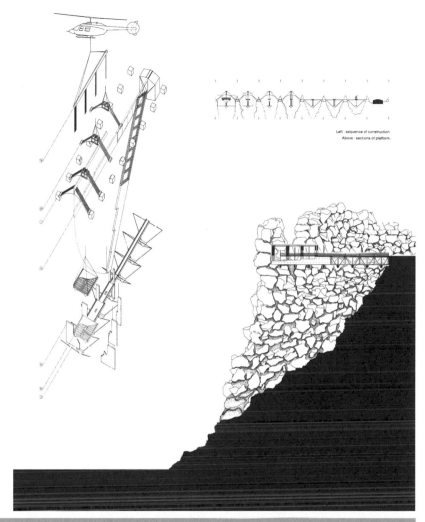

Left : sequence of construction.
Above : sections of platform.

The site for this project, which is a rocky crevasse on the face of a mountain, suggests the need for a process which is endemic to the notion of inaccessibility and fabrication. The observation platform is conceived as a floating space or floor within the natural room of the ravine. Constructed completely of prefabricated parts, the assembly of these elements becomes the essence of the drawing and of the building design itself. The drawing attempts to encourage the imagination to completion; to evoke a system of thinking that is tangible. Additional sections through the project inform the idea of site and assembly. The drawings are hand-drawn ink on mylar with extra black adhesive film in the opaque areas of the section.

Courtesy: Christopher Rose Architect.
Rose Architecture.
Observation Platform, Eggleston, Virginia.

Assembled-Disassembled Axonometric

- Assemblage of all components
- Assemblage of specific segment to the whole
- Assemblage of components in various groups

Assembled-Disassembled Axonometric

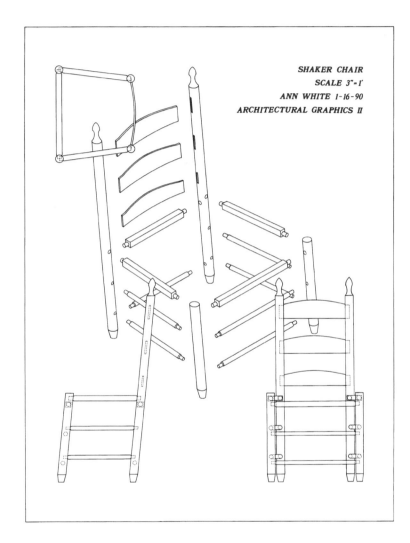

SHAKER CHAIR
SCALE 3" = 1'
ANN WHITE 1-16-90
ARCHITECTURAL GRAPHICS II

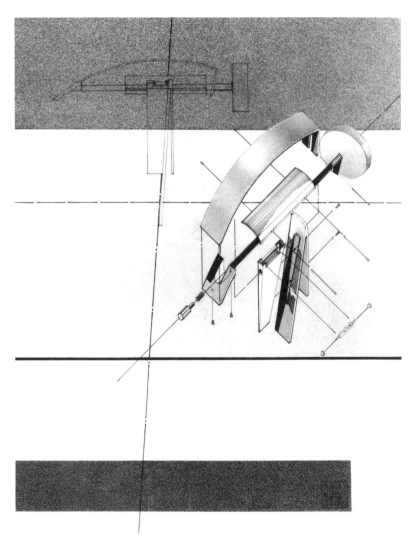

Components of a Shaker chair. The above drawing shows assembled views in orthographic elevations and a disassembled view in an axonometric. Ink line drawing on vellum.

Courtesy: Savannah College of Art and Design.
Student: Ann White. Studio Critic: Andrew Chandler.

Components of a Gallery installation. This drawing shows individual elements and their interrelationships. Adhesive screen and airbrush on ink line drawing.

Courtesy: Paul Westlake and Ronn Yong.
Prototype Installation 'Stratification.'

THE PIER

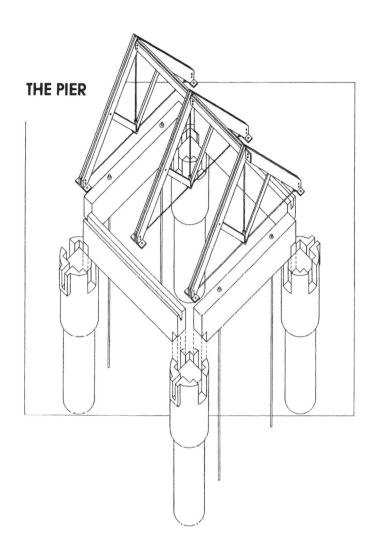

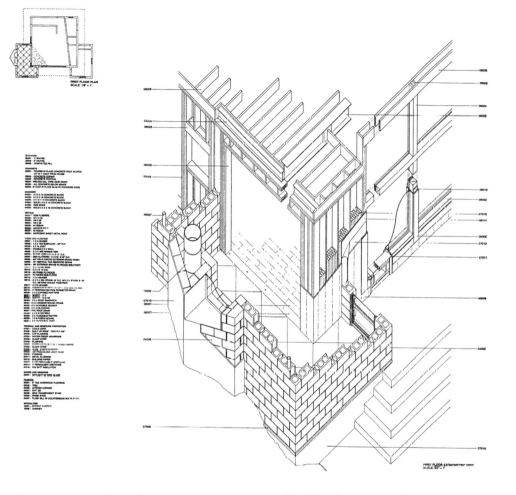

The drawing above illustrates the articulation of conditions of materiality, detail, and assemblage. Components are pulled apart at a larger scale to reveal the details of their connections. This drawing, part of a larger set of drawings, attempts to represent/document a mode of operation which exposes the structural interrelationships and dependencies inherent to each component. Hand-drawn ink line drawing on mylar.

Courtesy: Studio Concepcion.
Drawing: Carlos E. Concepcion.

The axonometric above shows the construction assembly of the front corner of the house dealing with masonry construction of the fireplace nook and wood framing of the roof and side walls. The intent of this drawing is to explore the structural and material connections between two building systems: wood frame and masonry. The drawing clarified the construction of the fireplace, explained the framing around the large south facing window, and assisted the structural engineer in detailing this complex corner.

Courtesy: Ross Anderson,
Anderson/Schwartz Architects.
Napa Valley House, Rutherford, California.

Exploration and Point-of-View . . . 5

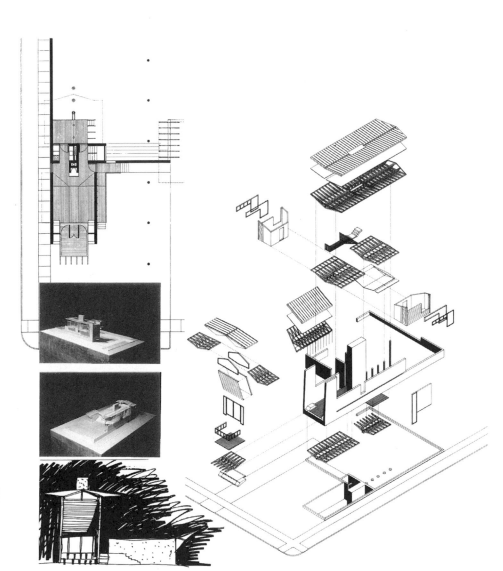

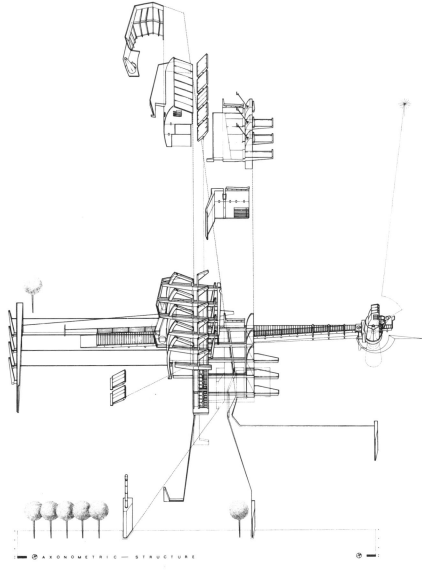

⊕ A X O N O M E T R I C — S T R U C T U R E   ⊕

In aspects of assembly, the economy of the house is the notion of separated building elements and systems. The drawings above address the identification of these elements by separating them with respect to their relationship with the primary masonry wall. The plan and elevation drawings describe specific ideas about the configuration of building elements, and both refer to the axonometric for clarity. The design addresses many issues of economy in construction prefabrication techniques and ready made materials use in a variety of configurations. All drawings are hand-drawn ink on mylar.

Courtesy: Christopher Rose Architect, Rose Architecture.
The Wall House.

This ink drawing on 32 x 40-in transparent mylar axonometric demonstrates the geometric compatibility between the framework and surface elements. The method of representation provides a pictorial field in which functional elements and detailed joinery are related to the structural configuration-- the part to the whole relationships are defined. The interpretive use of line weight further clarifies the structural congruency to the overall building form.

Courtesy: Robert J. Fakelmann, Associate Professor, Louisiana Tech University.
The Banqueting House: A Speculative Utopia.
Open flat Mississippi Delta landscape near the town of Poverty Point, Louisiana.

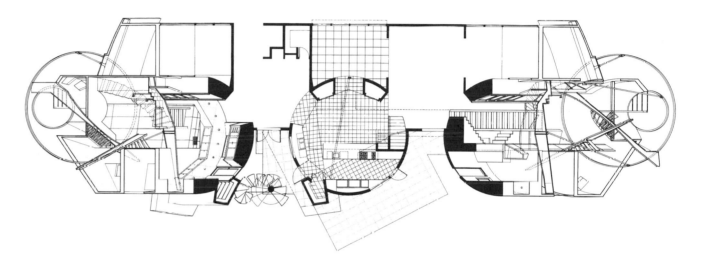

Plan with split worm's-eye axonometric.
Courtesy: Eric Owen Moss Architects, California. Lawson/Westen House, Los Angeles, California.

Split-Segmented Axonometric

- Vertical split
- Horizontal split
- Multiple split
- Split with rotation

Split-Segmented Axonometric

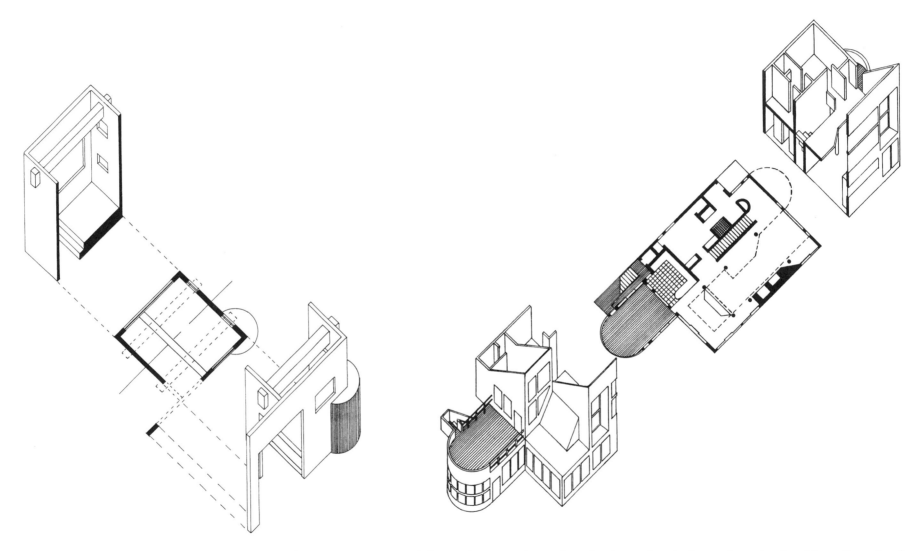

These drawings show 45-degree/45-degree plan oblique views cut into two halves and are moved away from the plan to show both two-dimensional and three-dimensional space arrangements. This type of split emphasizes the exterior in one half and the interior in the other half. Pen-and-ink line drawing on vellum.

Courtesy: Southern University, Baton Rouge, Louisiana.
Students: Michael Anthony and Nick Earls. Studio Critic: M. Saleh Uddin.

Split-Segmented Axonometric

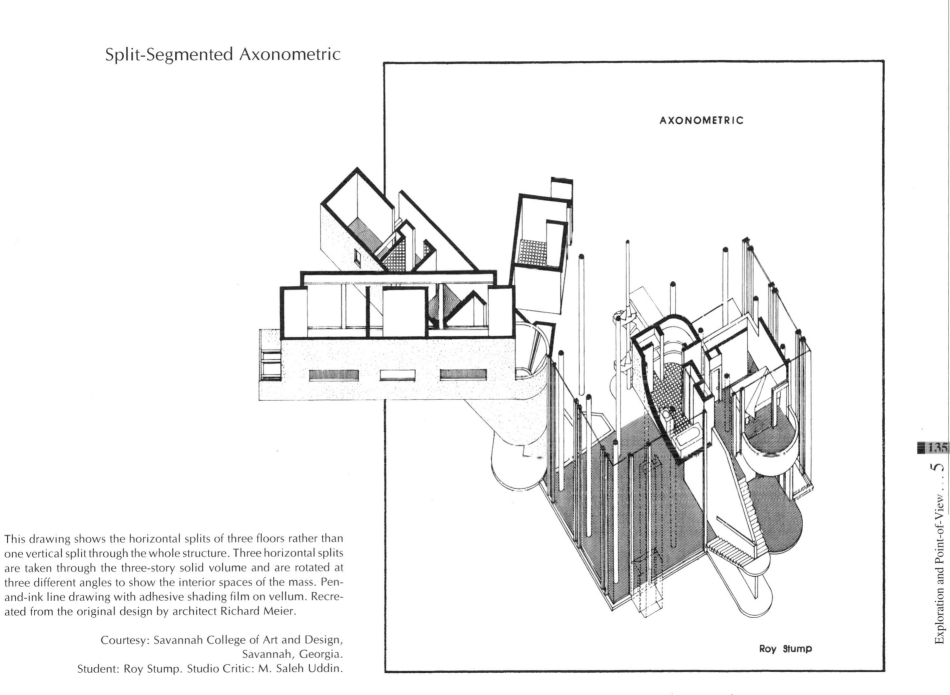

AXONOMETRIC

Roy Stump

This drawing shows the horizontal splits of three floors rather than one vertical split through the whole structure. Three horizontal splits are taken through the three-story solid volume and are rotated at three different angles to show the interior spaces of the mass. Pen-and-ink line drawing with adhesive shading film on vellum. Recreated from the original design by architect Richard Meier.

Courtesy: Savannah College of Art and Design, Savannah, Georgia.
Student: Roy Stump. Studio Critic: M. Saleh Uddin.

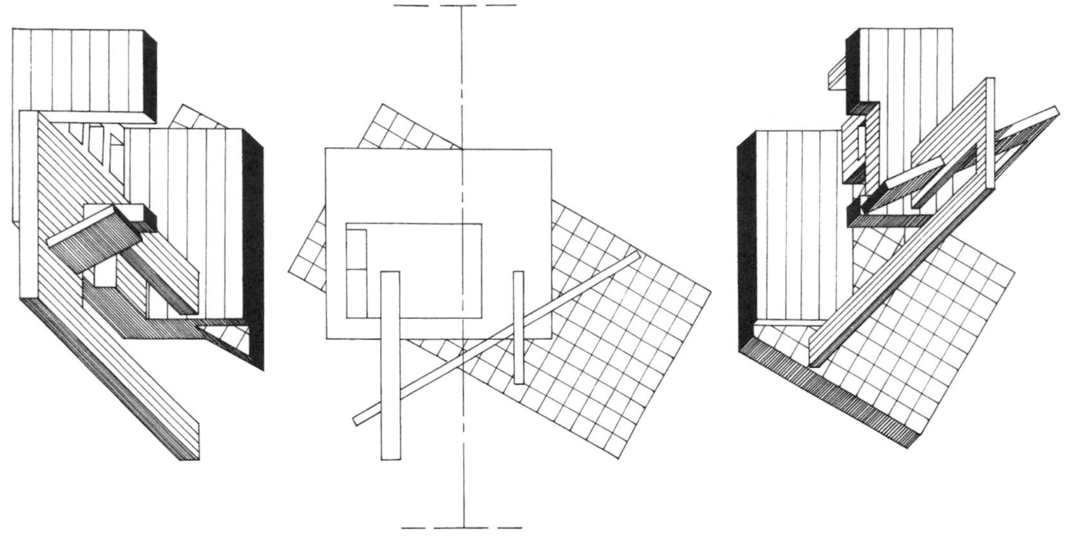

Split-Segmented Axonometric

The drawings to the left show 90-degree/0-degree plan oblique views cut into two halves and moved away from the plan. Vertical lines are projected upward at 45-degrees clockwise and counter-clockwise to show inside spaces of both segments. This type of split emphasizes the interior in both halves. Pen-and-ink line drawing on vellum.

Courtesy: Southern University, Baton Rouge, Louisiana.
Student: Gardenier Ware. Studio Critic: M. Saleh Uddin.

Split Segmented

Split AA

Split BB

A ← B

A ← B

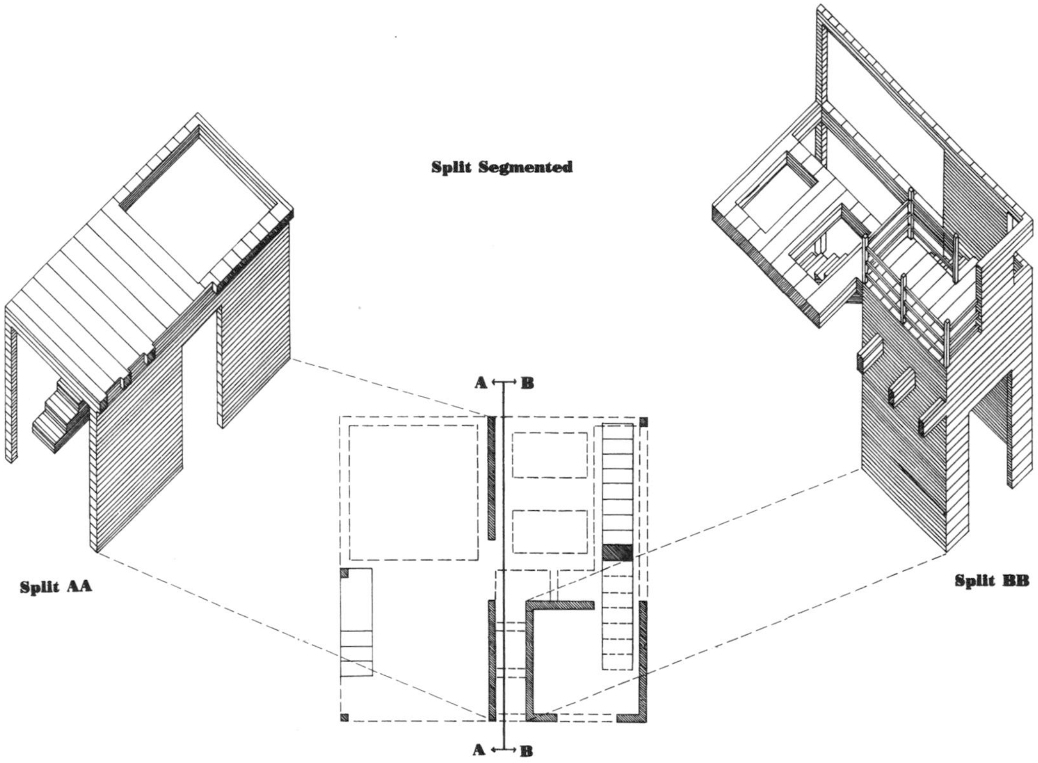

The adjacent drawings show 45-degree/45-degree plan oblique views cut into two halves and moved away from the plan. To keep vertical corners vertical, cut segments were rotated at 45 degrees for both split AA and split BB. This type of split emphasizes both the interior and exterior by skewing the plan obliques from their footprint plan. Pen-and-ink line drawing on vellum.

Courtesy: Southern University, Baton Rouge, Louisiana.
Student: Jason Lockhart. Studio Critic: M. Saleh Uddin.

Simultaneous Views Axonometric

- Sequential rotated views
- Combination of axonometrics types
- Combination of multiview and axonometric projection types

Simultaneous Views Axonometric

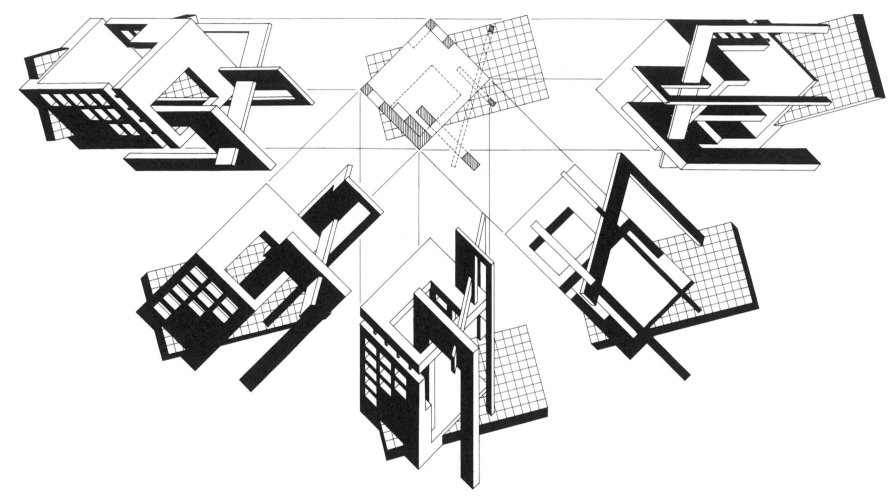

The simultaneous-views drawing above shows five sequential rotational views seen from the top. All rotational views are plan obliques; three 45-degree/45-degree and two 90-degree/0-degree to the primary cubical form. Each of the axonometric drawings have clear reference to the floor plan. The chosen views illustrate a clear overview of the exterior forms, as someone may see them from different viewpoints at the same altitude.

Courtesy: Southern University, Baton Rouge, Louisiana.
Student: Gardenier Ware. Studio Critic: M. Saleh Uddin.

5 . . . Exploration and Point-of-View

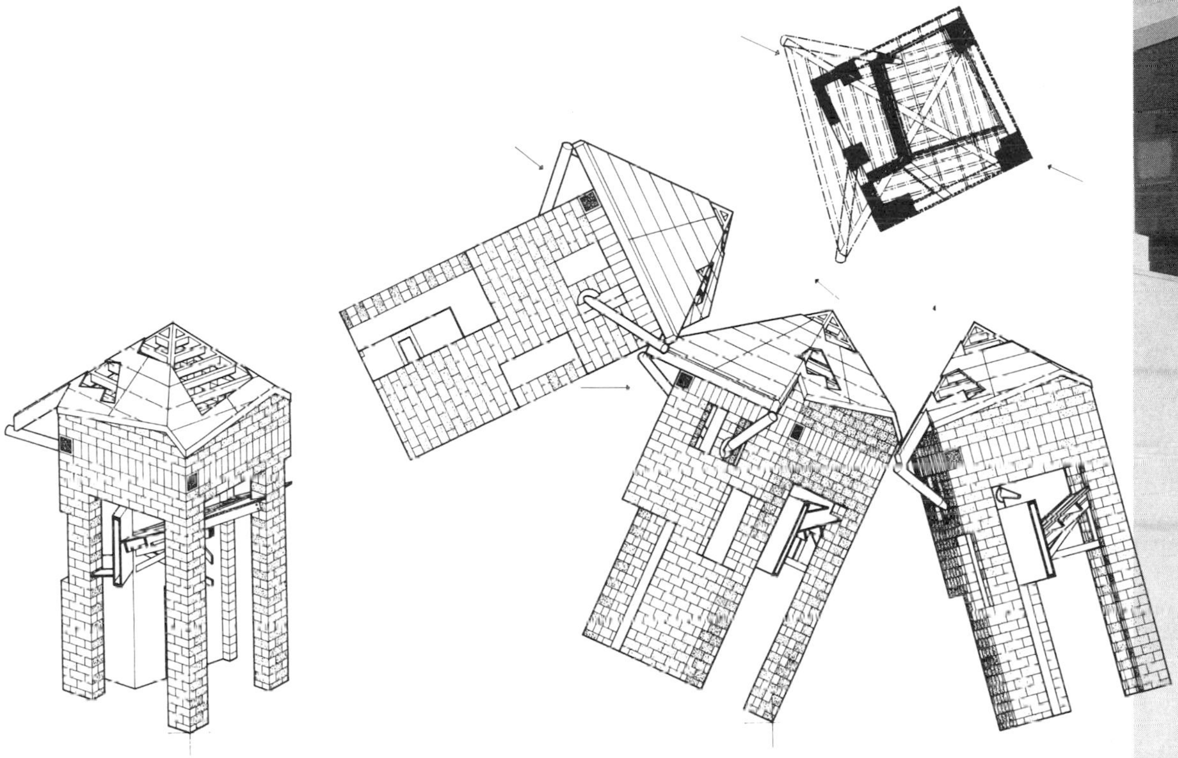

Plan and projected elevation, oblique, and auxiliary views.

Courtesy: Eric Owen Moss Architects, California. Lindblade Tower, Culver City, California.

Simultaneous Views Axonometric

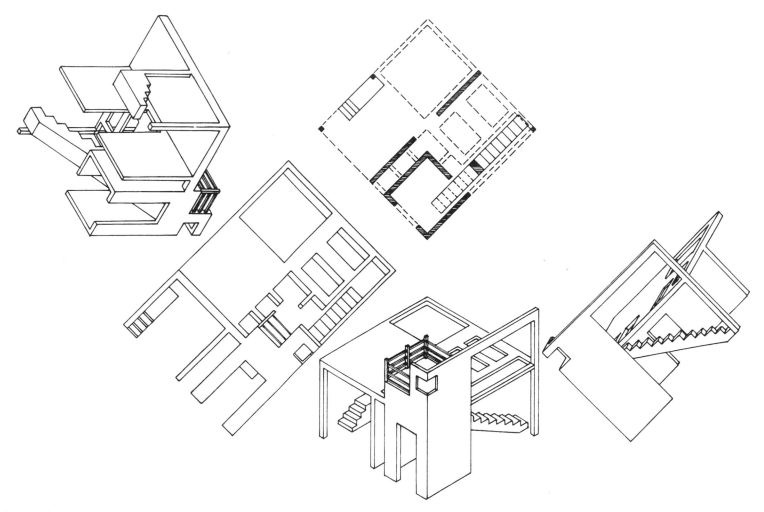

This simultaneous-views drawing shows four sequential rotational views; worm's eye, 90-degree/0-degree plan oblique, isometric, and elevation oblique. All axonometric projections have clear reference to the floor plan. The views illustrate a good overview of the structure as may be seen from different viewpoints and heights. The axonometrics in sequence from left to right are: Worm's-eye isometric highlighting the ceiling; frontal plan oblique emphasizing the roof and one facade; conventional isometric showing equally all three sides, two facades and the roof; and the low angle elevation oblique showing one facade and stair flight with the roof slab.

Courtesy: Southern University, Baton Rouge, Louisiana.
Student: Jason Lockhart. Studio Critic: M. Saleh Uddin.

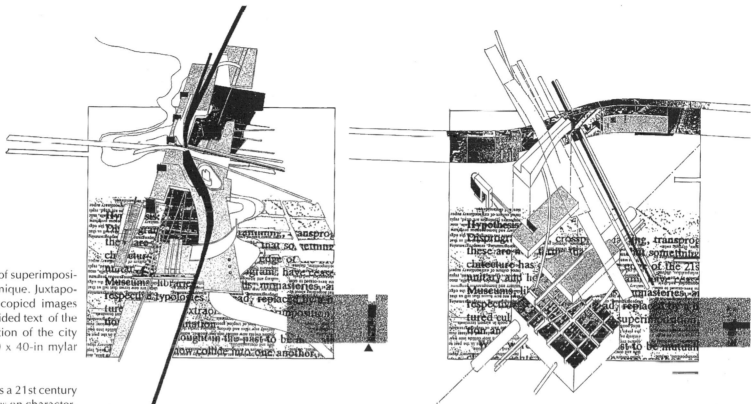

Hybrid axonometric as a result of superimposition of drawing media and technique. Juxtaposition of overlayering of photocopied images and collage tones from the provided text of the program as part of the abstraction of the city fabric on ink line drawings. 30 x 40-in mylar sheets.

The design investigation involves a 21st century linear megapolis city which takes on characteristics of an 'Urban Connector.' An infinitely long route with preceeding and succeeding cities linking to and from all forms of civilization, creating this new linear city. City configurations no longer radiate from a single source. Cities, towns, and suburbs are all linked, intertwined, superimposed, and weaved together in a stratified layer order, since a conservation of natural resources movement began in the 21st century. The Urban Connector progresses as a conveyor belt or aircraft carrier on a super-stratified level of platform consistently transprogramming and transforming existing resources.

Courtesy: Ronn W Yong + Sharlene Young. Project 'Urban Connector' Linear City.

Hybrid Axonometric

- Superimposition of media
- Superimposition of ideas
- Superimposition of techniques

Hybrid Axonometric

SITE

The Site is of the mind's construct > a dream scape located within the context of **geometric** memories. It consists of the wishes and fears exposed by the Dream of a House capable of accommodating our needs and articulating our desires. The condensation of hypothetical locations results in a virtual site existing in the very real space of our televisions, computers, and drafting boards.

The term hybrid is used when the drawing is as a result of sumperimposition of ideas and techniques. This "Dream House With No Style" uses the process of graphic abstraction by interpreting a three-dimensional model and transforming the regulating graphics of the model into an idea-generating schematic for the working design.

In an effort to simultaneously critique and supersede the style conventions of the contemporary developer house, one so steeped in style as to become unselfconsciously 'stylized,' a process for the design of a 'house with no style' must be devised which makes possible the selfconscious abandonment of all conventions of 'style.' That style conventions so subtly steep themselves into -- indeed, define, -- experience, the success of such a process, then, is solely determined by the degree to which its operative technique is freed to proceed beyond the language of style.

With stylelessness being the goal, the process employed in the design of the Dream House With No Style proceeds with the flattening of a three-dimensional object, via a line tracing of a photograph of a conventional house onto a two-dimensional surface. This new, flattened image thus becomes scaleless and abstract and, consequently, no longer likely to be understood in the style-tempered language of the conventional house.

OCEAN

OBJECT

MEADOW

LAKE

COUNTRY

CITY

BEACH   WOODS

MOUNTAINS

FIELD

SITE PLAN

Hybrid Axonometric

This flattened image is then reinterpreted and fleshed out to become a two-dimensional representation of a three-dimensional idea. In this way the dream house is formally derived not from the conventions of its often too-restrictive typology, but rather from the graphic abstractions (selfconsciously styleless) of a scaleless line drawing.

This new volumetric drawing is then reread as house that is, retrofitted with a program in the language of the house type. The result is a total critique of all house-type conventions: a critique not only of the formal language of the typology, but simultaneously, of its too infrequently interrogated programmatic organizations.

The production of this process is manifested through repeated ink on mylar overlays. The overlay technique is both essential to, and suggested by, this process as implicit in the critique is the recognition that only as blindly generative can the process successfully reveal prior imprints and tracings.

This house is a (non) design for America's "typical" family located within the constraints of suburbia. Acquiring one's own home is an expression of individuality. House after house, plot after plot, the self-same suburbs have become analogous to graveyards of complacency. The houses of America's suburbs conform to an unquestioned standard. They ask nothing of the inhabitants and mask any social, cultural, or formal deviation from the norm. Aligned in neat rows, these boxes have America in pseudo-packages. This house attempts to comment on the limited choices made by, and available to, the mass suburbanites. It can be seen as struggling to exist outside of the accepted idea of house, while located within the regulated mold of suburbia.

Courtesy: Resolution: 4 Architecture.
Joseph Tanney, Gary Shoemaker, and Robert Luntz.
Assistants: Casey S. Sherman, David Gissen.
Dream House With No Style,
Suburbia, USA.

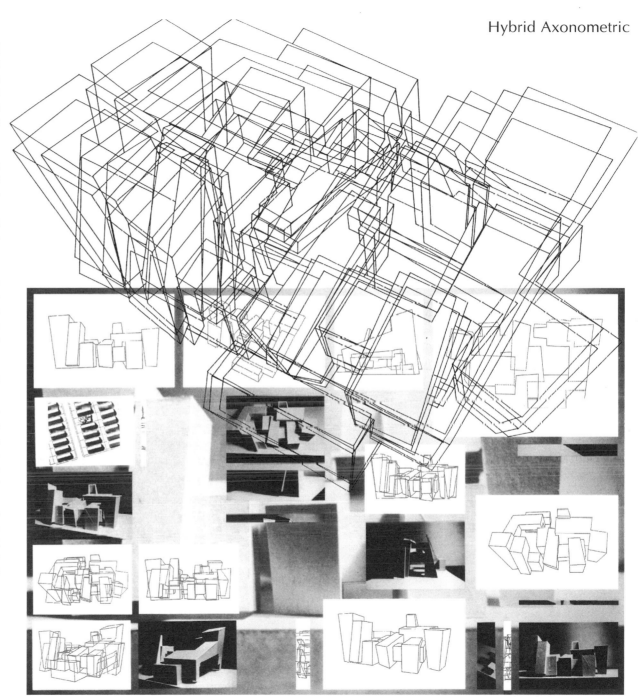

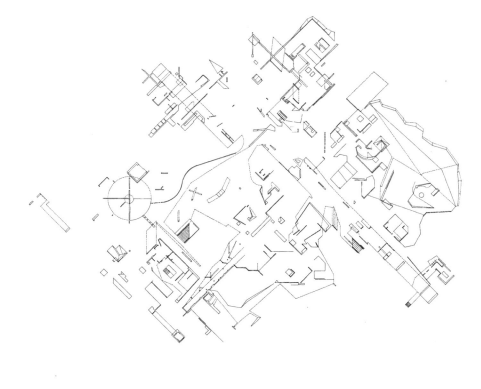

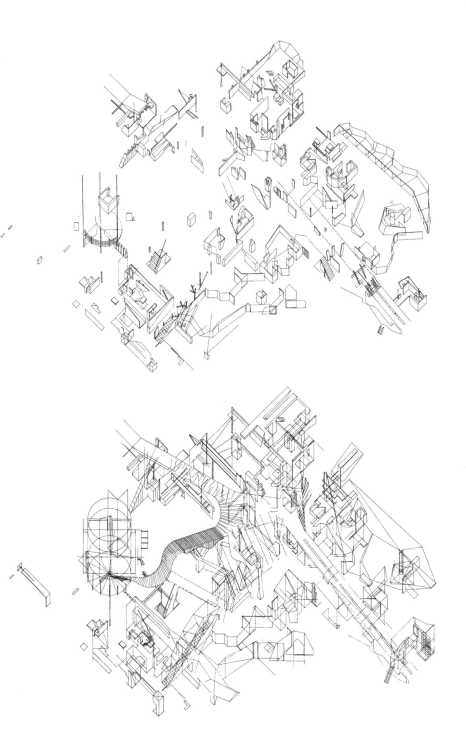

Hybrid Axonometric

The collaborators of a library design competition selected various programmatic requirements of the library and considered them independently. Discreet "ideal "architectural environments resulted from this procedure. These ideal environments were then placed in proximity with one another initiating a series of studies of a variety of spatial and programmatic relationships.

Courtesy: David Leary.
Design: Mark Clary, David Leary, and Mark O'Bryan.
Drawings: David Leary.
Matteson Public Library National Design Competition.

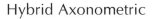

Axonometric in Design Analysis

AXONOMETRIC IN DESIGN ANALYSIS

ANALYSIS

In architecture the primary goal of a design analysis is to expose the underlying concept, organizational pattern, and execution process of the whole system. An analysis is an abstract process of simplification that reduces a total work into its essential elements. A major concern of any design analysis is to investigate the formal and spatial characteristics of a design work in such a way that the building parti can be understood clearly.

Often an analysis is an attempt to reduce the written discussion of theories involved and to emphasize more clearly the design characteristics and architectonic means used in producing simplified diagrams or sketches.

All effective design activities involved with the act of analysis can be summarized in three steps of a total design process:

1. Predesign stage (research, theories, concept formation)
2. During design (formulation of architectonic means and organizational strategies)
3. After design (understanding a built work by separating components from the whole)

AXONOMETRIC IN BUILDING ANALYSIS

Analyzing existing buildings is significantly important in architectural education for the fact that one becomes familiar with the organizational strategies of a design work. Both the process and product of an analysis can be a valuable learning experience. In this regard a good learning experience may be to analyze architecturally distinguished buildings having significant merit.

Axonometric drawings particularly may become very useful in such an analysis because of their diagrammatic but three-dimensional nature in communicating the main idea in a straightforward manner.

To analyze a building, the first and foremost requirement is usually to gather all available information on hand and to review it carefully. This may include a written description of the project, explanation of the design concept, early sketches by the designer, site and

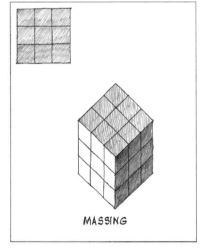

MASSING

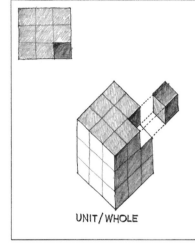

UNIT/WHOLE

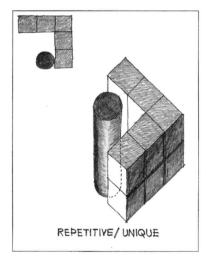

REPETITIVE/UNIQUE

SKELETAL/PLANER

6... Axonometric in Design Analysis

AXONOMETRIC IN DESIGN ANALYSIS

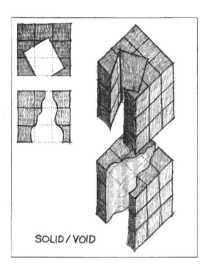

SOLID / VOID

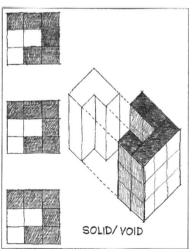

SOLID / VOID

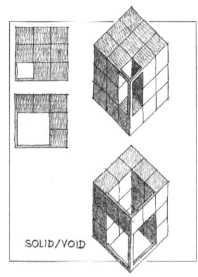

SOLID / VOID

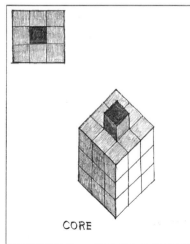

CORE

floor plans, building sections, elevations, and three-dimensional views. In addition, acquiring information on the architect in order to understand the designer's thought process and ideas is needed. Studying all available information and comprehending the spaces both in plan and 3-D is needed in order to interpret, analyze and represent the specific emphasis of the design.

After acquiring and studying all information, specific aspects of the various design principles and spatial organizational principles need to be analyzed in graphic format using three-dimensional axonometric drawings. The formulation of analysis should begin by studying the architect himself, his ideas and processes and how they shape the building. Only then can one begin to graphically expose those ideas within the building and explore other ideas that are present but not explained or discussed by the architect.

ANALYSIS HINTS

All information inventoried should be illustrated graphically. On the illustrations to the left important factors may be abstracted, or isolated and emphasized, to build a firm foundation from which to interrelate all known elements.

• First decide specific issues that will be illustrated in the analysis. Make a list of those issues (see the following section).

• Draw quick thumbnail sketches to get an overview of the effectiveness/appropriateness of your sketches in relation to the issues being analyzed. The same issues may be illustrated in several different ways. At this point the drawings may not be clear enough to be communicated to others.

• Using the thumbnail sketches as your base drawing, refine and redraw more developed illustrations emphasizing clearly each specific issue of the analysis. For instance, to show the structure of the building, highlight all support systems and show only the related enclosure.

• The technique of analysis should include the following procedures:

a. *Simplification:* Constructing drawings that remove all things not important to the analysis makes that particular issue more visible.
b. *Emphasis:* Through emphasis a part can be highlighted within the context of the whole. This can be done by varying the line types, line thicknesses, and shading.
c. *Reduction of graphic symbols:* Using a smaller set of symbols makes it easier to read and then understand the selected issue.
d. *Contrast in graphics:* Through contrast shades of graphics, a drawing may easily be read and differentiates the concern of the issue.

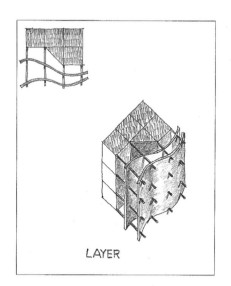

LAYER

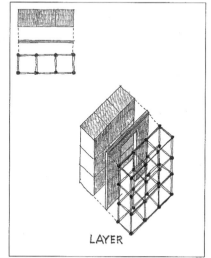

LAYER

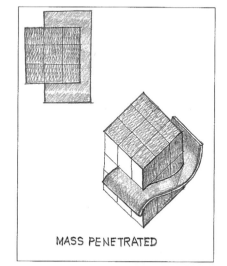

MASS PENETRATED

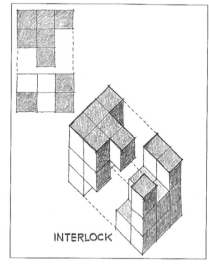

INTERLOCK

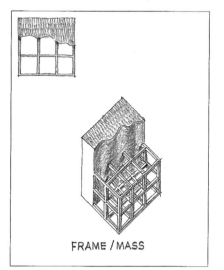

FRAME / MASS

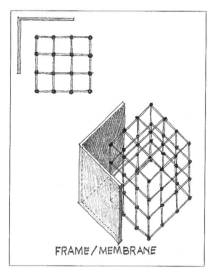

FRAME / MEMBRANE

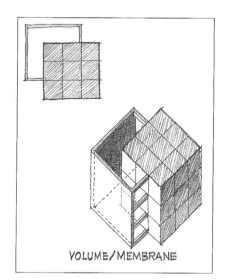

VOLUME / MEMBRANE

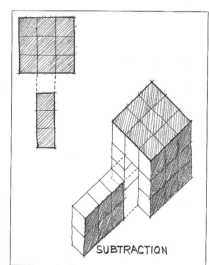

SUBTRACTION

ISSUES FOR ANALYSIS

In general, you may find that the following topics are only a few of the many issues to be considered for a building analysis:

A. CONTEXT
- Location, site, and contextual relationship
- Site implications
- Site forces
- Approach route
- Movement route
- Microclimate

B. BASIC UNDERSTANDING
- Theme and meaning
- Design principles
- Figure / Ground
- Parti diagram
- Zones
- Circulation sequence (entry-space-exit)
- Surrounding structures
- Spatial flow

C. VISIBLE COMPONENTS
- Form/Mass/Volume/Shape
- Related masses
- Cluster of units
- Mass penetrated
- Containment
- Form and space
- Volumes against membrane
- Frame against membrane
- Geometrical adaptation
- Structure
- Grid and frames
- Facades/Facade themes/Fenestration
- Envelope
- Enclosure
- Layers
- Planes
- Slabs and planes
- Penetration of planes
- Solid/Void
- Horizontal/Vertical features

D. PRINCIPLES/SYSTEMS
- Composition of form, space, and techniques
- Proportions in plan, section, elevation
- Geometric order: rhythm, repetition
- Light, color, shade, and shadow
- Transformation: Functional, Formal, Spatial, and Elemental
- Axes
- Core
- Datum
- Regulating lines
- Equilibrium/Hierarchy
- Thematic modulation
- Addition/Subtraction
- Contrast
- Tension
- Interlock

E. LEVELS OF PERCEPTION (PERCEPTUAL)
- Dynamism
- Visual shock
- Aesthetic
- View and vista
- Variety and drama
- Seasonal changes

In addition to deciding the issues, all collected information may be grouped under the following categories, and each category may have several subdivisions, which may then become the issues to be analyzed:

1) Natural features/factors/qualities
2) Physical elementss/factors/qualities
3) Aesthetic features/factors/qualities
4) Cultural features/factors/qualities
5) Social elements/factors/qualities
6) Visual features/factors/qualities
7) Perceptual features/qualities
8) Climatic factors
9) Circulation

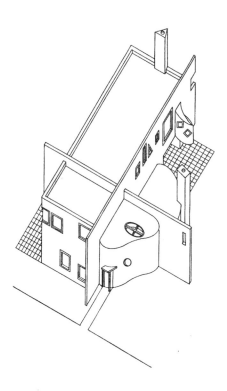

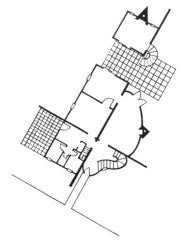

Analysis of Mulder House
Design: Architectonica.
Location: Lima, Peru.

• Two intersecting walls create the framework of the house dividing it into four quadrants, each with its own function, form, and orientation.

• The first quadrant is a sculptural form which serves as a two-story entry foyer.

• The second quadrant is the living room, that forms the shape of a segment of an ellipse and has floor-to-ceiling glass. A red fireplace supports the thin roof slab.

• The two stories in the third quadrant contain the family's sleeping quarters (upstairs) and a dining room and library (downstairs). The library is separated from the rest of the house by an exterior breezeway.

• The final quadrant consists of the kitchen and servants' quarters downstairs and a guest bedroom upstairs.

• The two intersecting walls extending out of the main volumes have sculptural cut-outs to emphasize their thinness and linear quality.

Courtesy: Southern University, Baton Rouge, Louisiana.
Student: Aaron Johnson.
Studio Critic: M. Saleh Uddin.

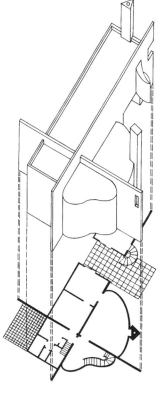

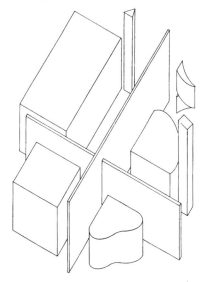

Forms of four quadrants separated by two intersecting planes at 90-degrees

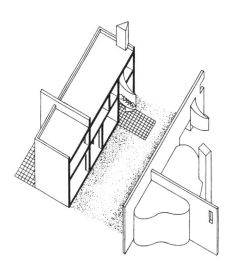

Cubical volumes containing smaller cubicles and sculptural forms containing larger single spaces

Pulled-up building envelope in relation to floor plan

Analysis of Garden Pavilion

Design: Anthony Ames.
Location: Atlanta, Georgia.

• The structure is rotated off the established grid of the residence and then elevated on pilotis to disassociate it from its surroundings.

• The elevated volume creates a sheltered car park space beneath the cubic form.

• The two major facades are treated differently: one a closed courtyard facade with a basketball hoop, and the other a translucent wall facing the garden.

• The dense freestanding core housing all service spaces may be read both as an object isolated by its figural qualities on an open floor plane and as poche creating edges for the open negative spaces.

• A sense of movement results in the ancillary spaces that helps to heighten the sense of repose that exists in the major space through contrast and juxtaposition.

Courtesy: Southern University, Baton Rouge, Louisiana.
Student: Jason Lockhart.
Studio Critic: M. Saleh Uddin.

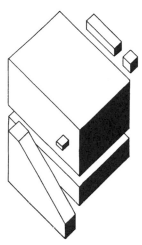

Form-Mass

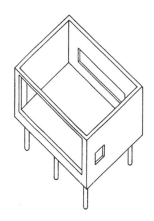

3 D Solid-Void: Exterior

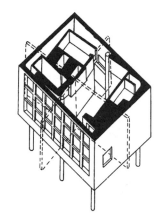

Axes: Interior organization 12-degree offset with the exterior axes

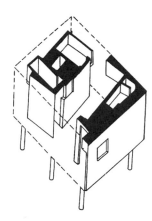

3-D Solid-Void: Interior

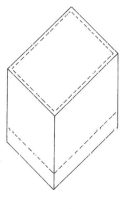

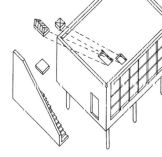

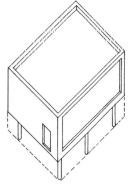

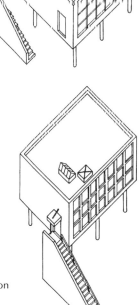

Form-Transformation

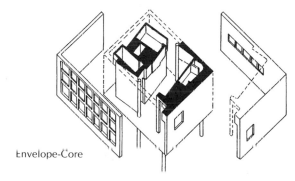

Envelope-Core

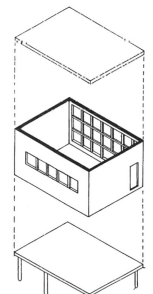

Enclosure-Boundary

Axonometric in Design Analysis . . . 6

6... Axonometric in Design Analysis

Design process analysis of student-generated Cartesian model study of the Winton Guest House by Frank O. Gehry and Associates. Ink on mylar.

Beginning with a modeled interpretation of the building's challenging relationship to 9-square geometry, this drawing was composed to delineate the balance and grounding of its forms while expressing itself through asymmetry and contrast. An intersecting plan and elevation graphic is added behind the plan obliques which creates perceptible space between the two drawing conventions.

Courtesy: North Dakota State University, Fargo, North Dakota.
Student: Lisa Waldoch. Studio Critic: Christopher Monson.
"What's Theory Done For Me Lately?"

Design process analysis of student-generated Cartesian model study of the Berkowitz-Odgis House by Steven Holl. Ink on mylar.

Recognizing the linear qualities of the Berkowitz-Odgis house, this analysis composition grows from a pair of plan obliques outward toward the signature detail elements of the architecture -- squared windows and "stick" framing. Like the house, the drawing itself is anchored by the vertical chimney form.

Courtesy: North Dakota State University, Fargo, North Dakota.
Student: Lee Swanson. Studio Critic: Christopher Monson.
"What's Theory Done For Me Lately?"

Axonometric in Design Analysis

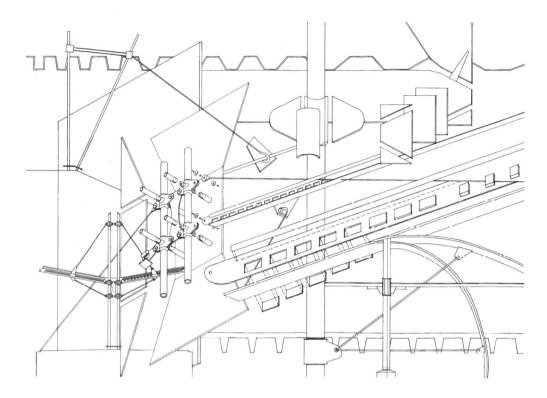

An analytic drawing based on a detailed study of the Overseas Passenger Terminal (New South Wales Government) designed by Lawrence Nield & Partners, Architects. Ink on mylar.

A sequence of fragmented and layered axonometrics begins to analyze the conditions of structural connections. The repetitive detail is examined by inventing a set of spatial characteristics between its constituent parts which would define both the process of its making and the materiality of its construction.

Courtesy: North Dakota State University, North Dakota.
Student: Jody Phenning.
Studio Critic: Christopher Monson.
"Object Making Being."

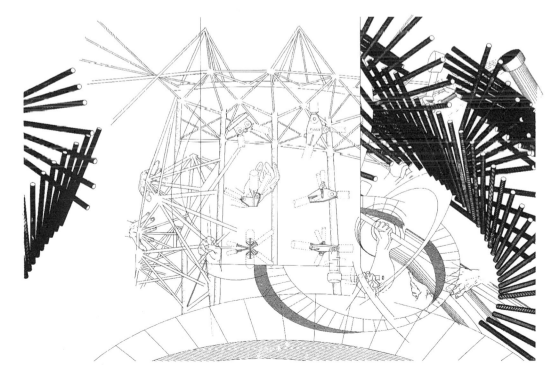

An analytic drawing based on a detailed study of the Sydney Football Stadium by Philip Cox Richardson Taylor & Partners. Ink on mylar.

Referred to an analytic image as "stretched muscles," the reality of detail invites the illustration of its parts as a construction "made" by the pattern of the hand and its movement.

Courtesy: North Dakota State University, North Dakota.
Student: Suzie Mertes.
Studio Critic: Christopher Monson.
"Object Making Being."

Axonometric in Design Analysis

A sequence of axonometrics analyzing *Circulation + Volumetric + Structure + Envelope*. The repetitive overall building outlines help identify constituent parts of the building in relation to its overall three-dimensional profile. Graphite on 30 x 42-in watercolor paper.

Courtesy: Carnegie Mellon University, Pittsburgh.
Student: Jason Alden. Studio Critic: Dana Buntrock.
Project for New Offices and Studios for the Pittsburgh Filmmakers.

These analytical drawings of the Children's Museum in Hyogo, Japan, designed by Tadao Ando, are part of a comprehensive study of the spatial and experiential characteristics of the building for a research project entitled *Through the Looking Glass: Rediscovering Museums with Children*, funded by The Pennsylvania State University and the National Endowment for the Arts.

The drawings were first drawn to scale freehand in ink from photographs and other sources. Digital images of the hand-drawn sketches were then created by a scanner and the images were edited on the Macintosh computer with an Adobe Photoshop graphics application program. Color was added to highlight the salient characteristics of the building design. Finally, the images were modified and composed with text using QuarkXPress, a publication layout software. The result is a hybrid active and dynamic analytical drawings which combine the softness of traditional free-hand drawing with the versatility of the computer.

Courtesy:Pennsylvania State University.
Jawaid Haider, Ph.D.,
Associate Professor of Architecture.
Lara Glembock and Husain B. Alam,
Student Assistants.
Children's Museum in Hyogo, Japan.

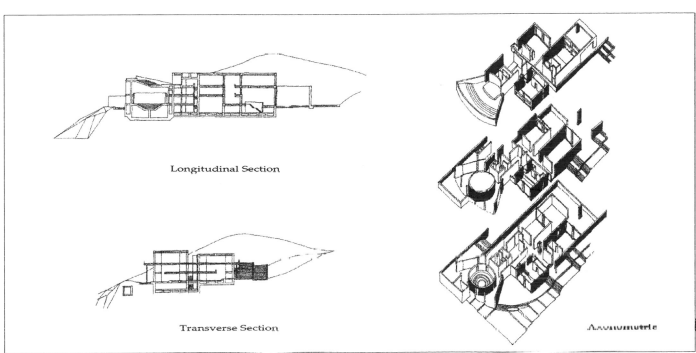

Longitudinal Section

Transverse Section

Axonometric

The main building is divided into two rectangles. It houses workshops, open-air spaces, and two theaters.

One side of the building is accentuated by sets of staircases; one of them ends poetically, in a pool of light

The poetry of light and the interplay of landscape, form, and spaces enhance the understanding of nature

A square block containing a grid of columns is connected to main building and children's workshop on sides.

ENCLOSURE

AXIS

BASE

Axonometric in Design Analysis

These drawings (this page and the next page) are part of a sequence [total 8] of 3-D wire-frame analytical drawings which attempt to represent/document more than an architectural proposal, a process, a mode of operation which exposes the [spatial and formal] complexities and interrelationships, dependencies and independencies, inherent to the design process.

This juxtaposition of information [enclosure/structural/spatial/circulatory] implicates a process which assumes a collaborative effort/involvement amongst the parts in the development of the [whole] project, by introducing critical [architectural] conditions which might otherwise postpone or go undetected in the design process, rendering them virtually inconsequential in the making of architecture.

The drawing to the left, first in the sequence, attempts to isolate three particular systems/conditions of inquiry specific to the project: enclosure, structural axis, and the base as a mediating agent between site and subject. The transparent or wire-frame nature of the drawing [axon] corroborates the inherent dialectic relationship between the systems/components/elements and the whole.

Axonometric in Design Analysis

The drawing to the right, third in the sequence, attempts to isolate spatial/programmatic and circulatory conditions of one of the components of the project for closer scrutiny. The series of smaller diagrams [right of the axonometric], attempts to map the process, situating the work/project within its contested territory by appropriating a number of contextual references/conditions, i.e., axial relationships, intersections, extracted urban module, and the subsequent geometric articulation of this information, informed by program. Once again, the wire-frame nature of the larger axonometric drawing corroborates the layering process of juxtaposed information.

All drawings were hand-drawn using technical pens, ink on mylar.

Courtesy: Studio Concepcion.
Carlos Concepcion.
The Island.

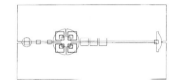

The Island is defined by two intersecting axis, Main Street axis, balanced by Church Circle and a perpendicular axis, balanced by the Marina Tower.

Form is based on the juxtaposition of Geometry and the tension created by these axis. The articulation of the volumes, layering of materials and movement through the spaces, is determined by internal and external forces.

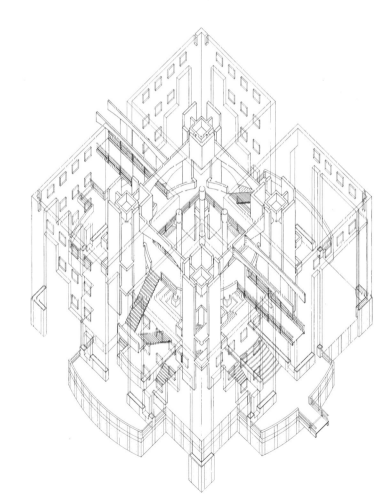

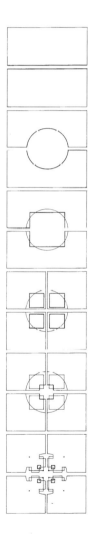

Axonometric in Design Analysis

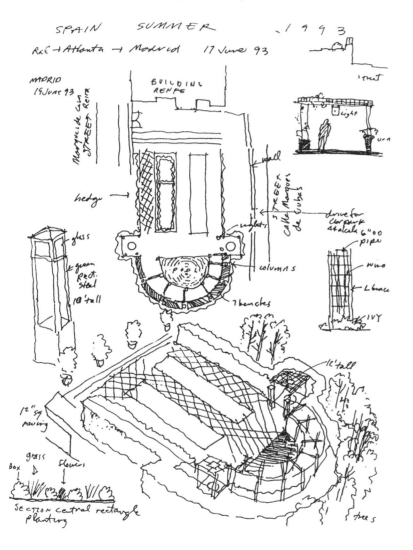

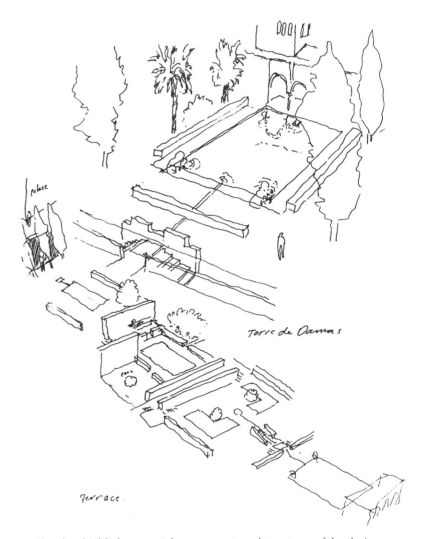

On-site free-hand sketches document and analyze public spaces and gardens in Spanish architecture. Sketches highlight essential components and structures of the design as experienced in the field. Details are eliminated except for its basic structure, shape, edges, relative scale, and planes. Part of a sketch series drawn on 8 -1/2 x 11-in travel sketchbook. Niji stylus pen on beige calligraphy paper.

Courtesy: Fernando Magallanes, Assistant Professor.
North Carolina State University, Raleigh, North Carolina.

Axonometric in Design Process

AXONOMETRIC IN DESIGN PROCESS

Each and every design project has a common goal: translating the client's program or needs into a specific functional building or edifice. In an architectural design the total scope of a project involves several steps. The following seven stages may easily be identified in such a project.

At each level of these steps, a certain amount of problem solving needs to be exercised in order to achieve a satisfactory result. The process itself may be viewed in general as the activities or actions that are taken to test appropriate and alternate ideas. The process also means the sequences or course of actions taken to execute a specific task.

The major activities involved in a creative design process deal with conceptualization, visualization, and expression of alternate ideas through drawings. The total process is an interactive one that goes back and forth with extensive cross-referencing. The interactive process of conceptualization, visualization, and expression through drawings becomes especially evident in the second, third, and fourth steps of a design activity (schematic design, preliminary design, and design development).

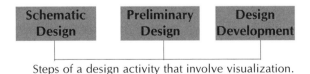

Steps of a design activity that involve visualization.

Paraline drawing may become a very useful tool in all of the above three stages, but perhaps most importantly in the schematic and preliminary design phase in a total design process. The following pages in this chapter illustrate several built and hypothetical projects that have used three-dimensional axonometric drawings in the design process to comprehend the final design.

Below:
One of the four urban design schemes drawn in a community participatory urban design charrette. Concept sketches were used to illustrate the contextual urban relationships of the proposed community center and its surroundings.

Right:
This first design study proposal of the east bank scheme illustrates the scheme's relationship to Main Street, Civic Plaza, Elkhart River, and the proposed river housing. Felt tip pen, fine point color marker & pencil.

Courtesy: Michel A. Mounayar, Professor of Architecture.
Ball State University, Muncie, Indiana.
Elkhart Community Center Charrette.
East Bank Scheme (Scheme 1 of 4).

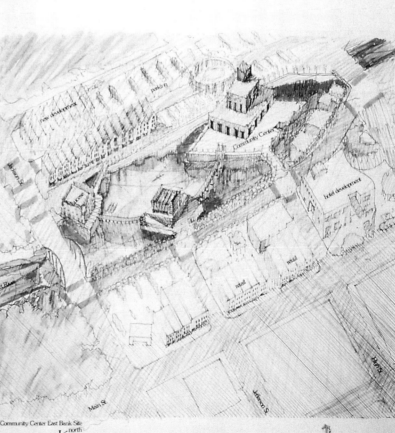

Community Center East Bank Site
north

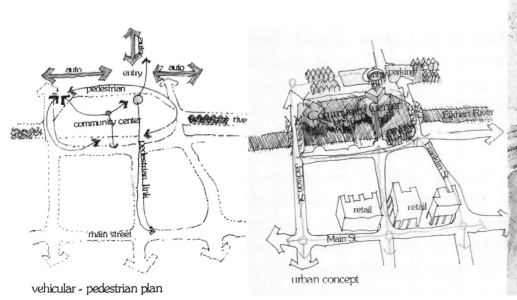

vehicular - pedestrian plan

urban concept

AXONOMETRIC IN DESIGN PROCESS

Alternate concept sketch of the same project (on previous page) shows the community center as an urban transition form linking the river to Main Street in a diagrammatic fashion. This East Bank Community Center Scheme developed the river edge, linked it to the east bank park, and integrated it into the Main Street commercial fabric. Felt tip pen, fine point color marker, and pencil.

Courtesy: Harry A. Eggink, Professor of Architecture, Ball State University, Muncie, Indiana. Elkhart Community Center Charrette. East Bank Scheme (Scheme 3 of 4).

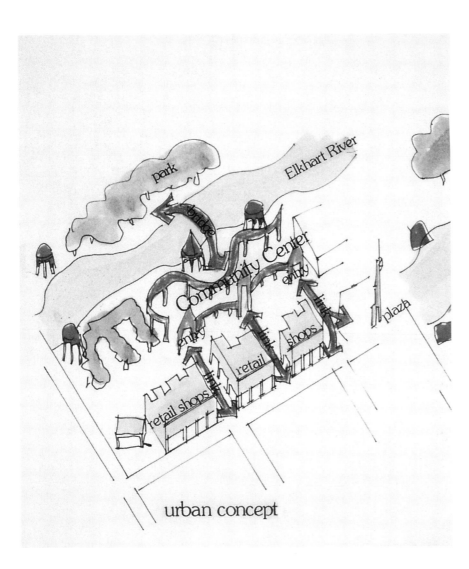

AXONOMETRIC IN DESIGN PROCESS

Design Study

These drawings are development sketches exploring massing, spatial occupation, and system relationships. The small sketches examine early form composition; the larger drawing is an axon composite, allowing each component its individual axis for the drawing type. Ink on paper.

These sketches were part of a study for an urban variant prototype of a public restroom. They respond to a dense context of urban flux. The project stands as an urban sculpture until users interactivate the architecture from folding wall panels within the core and sidewalk. The facilities are examples of self-sustainable architecture, and include two user-interactive information/entertainment screens with a communications port for going "on line." They were designed to be completely self-cleaning and thwart graffiti and vandalism. This project is considered to be an architextural experiment of information distribution.

Courtesy: Bryan Cantley + Kevin O'Donnell.
Outhouse Prototype no. 93.7.

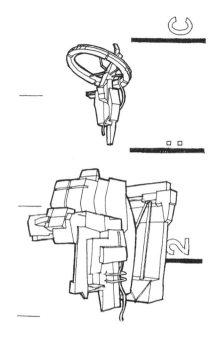

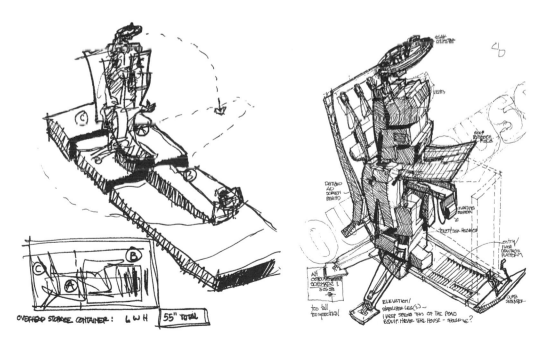

OVERHEAD STORAGE CONTAINER: L W H — 55" TOTAL

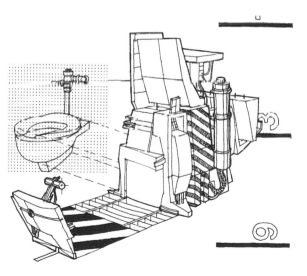

163

RAIN

ROOF-TOP GARDEN

spiraling system of sky-courts

WIND

TERRACES AS WIND-CATCHERS

PLANTING

RAIN

CONTINUOUS PLANTING SPIRALING UP.

planting

rain water can be used to water the planters.

BALANCE OF RAIN WATER RETURNED TO GROUND WATER.

Sun-roof

gymnasium pool

executive floors

RECESSED WALL CAN BE CURTAIN WALL

TERRACES

INTERSTITIAL SPACES TO BE FILLED UP FOR FUTURE EXTENSION

BUILT FORM   **PLANTING AND TERRACES**   **ORIENTATION**   **GLAZING AND SHADING**

N W E S

Axonometric showing bioclimatic principles

Concept Sketches

These drawings show the concept sketches, analytic-emphasizing bioclimatic principles, and the final design in a down-view perspective and a photographic view of the built structure.

The process not only brings together the architect's bioclimatic principles for the design of tall buildings (developed by the architect) but also interprets poetically the bioclimatic principles as being useful theoretical armatures for design.

This building has vertical landscaping (planting) integrated into the facade and at the predominant skycourts faced with variable bands of sunshading. It incorporates a number of passive low-energy features: all windows facing the hot sides (i.e., east and west sides) have external louvers as solar-shading to reduce solar heat gain into the internal spaces. Those sides without direct solar insulation (i.e., north and south sides) have full curtain-walled glazing for better views and opportunities for natural ventilation.

The building has elevator lobbies which are again naturally ventilated and naturally sunlit with views to the outside for awareness of place by its users. At the building's uppermost recreational floor is a sun-roof which provides panel space for possible future placement of solar-cells to provide background sources of ambient energy to serve the escape stairs and lift lobbies.

The building site is within the direct flight path into Kuala Lumpur International Airport and thus has a height restriction. In its built form, there are 13 stories, giving a total area of 12,345 square meters.

Courtesy: Ken Yeang.
T.R. Hamzah & Yeang, Selangor, Malaysia.
Menara Mesiniaga (IBM Malaysia),
Kuala Lumpur, Malaysia   1989 - 1992.

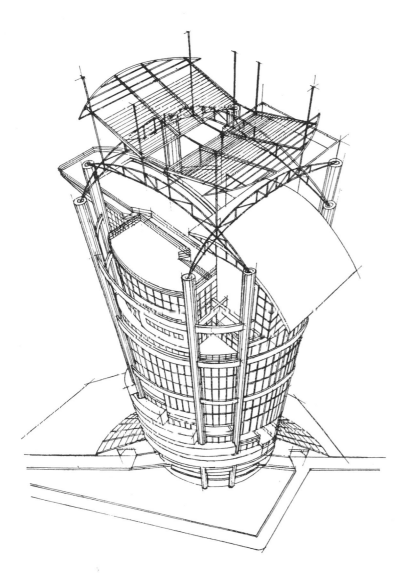

Original drawing and actual constructed building. Menara Mesiniaga (IBM Malaysia), Kuala Lumpur, Malaysia.

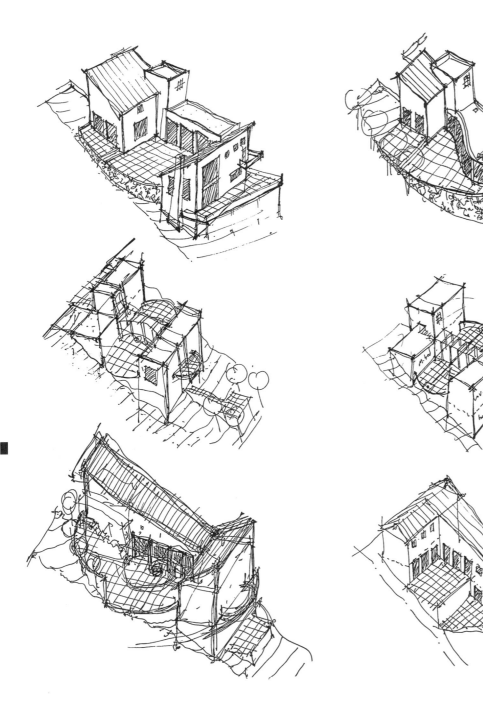

7 . . . Axonometric in Design Process

AXONOMETRIC STUDY SKETCHES

This house was designed to replace one which was destroyed in Oakland's tragic firestorm. The architects began the design process by carefully analyzing the site -- which in this case was a steep, narrow, down-hill lot. The designers produced a series of relationship diagrams which studied circulation and spaces in relation to the site. Simple three-dimensional study models were also built to investigate the impact of various massing alternatives. This series of axonometric-sketch studies was done concurrently during the early schematic design process to analyze the building's roof shapes, open space, massing, fenestration, and scale. These studies were presented to the client along with plans and models to convey the design process. The designers found this method of axonometric sketch a most valuable design tool.

Courtesy: House + House Architects.
Study Sketches: David Thompson.
Hammonds Residence, Oakland, California.

AXONOMETRIC IN DESIGN PROCESS

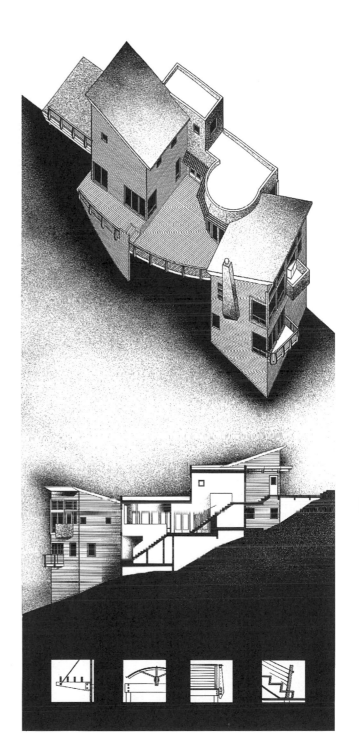

FINAL PRESENTATION AXONOMETRIC

Axonometric, section and details composite. India ink and airbrush on mylar. 30 x 64-in.

At the conclusion of the project the designers decided to produce a formal rendering of the project. The final drawing consisted of three parts -- an axonometric view of the house, a cross-section through the house, and a series of details. Various angles were studied for the axonometric in order to best convey the building's form. When the overall layout was finalized, the final rendering was drawn with ink on mylar. Airbrush was later applied to provide background tones and building shadows. The rendering successfully conveys the building's relationship to the land and its use of form and materials.

Courtesy: House + House Architects.
Rendering: Michael Baushke and Mark English.
Hammonds Residence, Oakland, California.

AXONOMETRIC IN DESIGN PROCESS

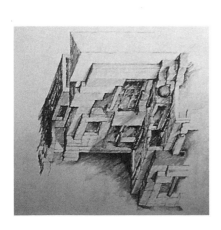

7 . . . Axonometric in Design Process

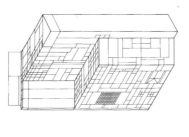

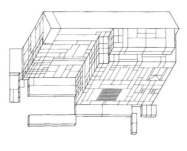

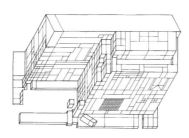

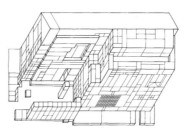

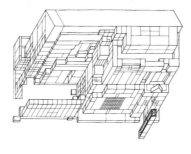

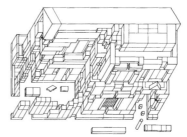

STUDY SKETCHES
AND PROCESS DRAWINGS

Preliminary study sketches in pencil and process drawings in ink line. The images show progression from study drawings to finished building.

The idea behind this house by Takefumi Aida is not the building-up of toy blocks like his earlier projects but instead their demolition or dissolution.

A box-shaped configuration of toy blocks is gradually destroyed in the conceptual process of design. Pieces move from the northeast to the southwest, suggesting a flow, as blocks push outward to create interior space. Spaces shift while set-back regulations, natural lighting requirements, and the need for rooms of certain sizes are satisfied.

A sphere symbolizing the moment at which the process of destruction is halted stands in the center of this house (see photograph of the exterior view on the next page). A momentary equilibrium between the forces of construction and destruction has been reached, and the sphere emphasizes the nature of this instant. The sphere in itself is a stable figure but expresses instability in the way it implies that it might roll off at any time.

Courtesy: Takefumi Aida.
Takefumi Aida Architects & Associates,
Japan.
Toy Block House X, Shibuya, Tokyo, Japan.

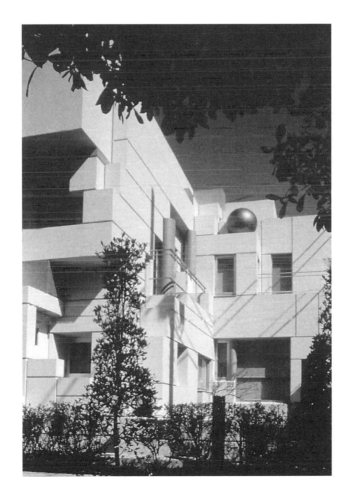

Courtesy: Takefumi Aida.
Takefumi Aida Architects & Associates, Japan.
Toy Block House X, Shibuya, Tokyo, Japan.

AXONOMETRIC IN DESIGN PROCESS

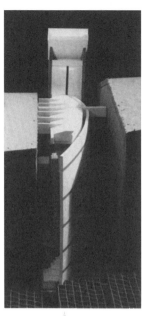

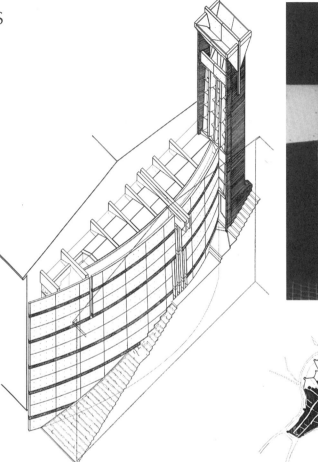

AXONOMETRIC IN VISUALIZATION PROCESS

The importance of a three-dimensional visualization was paramount in developing the conceptual idea of this project. Through the integration of axonometric drawing and modeling of the building in wood and cardboard, the scale of the project could be visualized and studied. The formats of physical modeling and drawing address very separate notions of space and yet are very interrelated in the depiction of the project. The cut-away axonometric drawing allowed a visual planometric tracking of internal space along the passage up the street. The model afforded a comprehensive sectional analysis of the interior and exterior spaces. The synthesis of the two media describe the ambiguity of the street and its relationship to the city and the museum spaces.

axonometrics.

First floor.

Third floor.

Second floor

Above : axonometric.
Above right : urban plan.
Right : view with adjacent buildings removed.

Fourth floor.

Courtesy: Christopher Rose, Architect,
Rose Architecture.
Museum of Historic Art, San Gimignano, Italy.

AXONOMETRIC IN DESIGN PROCESS

The Starbright Pediatric Network is creating an interactive computer network to allow children and teenagers in hospitals to travel through virtual worlds and teleconference each other across the nation. The Starbright Foundation commissioned ESI to develop a prototype unit (the PC Pal) with a distinctive identity for use in a hospital environment. The prototype needed to address issues of compactness, cleanliness, maneuverability, and security. Most importantly, it needed to adjust easily to a wide range of individual user needs.

The following isometric drawings represent the unit that was approved for production as a prototype. The unit was designed based on the concept of a "magic box" that transforms from a compact secure form into a fully adjustable computer station. The drawings were a tool to help visualize the sequential process of transformation. They also enabled ESI to communicate with both the client and fabicator in a three-dimensional format, which was crucial given the complexity of the object. The original drawings were done in pencil on 8 1/2 x 11-in sheets which allowed them to be faxed.

Client : Starbright Foundation (Los Angeles, California).
Design Firm: Edwin Schlossberg Incorporated (New York, NY).

Design Team: Edwin Schlossberg (principal designer), Diane Klein (project manager), Matthew Moore (project designer), Fred Amey (project designer), Joe Mayer (graphic designer), Dean Markosian (production/technical manager)

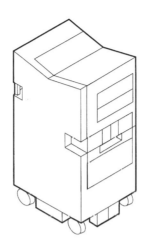

Drawling #1 represents the unit in its fully closed, locked position. In this position the unit can be easily moved and stored. This is the configuration of the unit when it enters the child's hospital room.

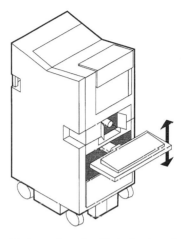

Drawing #2 shows the unit with the keyboard tray extended and the monitor screen cover open. In this compact position the unit can accommodate a user ir a chair or wheelchair.

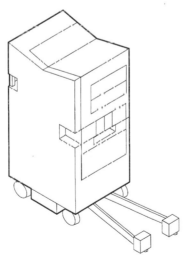

Drawing #3 shows the unit with the outriggers extended. The outriggers serve to provide a larger, more stable base prior to the extension of the monitor enclosure above. The monitor enclosure remains locked until the outriggers are extended.

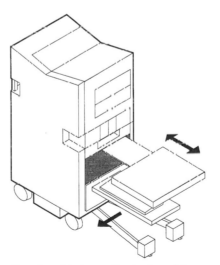

Drawing #4 shows the keyboard tray pulled clear of the unit, but not yet fully extended or rotated for use.

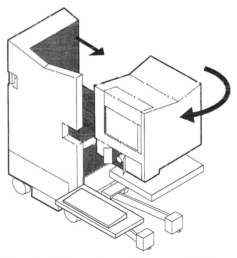

Drawing #5 shows the monitor cover rotated, the screen cover open, and the keyboard fully extended. In this position the keyboard and monitor can be raised and lowered to allow them to be used by a child in a hospital bed.

a.

b.

c.

d.

e.

F.

G.

h.

7 . . . Axonometric in Design Process

CONCEPT SKETCHES TO FINAL DRAWING IN THE DESIGN PROCESS

The use of axonometric sketches throughout the design process dominated as a means of exploration in a sequential manner. A volumetric "ideogram" of the site and solution direction was produced on-site during the second site visit. (a) This initial diagram developed into a plan with a series of very quick axonometric studies of major building portions. (b) Further development axonometrics of alternate solutions of specific small-scale elements such as the family room fireplace, (c & d) and master bath layout, (e) followed. Eventually individual details were also explored (f & g). Finally, several carefully delineated layouts were produced as a base for the rendered drawing. The example shown is one view that was rejected because of an inadequate view of the curving family wall (h).

The finished drawing indicates the important axis lines and foci, as well as circular traces where helpful. All curving surfaces are rendered with airbrush tones to accent the resultant enclosed space. The fireplace elements, which would normally be obscured, are pulled up and rotated for clear viewing.

The final drawing is a split-segmented/ composite axonometric. Pen-and-ink line work with india-ink airbrush tone on 40 x 40-in mylar.

Courtesy: Mark English.
Inglese Architecture.
Drawing: Mark English & Jeff Gard.
The Devitt Residence,
Los Altos, California.

Axonometric in Integrated Presentation

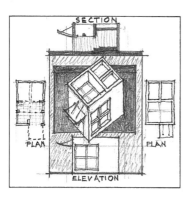

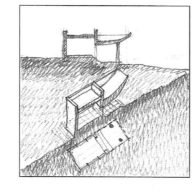

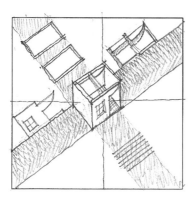

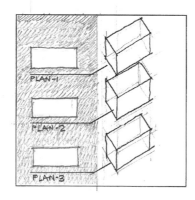

PARALINES IN INTEGRATED PRESENTATION

AXONOMETRIC AND PRESENTATION LAYOUT

Because of the three-dimensional nature of both the paraline and perspective drawing types, they can generate significant impact in an integrated presentation, where several different types of drawings are represented in one layout. The perspective drawings have a tendency to stay independent in a layout because of their central projection. On the other hand paraline drawings may become very complementary to other orthographic multiview drawings (plan, section, and elevation), since there are no vanishing points and convergence of lines to focus on other areas beyond the building. With prior planning, paraline drawings can be used very effectively to integrate all other drawings to create a total presentation layout where drawings refer to each other to better communicate the design idea.

Traditional forms of presentation layout consist of a series of multiviews (plan, elevation, section) and three-dimensional single-views (paraline, perspective), which are perceived as independent informative drawings. For a quick overview or an evaluation of the design by an external reviewer, this type of fragmentation of information may seem very awkward. Since presentation drawings are not working or construction drawings, all of the drawings should have clear cross-references between and from one drawing to another.

The direct relationship of the plan-elevation-section with the axonometric creates a logical opportunity to combine them, so that they cross back and forth, one to another.

Architectural design competitions have always been a fertile ground for innovative presentation layout. Significant experimentation with layout is noticeable in recent architectural competition projects where each participant tries to arrange the maximum amount of information within a limited specified area. Taking advantage of digital technology and combining CAD and desktop platforms, the options to manipulate layout and it's effects go several steps further.

Rather than be left to chance or become a coincidence, a presentation layout should be preplanned as a total composition. To do a preplanned composition all graphic components to be used in the layout must be known before executing the final layout. Another important aspect of creating a professional layout is to know the reprographic techniques involved and their effects in the layout. This may include conventional cut-and-paste and blue or black line print, adding color on prints, positive or negative film or paper prints, copy on translucent paper, reproducing in reverse or negative lines, and changing shades digitally with photo-retouching softwares.

Following are the chronological steps that are usually used in the process of preparing a design layout:

- gathering all graphic components that will be used in the layout
- determining primary and secondary drawings to create emphasis or deemphasis
- preparing quick thumbnail sketches of composition layout using all drawings and texts.
- comparing alternate composition schemes to those complying with the theme of the design
- preparing a full-size mock-up using scaled drawings
- deciding the type of techniques to be used to create the end product
- familiarizing oneself with the reprographic techniques involved in the total process
- producing and reproducing the finished layout

COMPOSITION OF THE LAYOUT

Five important points need to considered for the composition of a presentation layout.
1. SHAPE AND SIZE OF THE PRESENTATION BOARD
2. KEY DRAWING AND SECONDARY DRAWINGS
3. BOUNDARY AND RELATIONSHIP OF COMPONENT DRAWINGS
4. COMPOSITION MOTIF
5. TECHNIQUES OF COMBINING DRAWINGS

1. SHAPE AND SIZE OF THE PRESENTATION BOARD

All thumbnail sketches should be approximately proportional to the final shape of the layout. It is better to follow a recognizable shape, for example to make a true square or a linear rectangle rather than making it in between. Usually the size of the presentation board may be kept bigger so that it can be trimmed down to it's final size.

2. KEY DRAWING AND SECONDARY DRAWINGS

The key drawing should support the other drawings in the layout to complete the composition. Axonometric or similar three-dimensional drawings may take the role of a key drawing. Usually the key drawing becomes the central communicating vehicle of the concept of the design. An exploded axonometric by its nature of interrelated elements shown in components may inherently demand to become the key drawing in a layout. Even though there are no set rules, plan, elevation, and section drawings tend to act as secondary drawings to support an axonometric or perspective drawing. The key drawing usually serves the purpose of summarization of the project.

COMPOSITION MOTIF

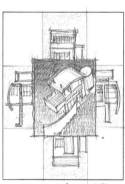
FIGURE/GROUND

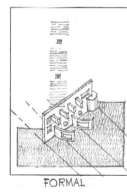
FORMAL

LINEAR/ANGULAR

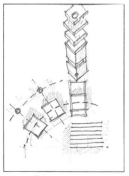
RADIATION

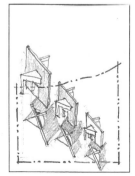
REPETITIVE

EMPHASIS ON ONE AREA

TECHNIQUES OF COMBINING DRAWINGS

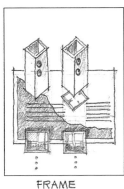

FRAME

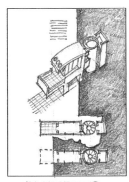

BACKGROUND

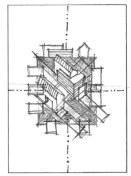

FRAME AND BACKGROUND

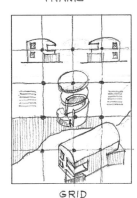

GRID

SCALE VARIATION

DESIGN ELEMENT

3. BOUNDARY AND RELATIONSHIP OF COMPONENT DRAWINGS

Boundary plays a significant role in the composition. Boundaries may be drawn as actual boundary lines or may be implied boundaries that would be created by the drawings and their fields. Boundaries may contribute to the following:

- demarcate periphery of the layout by arranging drawings within the boundary
- highlight certain portions of the layout by creating an implied boundary for a certain group of drawings
- disseminate by letting drawings grow outward, and
- integrate drawings by connecting them with frames or implied fields of background

4. COMPOSITION MOTIF

- figure-ground
- formal
- linear
- angular
- centralized
- radiation
- repetitive
- emphasis on one area

5. TECHNIQUES OF COMBINING DRAWINGS

- frame
- background
- frame and background
- grid
- hierarchy
- scale variation
- design element with a strong character

The following pages show examples of presentation layouts that have used axonometric drawing either as a key element to create the composition or as a means to integrate other drawings in the total composition.

AXONOMETRIC IN
INTEGRATED PRESENTATION

The axonometric being the primary drawing, the composition of the presentation uses a rectangular frame to arrange four orthographic elevation drawings in a formal way.

Courtesy: Savannah College of Art and Design.
Student: Richard Fisher.

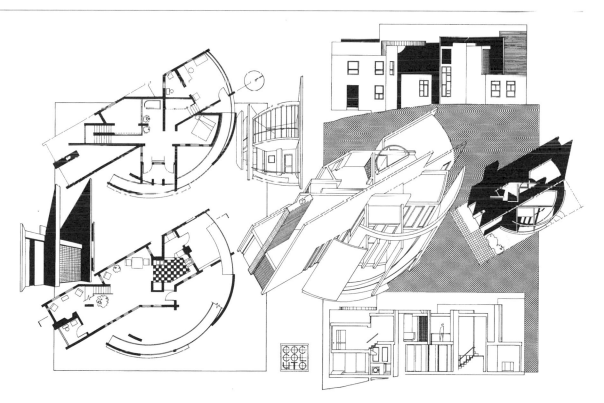

WEST ELEVATION

NORTH ELEVATION

SOUTH ELEVATION

EAST ELEVATION

Integrated presentation uses two squarish frames to arrange all drawings in one board. The left frame primarily holds two floor plans within it while the right frame arranges an elevation and a section at the edges of the frame. The inclined lines of the frame are the profile of the site altitude that becomes part of the elevation and section. The three-dimensional axonometric combines both frames to create this total composition of the presentation.

Courtesy: Savannah College of Art and Design.
Student: Richard Fisher. Studio Critic: M. Saleh Uddin.
Dwelling with Walls.

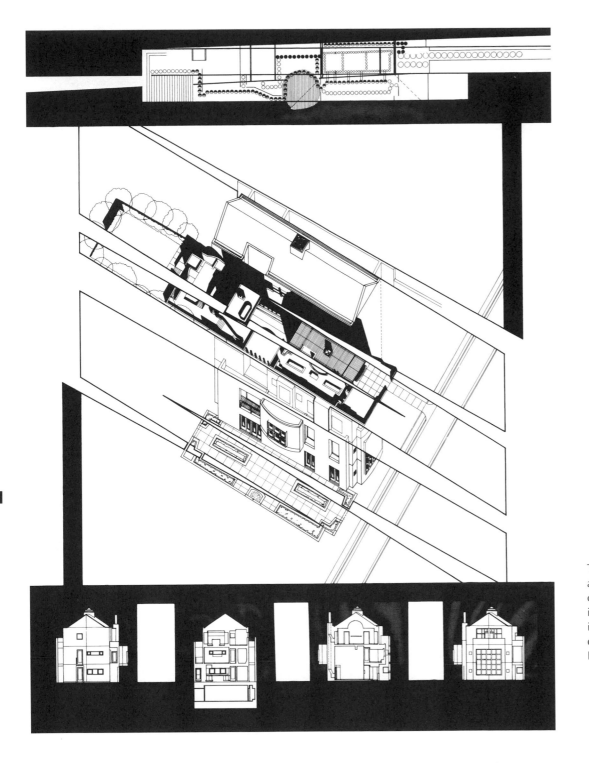

The composition makes use of separate simple drawings acting as top and base as well as complex overlay of information in the center, revealing site, elevation, plan, partial axonometric, interiors, roof, and sun orientation. The mechanism of the invisible border separating and fusing these diverse drawings is derived from an orientation shift in the design by the architect. Ink and adhesive film on mylar.

Courtesy: Savannah College of Art and Design.
Student: Darrin Davis. Studio Critic: Andrew Chandler.
Study of Hulse House by Anthony Ames.

AXONOMETRIC IN INTEGRATED PRESENTATION

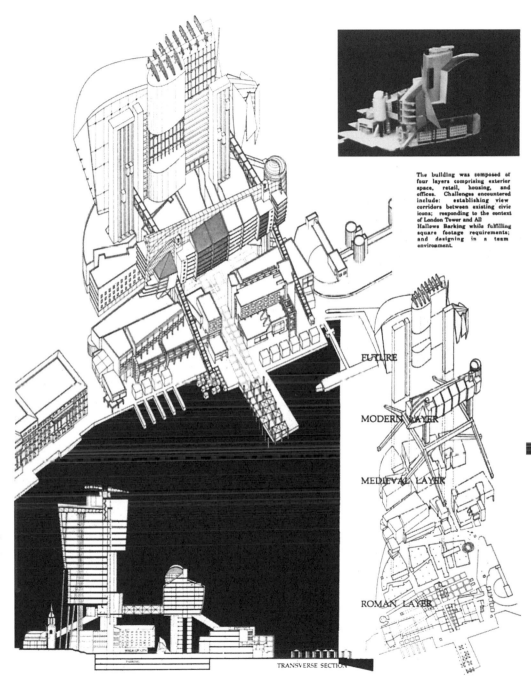

The building was composed of four layers comprising exterior space, retail, housing, and offices. Challenges encountered include: establishing view corridors between existing civic icons; responding to the context of London Tower and All Hallows Barking while fulfilling square footage requirements; and designing in a team environment.

FUTURE

MODERN LAYER

MEDIEVAL LAYER

ROMAN LAYER

TRANSVERSE SECTION

This drawing shows the layering of plan, section, and elevation, emulating the composite make-up of the design. The primary axonometric and its rendering becomes the central focal point as the colored film simultaneously represents water and sky. Ink on vellum, colored film, photographs, and text.

Hybrid building sited in the shadow of the Tower Bridge and next to the Tower of London. The design mirrors the rich layering of a highly contextual site and separates the layers into programmatic strata.

Courtesy: Kent State University, Kent, Ohio.
K. Andreyko, D. Brennan, C. Chen, B. Frolo, D. Lim,
T. Sofranko, W. Willoughby.
Studio Critic: Thomas Stauffer.
London; Designing in an Historic Context.

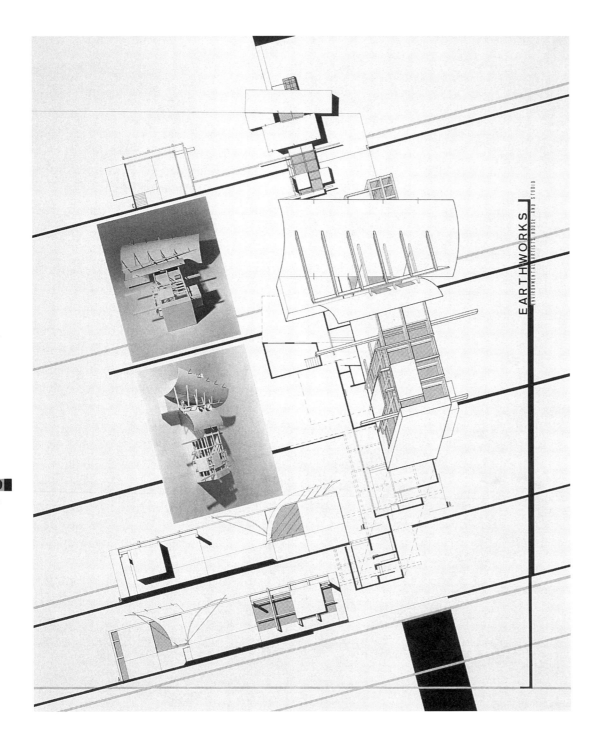

EARTHWORKS
ENVIRONMENTAL ARTISTS HOUSE AND STUDIO

AXONOMETRIC IN
INTEGRATED PRESENTATION

This drawing was created using ink on crescent board and photographs. The axonometric is floated over the plan and becomes the focal point. Strong transverse lines from the plan and axonometric are extended to organize the entire page by ordering elevations, site plan, and photographs.

The drawing is of a house and studio for an environmental artist. The cleft in the roof channels rain water into a trough next to the studio which eventually runs into a pool on the edge of the site. Rain is the artists inspiration.

Courtesy: Louisiana State University,
Baton Rouge, Louisiana.
Student: Lloyd Shenefelt.
Studio Critic: Thomas Sofranko.
Artist House & Studio.

AXONOMETRIC IN
INTEGRATED PRESENTATION

This is a 3-D relief drawing. Photocopies of drawings and models, white ink line drawings, colored paper and metal screen were used on a 40 x 40-in sheet. It is a documentation of the projects completed in one semester. Projects featured: American Film Institute in New York, A Conference Center in Barcelona, and Product Design.

Red background and exploded white line axonometric drawing work as the center of focus in the total composition. This axonometric drawing also helps anchor and stabilize other smaller drawings in the presentation board. Black horizontal bands with diagrams and model photographs work as the base of the composition. As the drawings move upward they become more independent and float on the gray background.

Courtesy: University of Southwestern
Louisiana, Lafayette, Louisiana.
Student: Ayoub Ashary.
Studio Critic: George S. Loli.
Portfolio Project: American Film Institute in
New York, A Conference Center in Barcelona,
and Product Design.

AXONOMETRIC IN INTEGRATED PRESENTATION

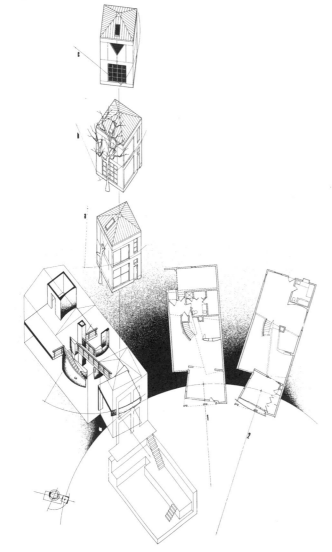

Composition using segmental radiation. Exploded axonometric and floor plans. India ink on mylar.

Courtesy: House + House Architects.
Renderer: Michael Baushke.
Chason Residence, San Francisco, California.

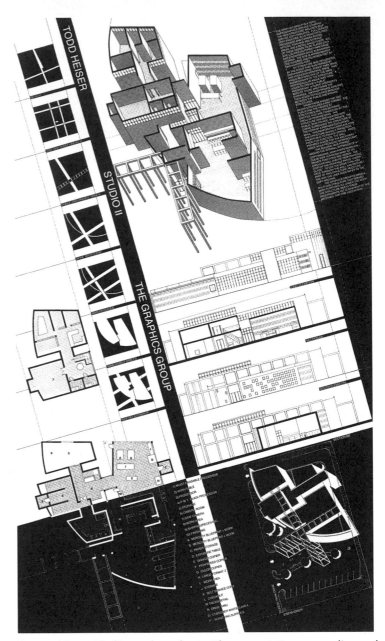

Composition with diagonal emphasis. The presentation uses a diagonal format that refers to the relationship between the new site and the existing site. Ink on vellum, positive-negative drawings.

Courtesy: Savannah College of Art and Design.
Student: Todd Heiser. Studio Critic: M. Saleh Uddin.
Savannah Blueprint and Reprographics.

AXONOMETRIC IN
INTEGRATED PRESENTATION

Plan and elevation oblique arranged in a formal layout. Pencil, prismacolor, and spray paint on 36 x 36-in vellum. The composition and the rendering technique were selected to emphasize the formal arrangement of the plan and the symmetrical nature of the front elevation. After the basic pencil work was completed, the back of the vellum was spray-painted black to provide a gray background. Prismacolor was used on the back and front to create a desired soft pastel effect on the house and on the front to highlight the landscape elements. Text font was selected carefully and spaced apart (justified to the width of the images) to complement the overall composition.

Courtesy: House+House Architects,
San Francisco.
Renderer: James Cathcart.
Cannizzaro Residence, Montara, California.

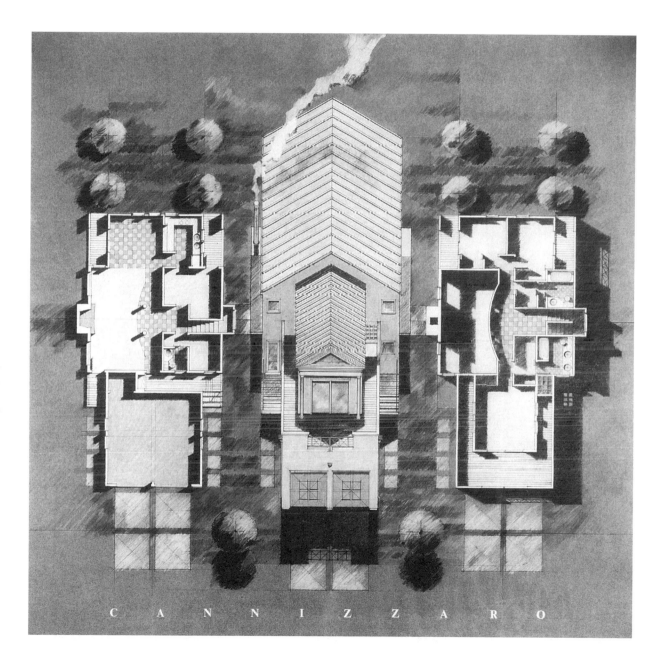

CANNIZZARO

AXONOMETRIC IN INTEGRATED PRESENTATION

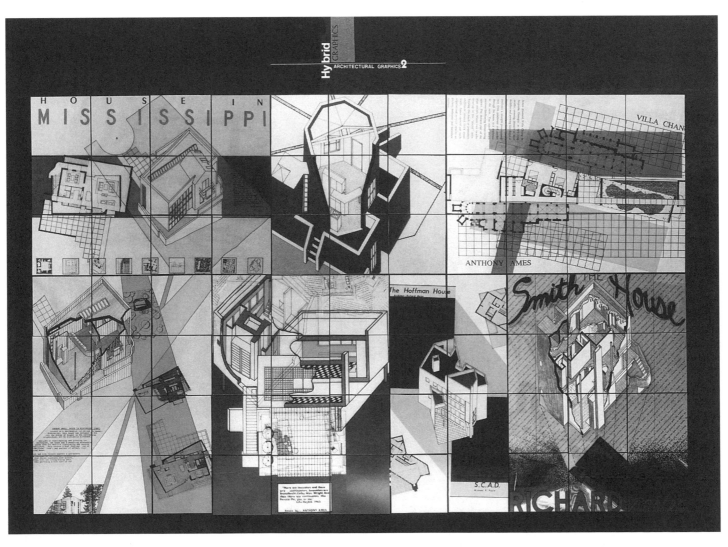

This drawing consists of various projects composed together in one 20 x 30-in presentation board. A pattern of formal grid combines projects in one composition. Each individual drawing/project was photographed with a 35mm camera and enlarged to an 8 x 12-in color print. The photographs were then cut and glued down on a black foam-core board. The grid pattern was created and determined by cutting out thin strips where one photograph touched the next one.

Courtesy: Savannah College of
Art and Design.
Projects from Architectural
Graphics Studio.
Studio Critic: M. Saleh Uddin.

Takefumi Aida Architects & Associates (Japan) • Anthony Ames Architect • Tadao Ando Architects & Associates (Japan) • Natalye Appel Architects • David Baker Associates Architects • R. L. Binder, F.A.I.A. Architecture & Planning • DO3 Bryan Cantley • Chung/Yates • Ellerbe Becket • Mark English • Robert Fakelmann • Richard B. Ferrier, F.A.I.A. • Gordon Grice (Canada) • Steven Holl Architects • House + House Architects • Murphy/Jahn Architects • Pollari X Somol • Krueck & Sexton Architects • Alexis Pontvik Arkitekt (Sweden) • Thomas Norman Rajkovich, Architect • Resolution: 4 Architecture • Rose Architecture • Joel Sanders, Architect • Shin Takamatsu Architects & Associates (Japan) • Minoru Takeyama (Japan) • Ventury Scott Brown and Associates

Axonometric in Contemporary Architects' Work

Takefumi Aida Architects
& Associates, Japan

Image/Technique: Inkline-drawn axonometrics showing the genesis of component blocks and their composition.

Design/Concept: Forms of individual blocks are intended to be an aid in understanding and composing architectural spaces. There are an invisible method and a visible method of employing toy blocks. The visible method used here attaches "toy blocks" to the surface of a cubical box. Toy Block House II is a mixed-use building in a commercial area; consequently its facade is particularly important. Rather than give the inside and outside the same "toy block" expression, the design attempts to express the feeling of toy blocks merely through surface treatment.

Courtesy: Takefumi Aida,
Takefumi Aida Architects & Associates, Japan.
Toy Block House II, Kawasaki, Japan.

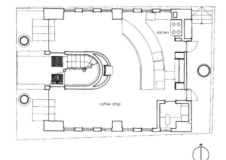

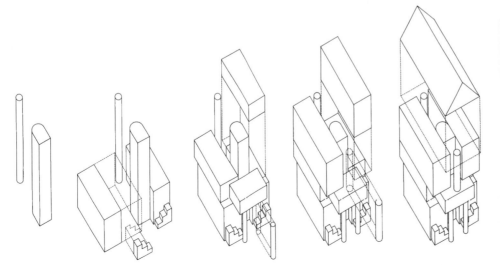

Anthony Ames Architect, Georgia

Image/Technique: Up view axonometric. Color pantone film on ink line drawing.

Design/Concept: The design strategy synthesizes two attitudes toward residential architecture: the first attitude is static, formal, and public with qualities reminiscent of Renaissance idealism; and the second attitude is dynamic, less formal, and more privately oriented. The major spaces, the living and dining areas, are oriented to the south. They are wrapped and protected from the northern exposure by a thickened "L" element that contains the other, more traditionally conceived spaces: bedrooms, bathrooms, library, and kitchen, and juxtaposes the modern spaces of the living/dining area. The fireplace nestles in the inside corner of the "L" and marks the physical and psychological center of the house.

Courtesy: Anthony Ames Architect.
Martinelli Residence, Roxbury, Connecticut.

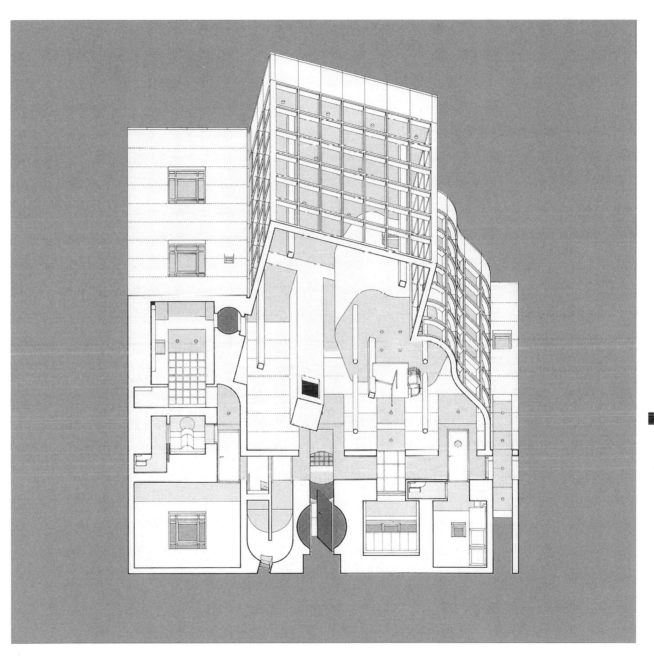

Tadao Ando Architects & Associates, Japan

Image/Technique: Cut-away axonometric. Line drawing in ink.

Design/Concept: Formally, the Galleria is a derivative of the architect's particular design method in which the encasement of the site within a concrete box denotes the primary act of making architecture. This operation is devised to eliminate the city as a physical context and produce an abstract void -- the site -- as a fixed place and a predictable context for the building into which meaning can be projected and reciprocated.

Courtesy: Tadao Ando Architects & Associates.
Galleria Akka, Osaka, Japan.

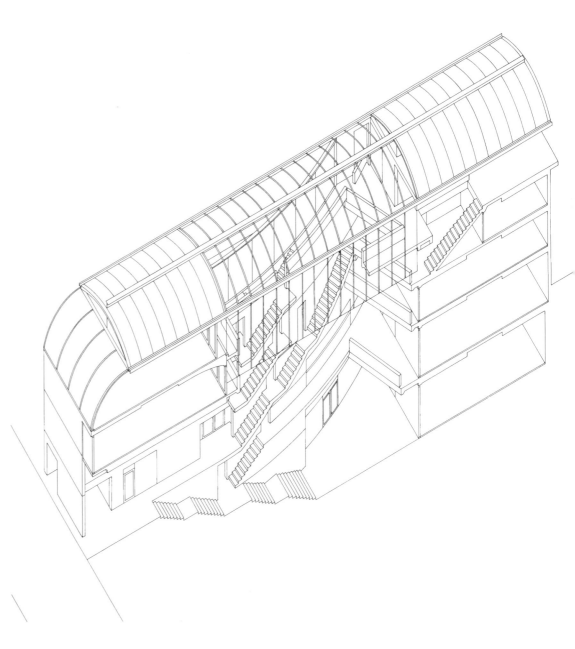

9... Axonometric in Contemporary Architects' Work

Image/Technique: Ink on mylar with color and shading film. The exploded axonometric illustrates the building's components and their specific relationships when viewed within the context of neighboring houses.

Design/Concept: A 50 x 105-ft lot faces Memorial Park, Houston's primary urban green space. Vehicular access is through an alley at the rear of the site. The owner has requested views of the park and pool from as much of the house as possible, yet wants to maintain privacy and security. Metal-clad, shed-roofed bedroom wings, lifted to the second story - views, relate to the scale and character of the neighborhood (an unzoned mixture of residential bungalows and prefab metal warehouses) as seen from both the park and alley sides of the site. The two-story, barrel-vaulted living wing bridges the bedrooms, as well as the kitchen and pool room below, with a glazed stucco skeleton allowing continuous views of the pool and sideyard. Circulation to the bedroom wings is provided by a freestanding metal stair and catwalk suspended from the bowstring trusses. The catwalk on the northwest and the fin-and-trellis sun control system on the southeast also provide lateral bracing for the 20-ft sidewalls.

Courtesy: Natalye Appel Architects.
Drawing: Natalye Appel, Jim Shelton.
Bavousett House, Houston, Texas.

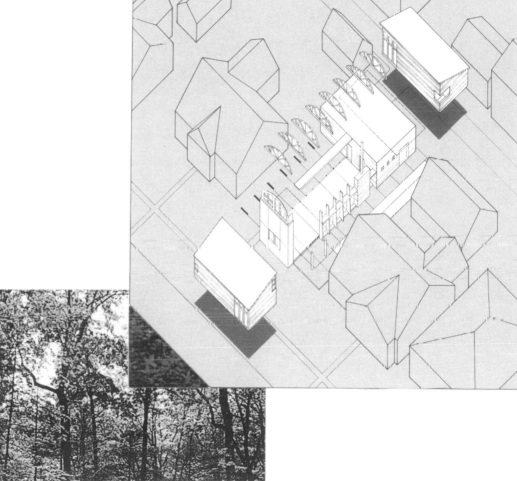

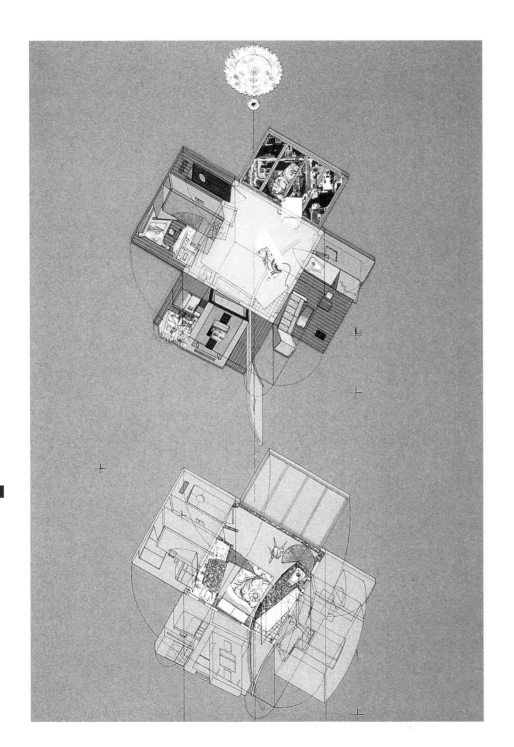

David Baker Associates Architects, California

Image/Technique: Color rendering scanned into computer, imported as a picture into Macintosh desktop publishing program, printed on ink-jet plotter.

Design/Concept: A commission from San Francisco Magazine to envision the condition of the house and the city in the year 2020. Concepts include a 16 x 16-ft Murphy Room and a nonnuclear family house for single parents.

Courtesy: David Baker Associates Architects, California.
David Baker.
2020 - House of the Future.

R. L. Binder, F.A.I.A. Architecture & Planning, California

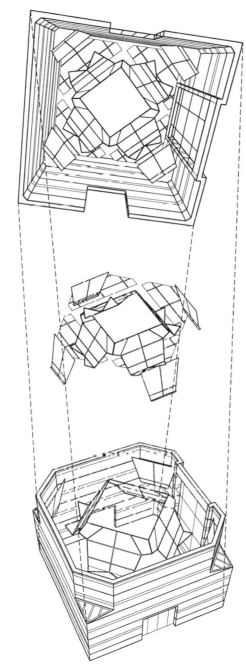
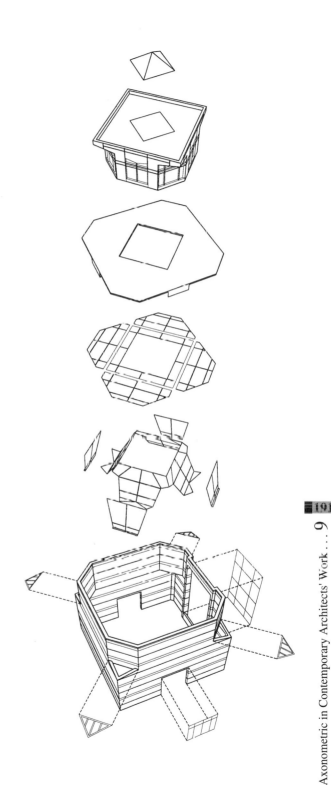

Image/Technique: Exploded axonometric provides a visual catalog of components composing the Reading Room space. Rotated axonometric unfolding (time lapse) view of the Reading Room seen at once from above and below.

Design/Concept: The overall building design incorporates expansion through the "lamination" of 40,000 square feet in two levels to the public facades of the 1960 UCLA Student Union. The reading room is sited prominently at the corner of the two "wings" defining and forming the edge of the newly configured Bruin Plaza.

Courtesy:
R. L. Binder, F.A.I.A. Architecture & Planning, California.
Drawing by: Chilin Huang.
UCLA, Ackerman Student Union Building,
Los Angeles, California.

DO3   Bryan Cantley, California

Image/Technique: Sequence axonometric views from Parti sketch through progressive development sketches. Since the piece is a singular NONMOTION machine, studies explain the evolving relationships of the more complex shielding components within the steel envelope. Ink on white paper.

Design/Concept: STUDY for the ALTAR of a "Temple of Laughter." Concept device that induces/deduces the notion of introspection and the SELF-LAUGH through altered video of the viewer. The large plane distorts reality, not philosophically unlike the concept of a funhouse mirror. The reference to laughter as a balance to the equation of sanity is expressed in the lateral support arm and the manipulated landscape.

Courtesy: DO3 Bryan Cantley.   Laughter icon-machine.

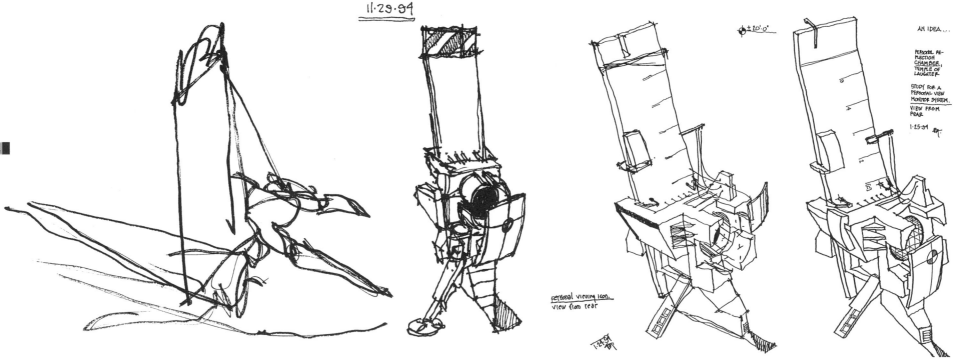

DO3   Bryan Cantley, California

Image/Technique: Finalized axons showing late development free-hand sketch to the finished product. Hard line shows the relationship of machine to immediate context [GROUND PLANE]. Sketch is ink on white paper; Final rendering is ink on mylar.

Courtesy: DO3 Bryan Cantley.   Laughter icon-machine.

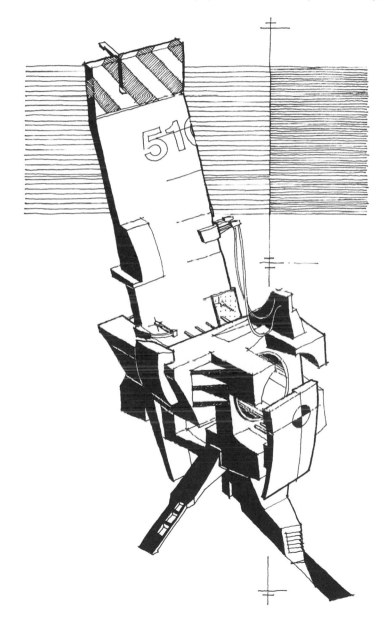

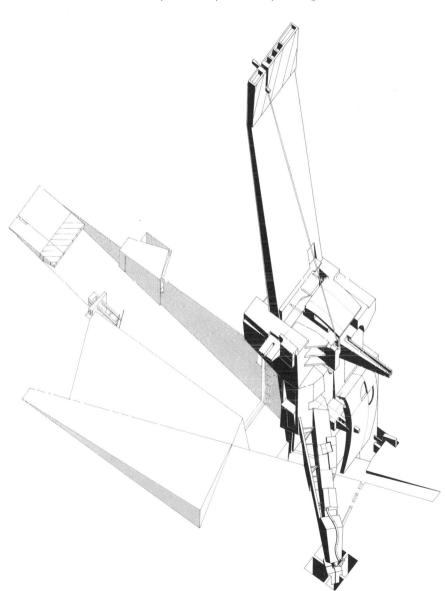

Stephen K. Chung of CHUNG/YATES, New York

Image/ Technique: Photographic prints were made from ink on mylar drawings. Transfer films were then applied to the prints. The cut-away frontal axonometric was a particularly effective drawing in communicating the design intentions.

Design / Concept: A sculptural wall is an essential characteristic of this project. It was conceived as a thick wall containing various niches for art objects, a fireplace as well as modulating incoming natural light. Plans and sections were unable to communicate the complexity of its volume.

Courtesy: Stephen K. Chung,
CHUNG / YATES, New York.
Drawing by: Stephen K. Chung.
Photograph: Eduard Hueber, Arch Photo Inc.
Bowman Residence, New Paltz, New York.

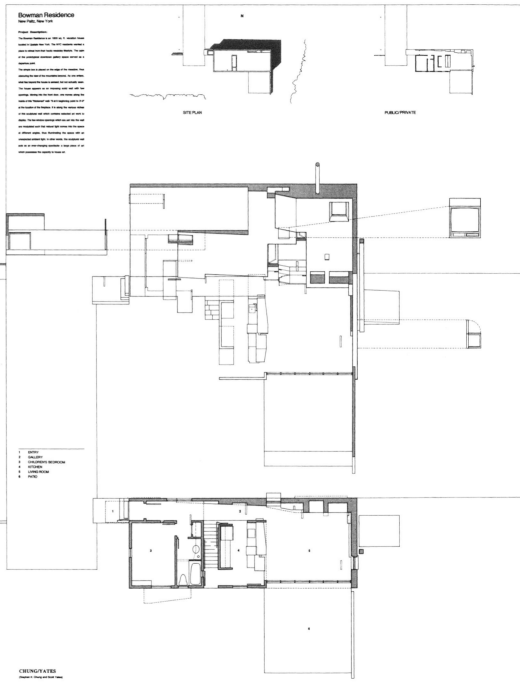

Bowman Residence
New Paltz, New York

Project Description:

The Bowman Residence is an 1800 sq. ft. vacation house located in Upstate New York. The NYC residents wanted a place to retreat from their hectic weekday lifestyle. The calm of the prototypical downtown gallery space served as a departure point.

The simple box is placed on the edge of the meadow, thus obscuring the view of the mountains beyond. As one enters, what lies beyond the house is sensed, but not actually seen. The house appears as an imposing solid wall with few openings. Moving into the front door, one moves along the inside of this "thickened" wall. It is along the various niches of this sculptural wall which contains selected art work to display. The few window openings which are set into the wall are modulated such that natural light comes into the space at different angles, thus illuminating the space with an unexpected ambient light. In other words, the sculptural wall acts as an ever-changing spectacle- a large piece of art which possesses the capacity to house art.

1	ENTRY
2	GALLERY
3	CHILDREN'S BEDROOM
4	KITCHEN
5	LIVING ROOM
6	PATIO

SITE PLAN

PUBLIC/PRIVATE

N

CHUNG/YATES
(Stephen K. Chung and Scott Yates)

Architecture ELLERBE BECKE
New Yo

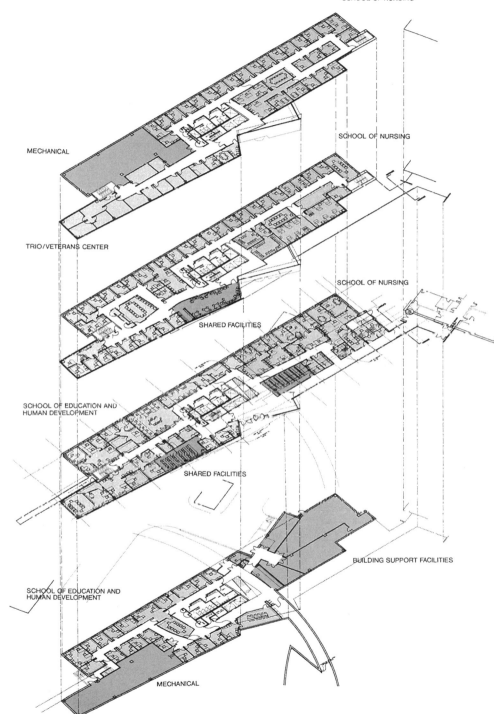

Third Floor

Second Floor

First Floor

Exploded plan axonometric.

Courtesy: Architecture ELLERBE BECKET, New York.
New Academic Buildings, Building B,
State University of New York,
Binghamton, New York.

Ground Floor

SCHOOL OF NURSING

MECHANICAL

SCHOOL OF NURSING

TRIO/VETERANS CENTER

SCHOOL OF NURSING

SHARED FACILITIES

SCHOOL OF EDUCATION AND
HUMAN DEVELOPMENT

SHARED FACILITIES

BUILDING SUPPORT FACILITIES

SCHOOL OF EDUCATION AND
HUMAN DEVELOPMENT

MECHANICAL

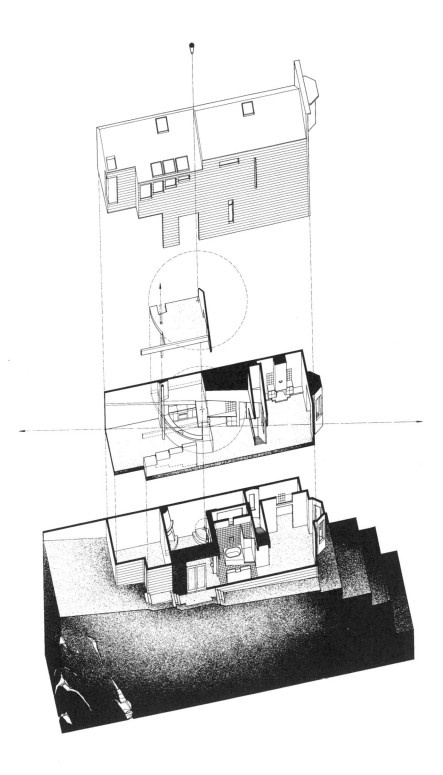

Mark English, California

Image/Technique: Exploded axonometric. Pen-and-ink line work with india-ink airbrush tone on mylar. 30 X 60-in.

The exploded axonometric allows conceptual differences between the Victorian-era container and its new architectural contents to be expressed. The interior axial and radial regulating lines are diagrammed for clarity. The heavy base gives a sense of the quake-fractured hillside building site.

Design/Concept: The site is part of a dense Victorian neighborhood in San Francisco's Noe Valley with 22-1/2 x 10-ft lots. Fire recently claimed the majority of the building and only the front facade was retained for civic context. The facade and new contextually-scaled envelope are used as a foil for a completely different set of spatial experiences within. A through-running diagonal axis extends the already substantial depth of the building, all spaces being arranged in a loft-like manner rather than in the typical pattern of separate rooms. A visitor at the main level can view unencumbered the San Francisco Bay beyond the scenic built environment to the east, and the nearby hills and gardens to the west. Carefully composed slits, high windows, and glass block walls allow only abstract views or interior lighting features at the north and south walls. The interior materials create a duality between "cool" (stainless steel, german silver, aluminum leaf, hammered cold steel, etched glass and glass block, mirror) and "warm," (maple flooring and cabinets, earth-toned granite details, special painted finishes).

Courtesy: Mark English,
Inglese Architecture.
Drawing by: Mark English.
The Robertson Residence, New House, San Francisco.

Robert J. Fakelmann, Louisiana

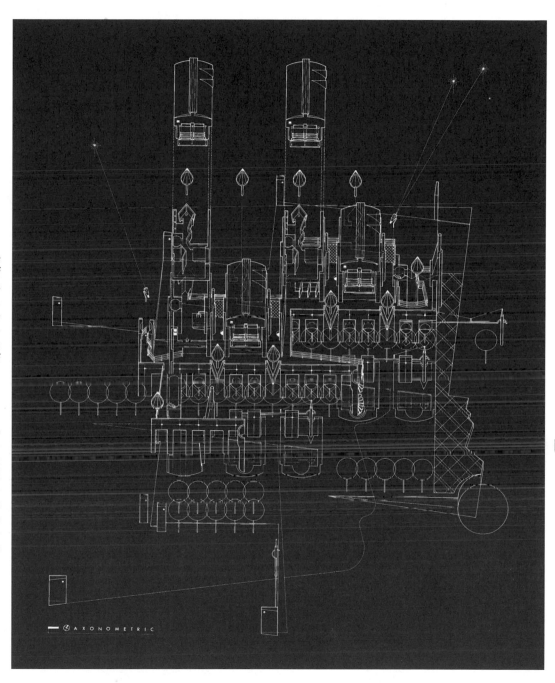

Image/Technique: Ink on 30 x 40-in transparent mylar. This zero-degree axonometric or frontal projection satisfies the combined needs of analysis and representation. Its precedence can be found in the paintings of Georges Braque which suggest viewing objects from the front and top, simultaneously. In architectural drawing this implication combines the two-dimensional qualities of the plan with the three-dimensional characteristics of the design. The compositional relationships in the plan can be analyzed while representing space and form. Additional elements of the form are exploded and removed to reveal interior components, allowing further representation of the interior-exterior relationships.

Design/Concept: This residential complex explores the relationship between architecture and landscape. It is intended to examine organizational constraints which architecture imposes on the landscape while acknowledging that elements of the landscape can be orchestrated according to principles of architectural composition. Rather than regarding architecture and landscape as discrete, separate entities, both are seen as being reciprocal and mutually interactive. Extensions of the building into the landscape are enhanced by the repetition of architectural and natural elements. Apertures in the walls acknowledge the merging of these elements and allow them to be experienced as one. From this perception architecture and landscape become synonymous.

Courtesy: Robert J. Fakelmann, Associate Professor,
Louisiana Tech University.
A Residential Complex for Visiting Faculty and University Dignitaries,
Ruston, Louisiana.

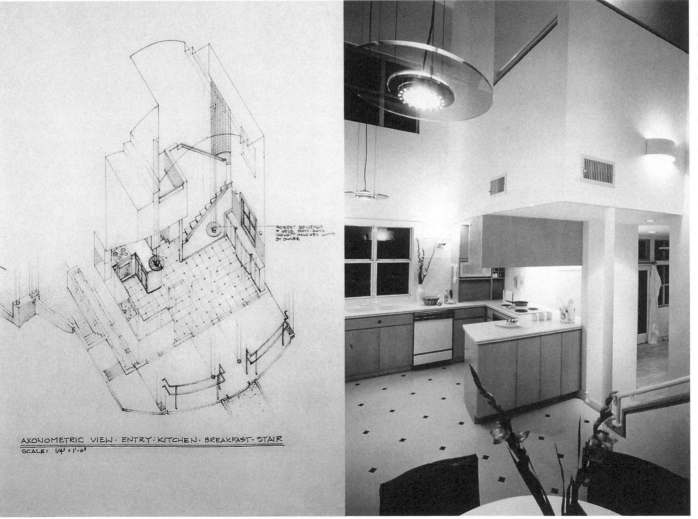

AXONOMETRIC VIEW · ENTRY · KITCHEN · BREAKFAST · STAIR
SCALE: 1/4" = 1'-0"

Image/Technique: Axonometric and photograph of kitchen. The drawing depicts the entry porch and the vertical yet narrow kitchen/dining area with stair and balcony above. This axonometric drawing reflects the final design and was utilized for the construction documents. Notice how clearly it describes the rather complex vaulted ceiling and the suspended lighting fixtures. The photograph offers a view from the dining area adjacent to the stairs looking into the kitchen area. Such axonometric drawings can describe to the client and the contractor the interrelationship of all the component parts so difficult to comprehend when viewed separately in plan, section, and elevation.

Design/Concept: The client had purchased and used an old cabin located on this site which was destroyed. We elected to recall the existing plan and respect the original dimensions of the structure. With this strategy, we did not block previously existing views to the lake by adjacent property owners. The original plan was simple and direct. One enters the kitchen/dining area, traverses a few steps down to the living room and fireplace, then out through glass doors to a wood deck overlooking the lake.

Courtesy: Richard B. Ferrier, FAIA.
Photographer: C. Kuhner.
GBC Douglas Lake House.

Gordon Grice, Canada

Image/Technique: Exploded axonometric view. The drawing was done freehand, using a triple-zero rapidograph jewel-tipped pen on mylar film. Reference material was provided in the form of design drawings, measured drawings, and aerial and ground-level photographs. Since much of the redevelopment work was, of necessity, subterranean, an exploded axonometric view was required that would explain the interrelationhips among the proposed areas and between the new and existing structures.

Design/Concept: The intent of the plan was to expand and upgrade the historic Canadian Parliament buildings and environs without compromising the existing visual aesthetics and integrity of the precinct. The plan has been tabled in the House of Commons and approved as policy by the NCC. (This planning project won several awards including AIA, 1991; Ontario Professional Planners Institute, 1990; Progressive Architectitre magazine, 1989; and Canadian Society of Landscape Architects, 1989.)

Courtesy: Gordon Crice + Associates.
Illustration: Gordon Grice.
Client: The National Capital Commission, Ottawa, Canada.
Planners and Architects: du Toit Allsopp Hillier, Toronto, Canada.
Parliamentary Precinct -- Long-Range Plan, Ottawa, Canada.

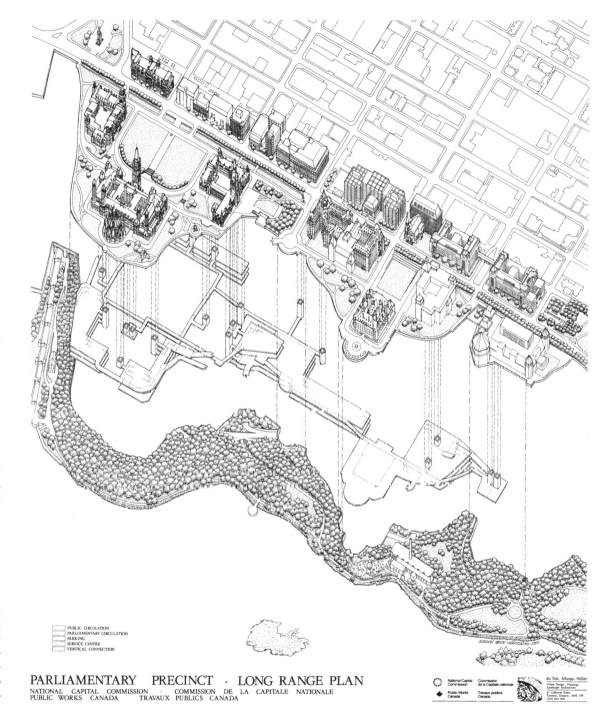

PUBLIC CIRCULATION
PARLIAMENTARY CIRCULATION
PARKING
SERVICE CENTRE
VERTICAL CONNECTION

PARLIAMENTARY PRECINCT · LONG RANGE PLAN
NATIONAL CAPITAL COMMISSION · COMMISSION DE LA CAPITALE NATIONALE
PUBLIC WORKS CANADA   TRAVAUX PUBLICS CANADA

National Capital Commission   Commission de la Capitale nationale

Public Works Canada   Travaux publics Canada

du Toit, Allsopp, Hillier
Urban Design, Planning, Landscape Architecture
47 Colborne Street
Toronto, Ontario, M5E 1P8
(416) 864-1876

Steven Holl Architects, New York

Image/Technique: Exploded axonometric and location plan. Pen and ink.

Design/Concept: Along with intensification of an urban condition, the building expresses the idea of a "society of strangers." The Hybrid Building combines retail, office, and residential uses. At the upper levels the building forms split into east and west types. Rooms facing the setting sun and central square are for boisterous types, late risers who enjoy watching the action, toasting the sunset, etc. Facing east to the rising sun are rooms for melancholic types. These individuals are early risers, inclined to silence and solitude. Melancholic types are imagined as a tragic poet, a musician, and a mathematician.

Courtesy: Steven Holl Architects.
Photohrapher: Author.
Hybrid Building, Seaside, Florida.

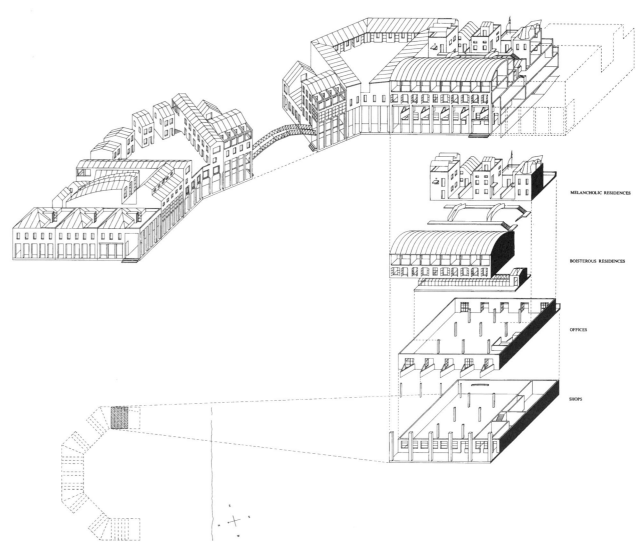

MELANCHOLIC RESIDENCES

BOISTEROUS RESIDENCES

OFFICES

SHOPS

House+House Architects, California

Image/Technique: Vertically exploded axonometric. Pen and ink with india-ink airbrush tone on 30 x 50-in mylar. The drawing is composed to best show both the boat-like form of the main body of the house and the vertical axis of the tower element. The partial cross-section rendered in black emphasizes the slope of the land and the subterranean location of the laboratory. In contrast the tower is pulled apart in pieces far above the ground plane to emphasize the skeletal armature within.

Design/Concept: The house, allowing for the varied interests of its scientist and inventor owners, is a backdrop for a large collection of fixed art and functions as a center for a far-flung group of performers and musicians. The curving form reflects an imaginary circle inscribed on a part of the heroic, daunting landscape to provide for a symbolic place of habitation. Building elements are arranged to mark the equinoxes and winter solstice when important holidays bring friends and family together.

Courtesy: House + House Architects.
Renderer: Mark English.
Photographer: Alan Weintraub.
Waldhauer Residence, Woodside, California.

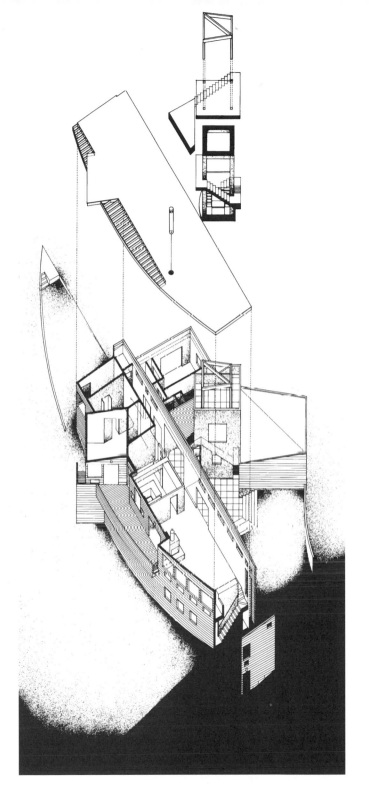

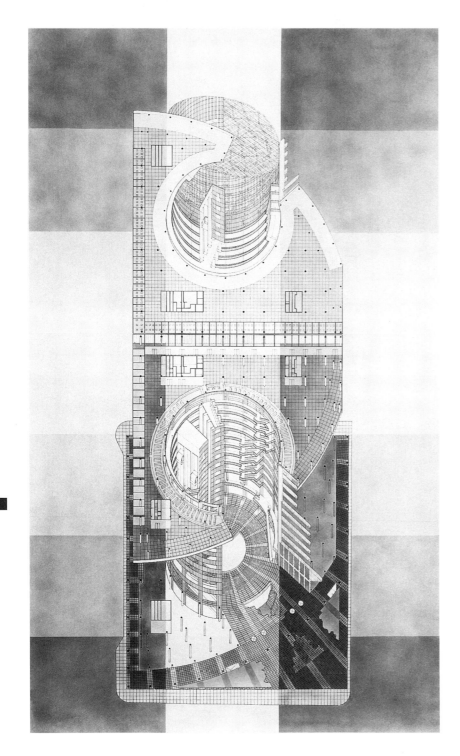

Murphy/Jahn Architects, Illinois

Image/Technique: Site plan oblique, floor plan oblique, and ceiling plan oblique showing central atrium space. Pen and ink with airbrush color on KP-5 paper.

Design/Concept: The unusual form of this state office building is a fusion of images: traditional ones from classical courthouses and capitols and contemporary images of a government building that seems accessible and inviting. The rounded facade and the immense public space within a circular skylit atrium, rising the full height of the building and thrusting through the roof are intended to recall the forms and embody the monumentality of traditional rotundas and domes.

Courtesy: Murphy/Jahn Architects, Illinois.
Helmut Jahn.
State of Illinois Center, Chicago, Illinois.

Murphy/Jahn Architects, Illinois

Image/Technique: Pull-apart or exploded axonometric showing entry level with site, main body of building blocks, and exterior enclosure systems. Pen-and-ink line drawing.

Design/Concept: Two rectangular blocks -- a 150,000 sft., eight-story bank and office building and a 300-room, nine-story hotel; are linked by a web of intersecting glass walls and trusses forming a prismatic, 27,000 sft. atrium between them. The atrium provides a grand entry hall for both buildings. The hotel restaurant spreads out under the glass canopy in the manner of a European street cafe.

Courtesy:
Murphy/Jahn Architects,
Illinois.
Designer: Helmut Jahn.
First Source Center,
South Bend, Indiana.

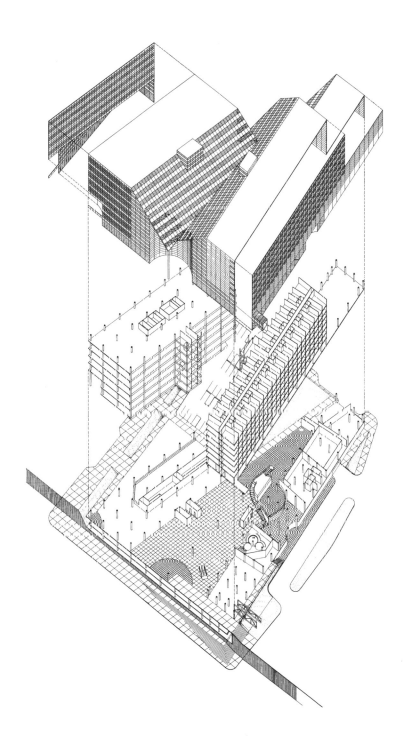

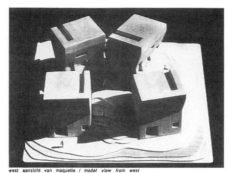

west aanzicht van maquette / model view from west

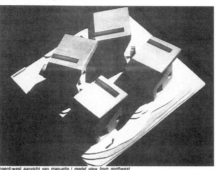

noord-west aanzicht van maquette / model view from northwest

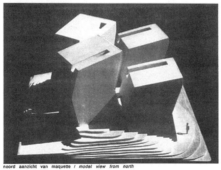

noord aanzicht van maquette / model view from north

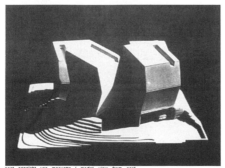

oost aanzicht van maquette / model view from east

isometrie woning IV / axonometric house IV 1:50

9… Axonometric in Contemporary Architects' Work

Pollari x Somol, Illinois

Image/Technique: Exploded axonometric and model views. An exploded axonometric view showing interior circulation and room layouts in House IV is combined with model views of the exterior grouping of all four houses. The axonometric is a black-ink line drawing while the model views are photocopies on adhesive film; all are applied to one sheet of mylar. 595 x 841 mm.

Design/Concept: This project develops an alternative to the modern architectural theme of the frame structure. Rather than operating through a Cartesian *infinite extrusion*, as in Le Corbusier's Dom-ino, these houses, located between an old village and a new development in Amsterdam, experiment with a Spinozan *finite extension* or "free section." The structure cantilevers to the convex and concave facades where the skin pulls away revealing a space poised between inside and outside. Operating between landscape and building, the houses display the casual disposition and anonymous appearance of various local tectonic elements such as the windmills that proliferate throughout the surroundings.

Courtesy: Pollari x Somol.
Linda Pollari.
Vrije Sektor/Free Section Houses.
Amsterdam, 1992.

Krueck & Sexton Architects, Illinois

Image/Technique: Pen and ink on mylar plan oblique drawing and photograph of the constructed project.

Design/Concept: The mass of the new building is broken into two wings arranged around a two-story atrium that serves as an entry and central core. The building enclosure, a curtain wall system of glass, aluminum, and granite, utilizes the mullions to break down the scale of the wall to proportions derived from the windows of the turn-of-the-century manor house that the client had restored within the site. Granite and glass of subdued color tones further relate the new building to the materials of the old building. The result is a contemporary response to the tudoresque-style of the mansion.

Courtesy: Krueck & Sexton Architects, Illinois.
Hewitt Associates -- Eastern Regional Center, Rowayton, Connecticut.

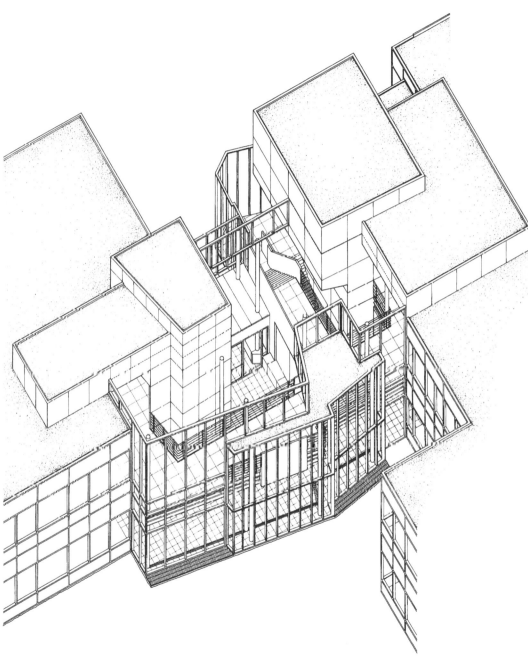

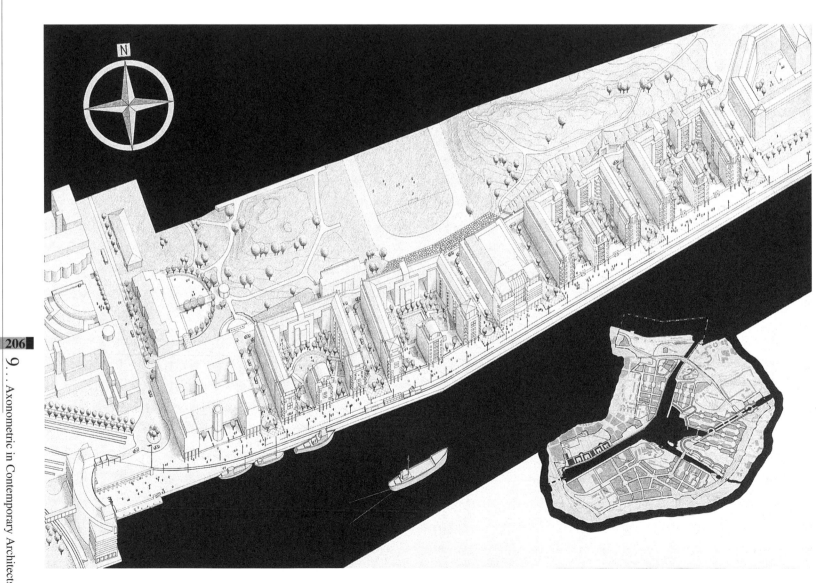

Image/Technique: Original ink on polyester film. Copied on watercolor paper and colored with Faber Castell Polychromos.

Design/Concept: An urban plan proposed for the city of Stockholm which is part of the development of Hammarby Sjostad, a new city at the edge of the water (shown in the smaller sketch). The buildings are a result of the local conditions: on one hand, continuing the city blocks and making a clear edge toward the water, a characteristic of Stockholm; on the other hand, providing views and equal living qualities for all the future inhabitants.

Courtesy: Alexis Pontvik. Alexis Pontvik Arkitekt, Sweden. 'KV Mjarden,' Stockholm Urban plan in collaboration with the Town Planning Office in Stockholm.

Image/Technique: Watercolor and ink wash over pencil linework. Proportion, outline, craft, and material are depicted as the primary considerations in the art of proper building. At once a representation of a single project and a more general essay in the architectural elaboration of vernacular building technique, the drawing serves an essentially didactic purpose.

Design/Concept: The fundamental compositional elements of architecture: column and beam (trabeation), wall and arch, and roof are combined in this proposal for a market loggia, which serves as a study in the tectonic origins of classical architecture. The artistic intervention which separates the ideal/representational from the real/necessary (and which distinguishes architecture from building) is evidenced in each element of the design. Architecture is here realized as the mythic representation of tectonic necessity codified over the millennia as the art of proper building.

Courtesy:
Thomas Norman Rajkovich,
Architect, Illinois.
Tuscan Market Loggia,
Evanston, Illinois.

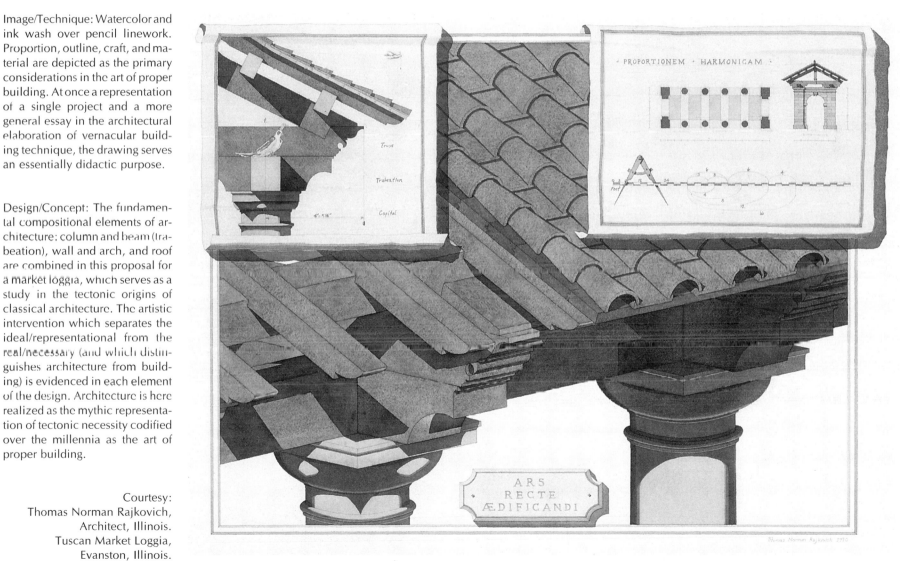

207

Resolution: 4 Architecture, New York

Image/Technique: Cut-away down-view axonometric and exploded perspective. Pen-and-ink line drawings and a photographic image.

Design/Concept: This total-health club concerns itself with all aspects of fitness, incorporating free-weight training, cardiovascular and Cybex machines, massage, testing, aerobics classes, and nutrition. The facility occupies a two-story space at the base of an II-story office building. The project's visual language uses a vocabulary of planes which wrap and carve space. The rhythms of these planes, which can veil, reveal, or reflect, bind the different areas into a single composition and frame the athletes in a dynamic setting. The incompletion of carved or exploded forms fosters ambiguity between adjacent spaces and allows the rhythm of planes to continue through all the spaces. Surface materials reflect the designers' interest in bringing inexpensive, off-the-shelf materials into a refined environment. One major wall is lacquered fiberboard while the others are textured gypsum board. A raked, low plywood ceiling defines a main corridor. Light is bright but softened by inverting the hung industrial fixtures to face the ceiling. The stair is a typical steel fabrication, but an illuminated landing and surrounding soffits and openings create a dramatic ascent.

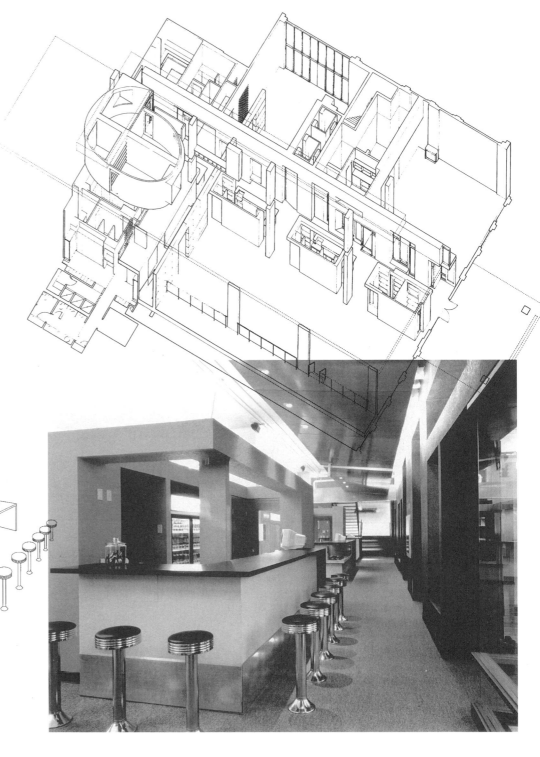

Courtesy: Resolution: 4 Architecture.
Joseph Tanney, Gary Shoemaker, and Robert Luntz.
Project Team: John Da Cruz, David Schilling, Markus Bader, Eric Liffin.
Premier Health Club, Hallandale, Florida.

Rose Architecture, California

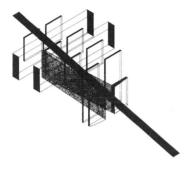

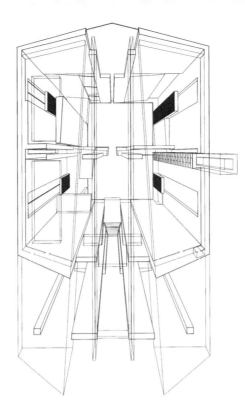

Image/Technique: The design solution of this relatively small enclosure required a spatial perception that extended beyond the limits of the building. Of this series of drawings, each one addresses a certain conceptual parameter of scale and building element. The aerial perspective encompasses the notion of spatial scale within the building envelope: the axon addresses interior elements and the apparent layers along the axis; and the conceptual diagram expresses the overall synthesis of passage and space. All drawings are hand-drawn ink on mylar with adhesive dot screen film.

Design/Concept: Starting with the existing foundation of a small carriage house, a new architecture of light and shadow was created. Situated at the center of a residential block, the house is set in a relative bucolic oasis of adjacent rear yards. Through the manipulation of perspective, scale, and vista, this originally small space assumes a new expansiveness. The progressive height of the walls and narrowness of the passages create an internal hierarchy of layers and privacy. The large windows are treated as frames that capture the views of the surrounding gardens and landscape.

Courtesy: Christopher Rose Architect,
Rose Architecture.
Blacksburg House, Virginia.

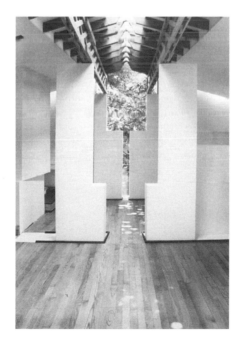

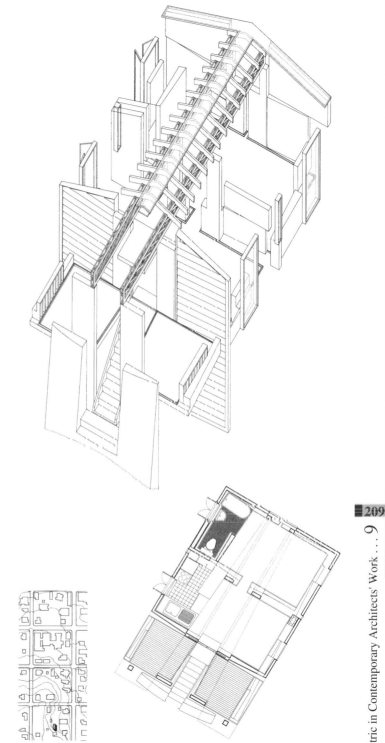

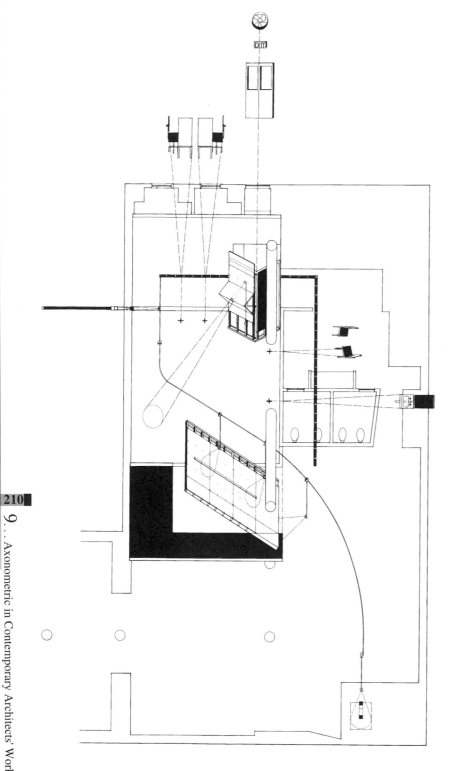

Joel Sanders, Architect, New York

Image/Technique: Composite plan/flip-up axonometric. Pen and ink, pantone on mylar. 24 x 36-in. This drawing uses flip-up axonometric projection in order to reinforce the insistent frontality of gallery architecture. It describes an overview of the installation; the spectator interacts with an inverted light track, brought down from the ceiling to the floor, which situates the viewer in front of the gallery wall and illuminates a zone of looking but not touching. Cuts in the once immaculate white wall frame views to places normally off-limits; the administrative offices, restrooms, and exit corridor.

Design/Concept: The installation calls into question the prevailing notion that the exhibition interior is a pure, neutral white space that does not interfere with the viewer's direct and uncontaminated perception of the work of art. Instead the project highlights how gallery architecture regulates the eye and body of the spectator.

Courtesy: Joel Sanders, Architect, New York.
Joel Sanders and Scott Sherk with Mark Tsurumaki.
"Sighting the Gallery," an installation at Artists Space, New York.

Shin Takamatsu Architects & Associates, Japan

Image/Technique: Frontal axonometric. Pencil on Kent paper.

Design/Concept: There are two ways to relate nature and architecture; one is by harmonizing them and the other is by taking scenery into the architecture. The latter is adopted in this museum. The museum building consists of four concrete blocks (exhibition rooms) and water spaces in-between. Each small pond between blocks reflects Mount Daisen which rises far behind the site. Vistors encounter beautiful sceneries when they move from one exhibition hall to another. By taking surrounding nature into the linear circulation the visitors experience the nature.

Courtesy: Shin Takamatsu Architects & Associates, Japan.
Drawing: Itsuki Takamatsu.
Shoji Ueda Museum of Photography, Tottori, Japan.

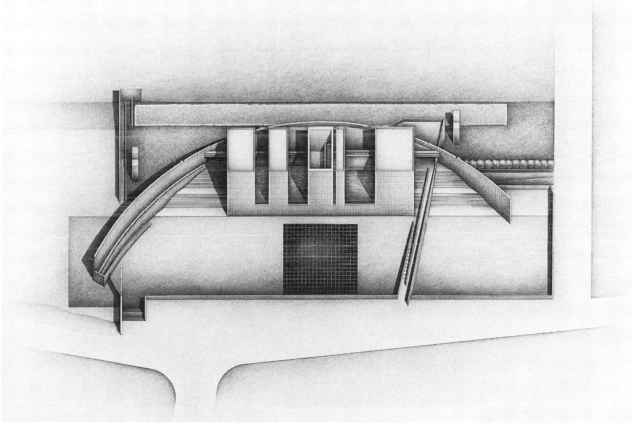

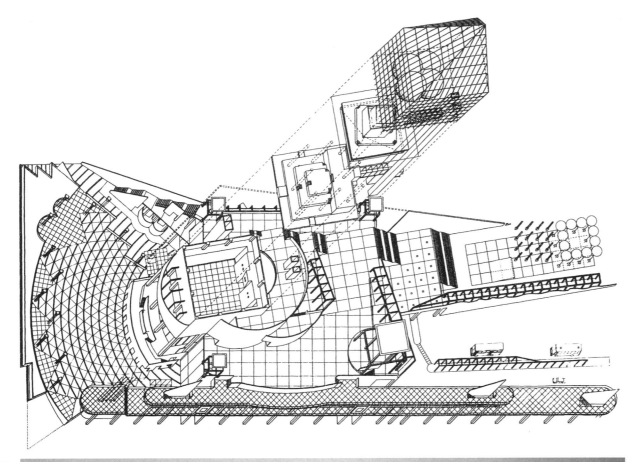

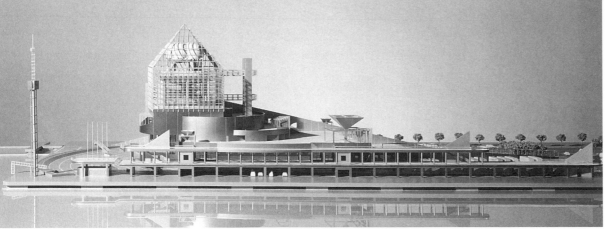

Minoru Takeyama, Japan

Image/Technique: Exploded xonometric. Pencil on illustration board. Ink for paving pattern. The drawing indicates the vertical orchestration of the different spaces which compose the port terminal building. The three lower floors are closely related by the open terraces, decks, stairs, and open corridor with similar floor patterns.

Design/Concept: The port terminal is primarily for international passenger boats. The site is on a reclaimed island located close to the center of the city and in the waterfront park. The form of "houseness" was conceived by creating a man-made hill, or multiple terraces of platforms, which covers the main body and cascades down to the street level. This is intended to be landmark and seamark which is simple, dominant, and identical from all directions. Visual interests are created (depending upon the viewing distance) by the solid-void of internal forms and external framework, scale, surface treatment, color, and light and shade.

Courtesy: Minoru Takeyama, Japan.
Tokyo International Port Terminal, Tokyo, Japan.

Ventury Scott Brown
and Associates, New York

Image/Technique: "Helicopter view" axonometric. A large (48 x 60-in) pencil on vellum axonometric drawing was projected from a plan of a section of the Westway State Park along the Hudson River in Greenwich Village. (A very light no.6H lead layout was overdrawn with a heavy no.2 Mongol pencil by Eberhard Faber.) A large scale was used for the drawing in order to show detail and realistically illustrate paving patterns, flower beds, trees, tall ships, and people walking, riding bicycles, sailing, and playing sports. The drawing was then photographed onto a full-size negative and contact printed at full-size on Kodak KC-5 paper (a high-contrast black-and-white paper) in order to preserve detail and line quality. The drawing was mounted on foam core and a combination of hand-cut color film overlay and ink-based air brush was used to color the drawing.

Design/Concept: The 100-acre Westway State Park was located along a 3-1/2 mile stretch of the Hudson River which connected Battery Park City with the Convention Center at 42nd Street. Particular care was taken in terms of view corridors and connections to the local neighbors in Chelsea, the West Village, and Tribeca. The design of the park featured a wide esplanade along the waterfront, passive and active play areas, a meandering bicycle path, playing fields, and multi-function piers at "gateway" areas such as Christopher Street.

Courtesy: Ventury Scott Brown and Associates.
Rendering: Frederic Schwartz, Miles Ritter, Simon Tickell, Robert Marker.
Westway at Christopher Street, Westway State Park, New York, New York.

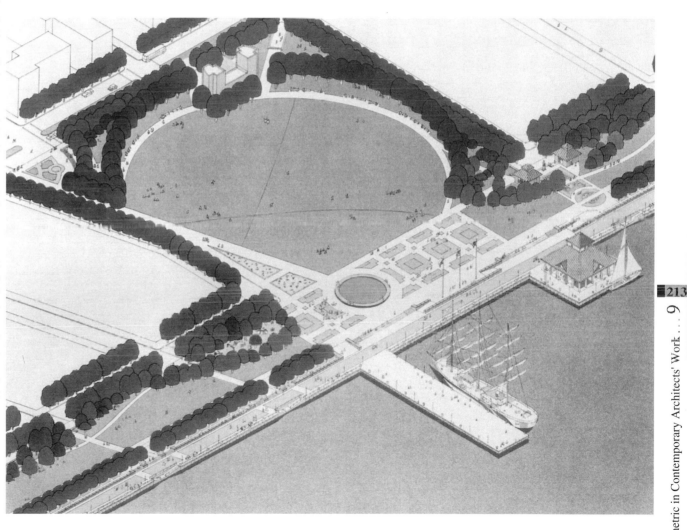

213

Axonometric in Contemporary Architects' Work . . . 9